Epidemiology and the Delivery of Health Care Services

Methods and Applications

Epidemiology and the Delivery of Health Care Services

Methods and Applications

Edited by

Denise M. Oleske

Rush University
Chicago, Illinois

Plenum Press • New York and London

Library of Congress Cataloging-in-Publication Data

On file

Epidemiology and the delivery of health care services : methods and
  applications / edited by Denise M. Oleske.
       p.   cm.
  Includes bibliographical references and index.
  ISBN 0-306-44968-4
  1. Health planning--Methodology. 2. Epidemiology. 3. Health
services administration.   I. Oleske, Denise.
  [DNLM: 1. Epidemiology. 2. Health Planning--methods. 3. Delivery
of Health Care--organization & administration. 4. Epidemiologic
Methods.   WA 105 E6433 1995]
RA394.9.E64 1995
614.4--dc20
DNLM/DLC
for Library of Congress   95-9426
                                                              CIP

ISBN 0-306-44968-4

© 1995 Plenum Press, New York
A Division of Plenum Publishing Corporation
233 Spring Street, New York, NY 10013

10 9 8 7 6 5 4 3 2

Printed in the United States of America

Contributors

Dolores Gurnick Clement
Department of Health Administration
Virginia Commonwealth University
Medical College of Virginia
Richmond, Virginia 23298

Frances J. Jaeger
University of Illinois Perinatal Center
and
Department of Health Systems Management
Rush University
Chicago, Illinois 60612

Andrew Kucharski
Department of Clinical Development
Immunex Corporation
Seattle, Washington 98101

Wayne M. Lerner
The Jewish Hospital of St. Louis
BJC Health System
and
Washington University School of Medicine
St. Louis, Missouri 63110

Karl A. Matuszewski
Technology Assessment Program
University Hospital Consortium
Clinical Practice Advancement Center
Oak Brook, Illinois 60521
and
Department of Health Systems Management
Rush University
Chicago, Illinois 60612

Robert Mittendorf
Department of Obstetrics and Gynecology
University of Chicago
Chicago, Illinois 60637

Kevin L. Najafi
Department of Health Systems Management
Rush University
and
ArcVentures, Inc.
Chicago, Illinois 60612

Denise M. Oleske
Departments of Health Systems Management and Preventive Medicine
Rush University
Chicago, Illinois 60612

Iris R. Shannon
Departments of Community Health Nursing and Health Systems Management
Rush University
Chicago, Illinois 60612

Marie E. Sinioris
Department of Health Systems Management
Rush University
and
Rush-Presbyterian-St. Luke's Medical Center
and
ArcVentures, Inc.
Chicago, Illinois 60612

MeriBeth Herzberg Stegall
Program in Healthcare Administration
University of Osteopathic Medicine and Health Sciences
Des Moines, Iowa 50312

Thomas T. H. Wan
Department of Health Administration
Virginia Commonwealth University
Medical College of Virginia
Richmond, Virginia 23298

Preface

With larger numbers of persons needing health care, competition for markets among health care providers, and the constantly changing social, economic, and political environments, a health care manager can no longer exclusively focus on the internal operations of an organization to be financially viable and achieve its mission. Health care providers must look to forming systems. Accompanying this change in organizational strategy requires a population-based perspective. Guiding a system to meet the health care needs of populations can be accomplished with a knowledge of epidemiology. Numerous textbooks exist that present an introductory approach to epidemiologic principles and methods for health care practitioners. Most of these present epidemiology from a classical orientation, namely, the investigation of the distribution and determinants of disease. In reality, few health care practitioners will be engaged in this type of endeavor.

This book describes the conceptual orientation and knowledge of techniques from epidemiology that health care providers must have in order to deliver health care to populations. It is intended for students aspiring to become health care managers and for those who currently hold such positions, regardless of if their primary disciplinary preparation is in business administration, medicine, nursing, or allied health. Specifically, the objectives of this book are oriented to provide a practical understanding of how epidemiologic concepts and methods can be used to: (1) assess the health status of populations served; (2) determine the need for health services; (3) understand the factors that influence the health status of populations served; (4) monitor system effectiveness; (5) plan and evaluate health services and technologies used; and (6) anticipate the effect of policy changes upon the delivery of health care services. The first three chapters of this book cover basic epidemiologic concepts and descriptive methods relevant to managing population-based health care. The remaining chapters emphasize the application of epidemiology in specific aspects of health care management that particularly necessitate a population-based perspective. Additional epidemiologic concepts, including selected analytic methods and designs, are discussed. A course in biostatistics prior to or concurrent with reading this book is advised.

The chapters are written by individuals who, as a matter of course, apply epidemiologic thinking and techniques in their current positions. Following each chapter, the reader is challenged with case studies relevant to the theme of the chapter that require epidemiologic concepts and techniques for their solution. Since the case studies are real-life or based upon real-life situations of the contributors, the reader will also gain insight and some experience with the practical aspects of epidemiology in health care management. Some of the cases have suggested answers provided in a separate chapter at the end of the book. It must be emphasized that these are suggested answers; different situations, depending on the context, resources, and time constraints, may require different approaches. Some of the cases have questions without suggested answers; this is intended so that users of this book can derive their own creative solutions using epidemiologic principles and methods. Readers are encouraged to share these with me as well as other case situations, which may be considered for future editions of this book.

Denise M. Oleske, Ph.D.

Chicago, Illinois

Contents

Chapter 6—Control of Transmissible Diseases in Health Care Organizations 101

Andrew Kucharski and Robert Mittendorf

1

An Epidemiologic Perspective for Health Care Management

Denise M. Oleske

An Epidemiologic Framework for Health Services Delivery

The organization and delivery of health care services in this last decade of the 20th century have been heavily influenced by two themes. One found in a substantial body of literature is the proposition that care delivered from high-volume providers can favorably affect the health status of patients served (Luft *et al.*, 1990). The other theme is associated with the growing importance of quality in health care. To achieve volume, health care organizations are forming into systems at a rapid pace. These systems can take on a variety of configurations, from loose affiliations among hospitals to systems that provide the full continuum of care, ranging from health promotion to hospice. Volume can provide economy-of-scale advantages in the delivery of services. Although it is desirable to achieve lower costs through volume, adequate volume is also necessary for a provider to gain a level of experience that enhances the quality of care. Quality is also linked to reducing health care costs because, in theory, the delivery of high-quality care avoids costs related to unnecessary procedures, unnecessary hospitalizations, and so forth.

In the face of these challenges, a number of questions are raised: Should all health care services be equally distributed among the population? Are all health services equally effective among population subgroups? To what degree do health services impact health status? A population-based focus is required to answer these questions. Such a focus classically directs attention on the general population in a defined geopolitical area (Last, 1988). Although private health care services have typically not undertaken responsibility for addressing the needs of geographically based populations, health care reform may change this. Health care systems may be charged with improving the health status of all individuals within a defined geographic area. Even if this is not the case, the continued growth of health care systems will result in large populations being under some form of active treatment, monitoring, or follow-

Denise M. Oleske   Departments of Health Systems Management and Preventive Medicine, Rush University, Chicago, Illinois 60612.

Epidemiology and the Delivery of Health Care Services: Methods and Applications, edited by Denise M. Oleske. Plenum Press, New York, 1995.

up. Epidemiology can be the pivotal link in assisting providers to align services more effectively to enhance health status. This balance needs to occur both at the point of delivery as well as at the level of public policy.

To represent the application of epidemiology in the new era of the delivery of health care services, the following definitional orientation is offered:

> **Epidemiology is the study of the distribution of health needs, including disease, impairments, disability, injuries, and other health problems in human populations, and factors contributing to their emergence, severity, and consequences. The ultimate goal of epidemiology is to identify the causal factors that could be eliminated or modified to prevent or control adverse health outcomes and apply the knowledge of these to improve the health status of populations.**

A population-based focus in the delivery of health care can influence health status. A model that represents how the orientation may be operationalized is displayed in Fig. 1.1. A discussion of the components of the model follows.

Population Characteristics

Fundamental to the epidemiologic model of health services delivery is an understanding of the characteristics of the population to which services are targeted. Populations considered can be those residing in communities, served by health systems or organizations (e.g., hospitals, companies), those in institutions (e.g., prisons, hospices), or selected for the purpose of conducting special studies. Populations are characterized in terms of trends in size, demographic and social characteristics, and distribution of exposures that could influence

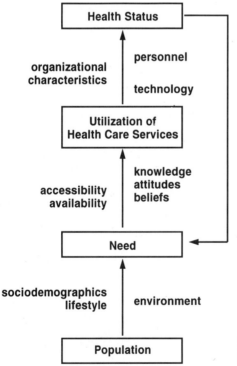

Figure 1.1. Epidemiologic model of the factors influencing health status.

health. The major components that affect trends in population size are birth rate, death rate, and, to a lesser extent, migration. The greatest amount of growth in a population over the short term is usually attributable to the difference between the birth rate and the death rate, whereas over time, migration contributes a major influence to population change. With respect to demographic and social characteristics, attributes of a population known to be related to health events include: age, gender, race, ethnicity, education, employment status, and income. Data from the decennial census provide the basic information on these and other characteristics of populations residing in the community. An Act of Congress delineated the provision for the 1990 census and was codified in Title 13, United States Code. The census provides basic information for all inhabitants of the United States. Administrative data, such as insurance claims files, hospital discharge abstracts, personnel files, and health plan membership files can provide information on populations served by organizations, systems, or institutions (Lauderdale *et al.*, 1993).

Populations may also be characterized in terms of the distribution of exposures or factors that may result in physical, emotional, or psychological harm. Epidemiologic studies can determine which of these exposures are risk factors. A risk factor is a characteristic that is known to be associated with a health-related condition. Risk factors may be personal characteristics, life-style features, or the environment. Epidemiologic measures can be used to characterize the distribution of the risk factors in the population, across geographic areas, and over time. Some characteristics are immutable (e.g., age, gender) and some are potentially modifiable (smoking, air pollution). The profound differences observed in the occurrence of health needs, use of health services, and health status are driven by features of a population. Thus, a knowledge of the population targeted for health services is essential to plan and deliver health care services that optimize health status.

Need for Health Care

Any perceived deviation from societal norms of health may be considered a "need." Health needs may be expressed as a global measure of perceived health, disease, impairments, injuries, psychological/emotional distress, or behaviors that prompt seeking preventive care, health information, or therapeutic intervention. The use of health care services is influenced by the degree of deficits produced by a health need and/or the amount of services required to produce maximum attainable functioning (Steinwachs, 1989).

There are several approaches for quantifying health needs. Inferences can be made from census and vital data (records of births, deaths, marriages, and divorces). A second approach is to measure self-report of perceived level of health, symptoms, diseases, injuries, and impairments. A third measurement of need is withdrawal behavior, such as absentee rates and work-loss days. A fourth approach is to assess the use of nonmedical services, such as nonprescription medications and treatments. A fifth measure is to evaluate levels of utilization of various types of formal health care services, with the assumption that increasing utilization rates reflect increasing levels of need. And, a sixth approach for quantifying need is through clinical measurements of such variables as physical function, blood pressure, cognitive impairment, or cholesterol level.

Where possible, physical measurements of need are desirable, as great variability exists in self-reported needs because of differences among individuals in the perception of needs and physiological and psychological distress caused by them (Mechanic, 1982). The level of need in the population among population subgroups, across geographic areas, and over time may be represented through epidemiologic measures. Figure 1.2 displays the variation in coronary heart disease (CHD) mortality rates across levels of the risk factors, serum cholesterol and

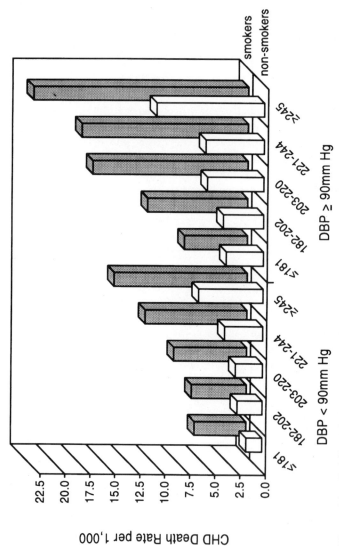

Figure 1.2. Relationship between coronary heart disease (CHD) mortality and cholesterol levels, smoking status and diastolic blood pressure (DBP) in Multiple Risk Factor Intervention Trial (MRFIT) screenees. Data from Stamler et al. (1986).

diastolic blood pressure, in a population of men recruited from the community for an intervention study aimed at reducing premature death from CHD. (Additional discussion on epidemiologic measures may be found in Chapter 3.) The selection of one measure of need over another for use in estimating the utilization of a health service depends on the type of health service under consideration. For example, perceived health status and morbidity are not strongly correlated with utilization of preventive care, whereas factors such as education and income are (Hulka and Wheat, 1985). It must also be kept in mind that some persons have a health care need but do not utilize health care services for reasons described below. Furthermore, some persons utilize health care services despite a lack of identified health care needs.

Utilization of Health Care Services

A considerable literature exists demonstrating that need influences utilization (Hulka and Wheat, 1985). In theory, regardless of the measure of need, utilization rates should vary with need, with the highest levels of need associated with the highest levels of utilization. Figure 1.3 illustrates this concept, showing that lower levels of perceived health are associated with increasing days of restricted activity, increasing physician contacts, and increasing hospital days. Utilization is influenced by an individual's attributes, age, gender, race, and poverty status as well as knowledge, attitudes, and beliefs regarding the efficacy of health services (Wissow *et al.*, 1988; Becker *et al.*, 1977). For example, knowledge of symptoms, their seriousness, and knowledge of a procedure being available are known to be positively associated with utilization of health care services. Beliefs about the curability of a condition may impede or promote the use of early detection. Attitudes are particularly important regarding influencing the action an individual takes regarding the utilization of health care if a symptom is not present. In addition, utilization is mitigated by accessibility and availability of services. Accessibility is the proportion or number of a population that use a service or facility given certain barriers that may be physical (distance, wheelchair access), economic (premium, fee charged), cultural (language barriers), or aspects of the health care system (waiting time for an appointment). Accessibility can be estimated from self-reports by the population on: the use of medical services for prevention and screening (percentage of the population having blood pressure checks, measles vaccine), use of treatment services, and physical barriers (e.g.,

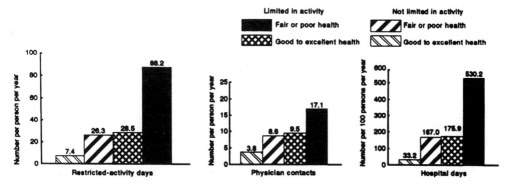

Figure 1.3. Relationship of perceived health status and limitation of activity, physician contacts, and short-stay hospital days, United States, 1985–1988. Unknown health status is excluded in calculating rates. Source: Ries and Brown (1991).

waiting time for an appointment). Availability is the ratio between the population of an administrative or geographic unit and the health facilities, personnel, and technology to support the delivery of health care. Greater utilization occurs with greater availability of resources.

Utilization of services does not necessarily mean that health needs are addressed or that utilization is appropriate. Variations in physician practice styles and intensity in the use of medical resources and technology exist across systems of care and geographic areas independent of health care needs (Every *et al.*, 1993; Greenfield *et al.*, 1992). Moreover, utilization of health care services does not always lead to improved health status. The appropriateness of utilization must also be considered. The goal of the health care manager should be to identify the best or most appropriate match between health needs and resource utilization within a specific population.

Health Status of Populations Served

Health is the optimal balance among physical, mental, and social functioning (WHO, 1948). A component of health status assessed after an intervention may also be referred to as a health outcome. Health status can be quantified with proxy measures (such as mortality or morbidity rates), determined by a health care provider, or be self-reported (see Chapter 2). The method used to measure and classify health status of populations depends on the nature of the health need, the goal of the assessment (e.g., to evaluate populations with or without interventions, with interventions requiring more detailed assessment), the validity and reliability of the measure, and the scope of the evaluation (international, national, local, or provider-specific). (More discussion of measurement issues may be found in Chapter 2.) International or other across-geographic-area comparisons of health status may be performed using the infant mortality rate (the number of deaths under 1 year of age per 1000 live births) and the life expectancy (the average number of years that an individual is expected to live assuming current mortality rates continue to apply) because of the universality of recording deaths among countries. Infant mortality is felt to be the most sensitive indicator for evaluating the health status of populations for short-term interventions such as immunization or prenatal care programs. Life expectancy is the preferred indicator of health status for long-term interventions, for interventions evaluating the availability of medical intervention, or for changes in the economic conditions. With the appropriate and timely use of health services, health status should be improved. Lack of achievement of optimal health status after health services use results in unmet needs and further utilization of health care services. For example, Steinwachs (1989) found that needs in the elderly not met during hospitalization were associated with high rates of hospital readmission. Epidemiologic measures such as unscheduled hospital readmission rates and postservice morbidity and mortality rates are commonly used to assess success or failure of achieving an optimal state of health following utilization of health care services.

Brief History of the Application of Epidemiology in the Delivery of Personal Health Services in the United States

The idea of applying epidemiologic methods to decision making in the delivery of personal health care services to populations in the United States is not new and has its origins in the development of public health. Selected key developments and studies are presented. One of the first individuals in the United States known to use epidemiologic measures in assessing the health status of a population was Lemuel Shattuck, a statistician. Shattuck collected morbidity and mortality data on the Massachusetts population as a means for drawing attention to variation in rates among geographic areas. Since the highest rates were found in urban areas, aspects of the environment, namely the unsanitary conditions created by population density, were believed to be responsible. Shattuck's 1850 *Report of the Massachusetts Sanitary Commission* included recommendations for the continued collection of data on health conditions and for the supervision of water supplies and waste disposal by the state. Using similar types of data-collection strategies and analyses, reports were prepared in other states that ultimately served as the justification for many public health agencies that emerged, with the first being the New York City Health Department in 1866 (Institute of Medicine, 1988).

In the late 1800s, the recognition that a biological organism can cause disease was advanced by discoveries made by Louis Pasteur (anthrax) and Robert Koch (the tubercle bacillus). Shortly thereafter, several other diseases were identified as originating from biological agents including cholera, diphtheria, typhoid, rabies, and yellow fever. From this knowledge, the means of producing immunity to these and other diseases was achieved through the development of vaccines. Simultaneous with this was the recognition that persons who were "healthier" and had clean environments suffered less morbidity and mortality than "slovenly" persons. The development of vaccines and the recognition that good personal hygiene and health status lowered the likelihood of outbreaks of infection provided the impetus for the addition of population-based personal health services to the responsibilities of public health agencies.

The documentation of disease was recognized as an important means of combating morbidity and mortality in populations served by public health agencies. In fact, some states had laws requiring the routine collection of data for a number of communicable diseases. Such data enabled identification of subgroups of the population with the greatest frequency of disease and the establishment of nearby clinics for the purpose of providing vaccines and treatments. The required reporting of these diseases also facilitated follow-up and health education of affected individuals and their contacts by public health nurses. In addition, the epidemiologic data maintained by local health departments could be used to evaluate community-based health initiatives. Winslow (1934) details how a demonstration program funded by the Milbank Memorial Fund to improve the health status of Syracuse, New York was evaluated using epidemiologic measures. The epidemiologic measures indicated that communicable diseases represented the most immediate needs of the community. Of the demonstration program components, almost all were directed toward personal care services such as increasing immunization activity for diphtheria and increasing the number of sessions and personnel for tuberculosis clinics. At the end of the demonstration period, the success of the program was documented by showing how the death rates for tuberculosis, other communicable diseases, and other conditions dramatically decreased.

The use of epidemiologic methods for planning and evaluation of health care services in other than public health agencies lagged, but it did finally emerge, with the earliest applications relying solely on descriptive epidemiologic measures. In 1952, Lembcke compared appendectomy rates among hospitals to the appendectomy death rates in their communities. Not finding any relationship between the rates of appendectomy in various hospital service areas and the death rates from appendicitis, he raised a question regarding the necessity of some of the procedures. Donabedian in 1973 described how epidemiologic measures in the form of rates could be used to assess the health needs of populations served by hospitals and to project resources required based upon those needs. In that same year, Wennberg and Gittelsohn demonstrated how highly variable health care resource utilization rates were and reported that this variability did not seem to relate to population need as measured by the proportion of the population in an area 65 years of age and over. This study was the seminal piece in the epidemiology of health care quality, introducing the concept that a high degree of variability in rates may signal inappropriate use of services.

Beginning in the mid-1970s, epidemiologic analytic studies of various aspects of the delivery of health care services began emerging. Analytic studies elucidate the understanding of the relationship between causes (exposures or interventions) and outcomes. (Analytic studies are discussed in detail in Chapter 5.) One of the earliest applications was in the evaluation of a comprehensive program for preventing rheumatic fever. In that study, Gordis (1973) compared the incidence rates for hospitalization for acute rheumatic fever between those populations eligible for comprehensive care programs and those who were not eligible. The eligibility for various programs was defined by census tract; hence, these geographic units served as the basis for defining the populations studied. The incidence rate of rheumatic fever was found to decrease significantly over time in areas where residents were eligible for the programs, whereas the rates in those areas not served by the programs increased. Laurence Branch was a leader in utilizing longitudinal study designs in evaluating the determinants of utilization of health care services in elderly persons. In particular, predictors of long-term care (LTC) institutionalization were investigated. Since long-term care is extremely expensive, the identification of potentially modifiable factors associated with LTC utilization can pose a great personal and societal savings. Among the findings were that living alone, physical disability, and mental/emotional disability were associated with an increased risk of LTC institution-alization (Branch and Jette, 1982; Branch, 1984).

During the 1970s, epidemiologic studies became more prominent in evaluating the effec-tiveness of health services with health promotion and screening targets of the early efforts. Population-based efforts initiated to evaluate the effectiveness of cardiovascular disease included the Stanford Heart Disease Prevention Program, the Minnesota Heart Health Pro-gram, and the Stanford Five-City Project (Maccoby et al., 1977; Farquhar et al., 1985; Black-burn et al., 1985). The objectives of these programs were varied, but all included strategies to increase participants' knowledge of risk factors for cardiovascular disease, in particular dietary modifications. Shapiro (1977) reported the value of periodic screening services for reducing breast cancer mortality based upon a randomized trial. In terms of the effectiveness of assessing the full range of services, Brook et al. (1983) examined the impact of options for health insurance premium payments upon health status. Health status was evaluated in terms of physical functioning, role functioning, mental health, social contacts, health perceptions and the risk of dying.

Until recently, an epidemiologic orientation to the delivery of health care services on a day-to-day basis outside the public sector or outside formal research and evaluation has not been widespread. One reason is that the question of "Who should be the population served?" has been a difficult question for private sector providers to address. In addition, resources were not available for the timely collection of information that would enable managers to monitor and characterize population exposures and health status using epidemiologic methods.

Reasons for Applying Epidemiology in Health Services Management

There are several reasons why it is essential that all health care managers have a basic knowledge of epidemiologic concepts and methods. These are: (1) the increasing size of populations served by health care providers, (2) the need to understand the characteristics and health status of these populations more precisely for planning services, (3) the need to understand the consequences of health care problems, (4) increasing evidence of the impact of the health care system and organizational characteristics upon the health status of persons served, (5) the necessity of monitoring health system, organizational, and program performance, (6) the continuous need to restructure the health care system, organization, and its processes to fit the changing environment, and (7) the development and evaluation of public policy affecting health care delivery. An explanation of the significance of each of these reasons follows.

Trends in Service Population Size

The primary role of the health care administrator is to manage resources with the goal of enhancing the health status of populations served. This function requires managers to have a population-based perspective and to be cognizant of trends affecting population size. The manager must understand the factors that influence population change in order to project resource needs of populations targeted for services. These factors include those resulting from sociodemographic changes (birth rate, death rate, and migration) and those caused by changes in the structure of the health care system (Table 1.1). An examination of trends in the United States reveals a substantial increase in the overall size of the population (Fig. 1.4), which is attributable to continued declines in mortality rates in all age groups, continued immigration into the country, and recent increases in the birth rate in certain age groups of women (USDHHS, 1991a). Other factors affect the size of a population to be served, such as the closure of inner-city and rural hospitals and the shifts of the population served by these facilities to facilities elsewhere. Another factor is implementation of strategic initiatives by health care providers. Vertical integration of organizations (e.g., an academic medical center aligns itself with community hospitals associated with an HMO), the formation of multihospital systems (e.g., Hospital Corporation of America), collaboration among providers and insurers (e.g., Uni-Health American and California Blue Shield), and joint ventures between providers and vendors (e.g., Caremark, Inc.) are examples of these initiatives. Larger populations also result from such trends as the emergence of health care purchasing coalitions of small businesses. The trend in increasing service population size will continue as it is viewed as consistent with achievement of cost-efficient care as a result of economies of scale. The substantial gains in enrollment in health maintenance organizations illustrates this

Table 1.1. Factors Affecting the Size of the Population Served by Health Care Systems

Birth rate
Mortality rate
Migration
Facility closures
Horizontal integration of organizations (e.g., affiliations, joint ventures)
Vertical integration of organizations (primary, secondary, and tertiary care)
Purchasing coalitions
New service configurations (provider–vendor; provider–insurer)

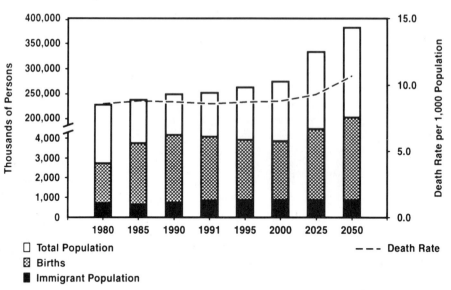

Figure 1.4. Components of population change, 1980–1991, and projections, 1995–2050, selected years, United States. Source: U.S. Department of Commerce (1993).

trend (Fig. 1.5). Thus, today the term population-based may be viewed as extending to large populations served by a health care system in which epidemiologic studies may be conducted.

Service Population Characteristics

As described earlier, a careful understanding of the characteristics of the populations served is essential. The population characteristics that must be taken into account when planning health services are demographic features and the distribution of risk factors, and health status. Epidemiologic measures enable the distribution of health needs in a population to be characterized in terms of "Who is affected?" "When?" and "Where?" For example, infectious disease is a priority concern in populations with a large percentage of individuals 5 years of age and under. The provision of immunization services would be an appropriate priority response. Mortality from heart disease is highest in those aged 65 years and over. Organizations within a community with a large proportion of elderly persons should provide services to address this health problem. Knowledge of service population characteristics not only help managers determine the types of services needed, but also the amount. An estimate of the frequency of occurrence of a particular condition in a population enables the projection of the amount of resources that would have to be expended. For example, diabetics have high rates of hospital utilization and experience a high incidence of various comorbidities such as myocardial infarction and diabetic retinopathy. Hospital rates for these comorbidities are increasing (Wetterhall *et al.*, 1992). Health maintenance organizations or other capitated programs that have a high proportion of diabetics may find it cost-effective to initiate screening programs to identify diabetics. Once identified, diabetics could be targeted for intense education and follow-up to optimize management of the diabetes and to avoid complications such as diabetic retinopathy and prevent unnecessary hospitalization. Another indicator of the consumption of health care resource is the proportion of smokers. Smokers,

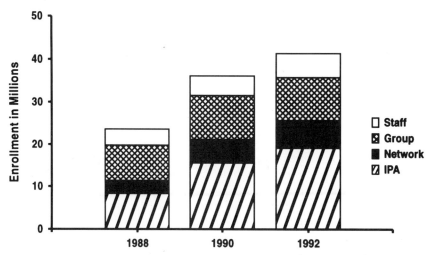

Figure 1.5.   Trends in enrollment in managed care plans. Source: Group Health Association of America (1991, 1993).

too, have a higher utilization of health care services than nonsmokers (Vogt and Schweitzer, 1985). Knowledge of the prevalence of risk factors may be applied in negotiating provider contracts. Epidemiologic information allows the manager to anticipate the resources to meet population needs, and the risks that may be incurred if the needs are not met may also be estimated. This information also allows managers to distribute resources and to assess the impact of developing affiliation and joint-venture agreements.

Understanding the Consequences of Health Problems

Risk factors, which are attributes or exposures that increase the chance of the occurrence of an outcome, are not known for many conditions. Even when they are known, individuals may or may not be able to take measures to avoid these factors, thereby reducing the likelihood of health problems arising. Thus, health care services must be available to address the resultant health problems and manage the consequences. Epidemiologic methods help identify prognostic factors, which are aspects of the disease or the individual from which the probability of recovery (or death) can be determined. To illustrate how knowledge of the consequences of health problems is useful in the delivery of health services, the problem of injuries from falls is described. Fall injuries are a major source of morbidity and mortality in the elderly (USDHHS, 1991a, b). However, limited information is available on potentially modifiable risk factors for which preventive interventions could be implemented on a wide scale to reduce significantly the occurrence of these injuries. Epidemiology can be used to investigate the causes of falls, but until these are well known, the identification of those factors that could affect the occurrence of consequences is important. In the case of fall injuries, those consequences frequently are hospitalization, nursing home placement, disability, or death (Alexander *et al.*, 1992). Epidemiology can also aid in understanding the factors that influence the course of hospitalization for those injured patients. Through survival analysis (see Chapter 5), an epidemiologic method, the onset of infection while hospitalized markedly increases the mortality in these persons (Myers *et al.*, 1991). The implications of this finding are that early diagnosis and treatment of infection may result in a more favorable survival.

Understanding the Relationship between Health System Characteristics and the Health Status of Populations Served

There is a growing body of literature indicating that features of a health system, its *organization*, its *personnel*, its *available technology*, and *programmatic efforts* have often been linked to changes in the health status of populations served, even when medical conditions and therapeutic regimes of the patients are considered. In drawing an analogy to classical epidemiology, these organizational features may be characterized as "risk factors." Examples of the impact of organizational features upon health status are plentiful. An **organization** is characterized by its volume, ownership (e.g., governmental, for-profit, not-for-profit), configuration (e.g., affiliation, system member), other features such as stay (e.g., outpatient, short-term stay, long-term care), and other factors such as number and types of accreditation and breadth of services (e.g., wellness programs, home care). The outcomes for females having hospital newborn deliveries differs according to organizational characteristics. Lower cesarean section rates are observed in hospitals that are members of the Council of Teaching Hospitals even when the characteristics of women delivering are taken into consideration (Oleske *et al.*, 1991).

Personnel considerations of an organization pertain to the number of staff, their qualifications and experience and other factors of manpower (e.g., age, volume, skills). The personnel associated with an organization can have a substantial affect on the health status of patients served. For example, hospitals with a higher percentage of physicians who are board-certified specialists and hospitals with a higher percentage of RNs on their nursing staff have a lower patient mortality (Hartz *et al.*, 1989). A low nurse–patient ratio in nursing homes has been linked to an increased likelihood of falls, medication errors, and other adverse outcomes (Spector and Takada, 1991).

The **technology** of an organization includes devices, procedures, and pharmaceuticals available to diagnose and treat populations served. The availability of technology generally improves the outcome of the care provided. For example, the technology of neonatal intensive care directly benefits select high-risk pregnancies and neonates, including those who are preterm or low-birth-weight or born to mothers with diabetes mellitus (Svenningsen, 1992). Mammography can be used for the early detection of breast cancer. If the cancer is identified in an early stage, the likelihood of death and high medical expenditures associated with the treatment of more advanced disease is reduced. For this reason, the prevalence of mammography screening in women served by health plans is a marker of organizational quality (NCQA, 1993). Managers can also use epidemiology to assess if the use of a particular technology is associated with any risks. Epidemiologic data are also useful in cost-benefit/cost-effectiveness evaluations of technology.

Programmatic efforts represent what services are provided, how these are organized, or the means by which they are delivered. Programmatic efforts include quality assurance programs, total quality management programs, and clinical guidelines. An example of a programmatic effort is an inpatient team management of geriatric patients. Such a program has been found to be associated with improvement in functional status of elderly persons as compared to those receiving routine care (Rubenstein *et al.*, 1984). Clinical management guidelines and provider feedback have been found to be associated with a decreased likelihood of birth by cesarean section (Myers and Gleicher, 1988). Although the strength of the association between organizational features and patient outcomes is of a lesser magnitude than demographic, social, and clinical factors, such associations continue to be discerned in most studies.

Monitoring Health Care Systems, Organizations, and Program Performance

The increased necessity for the continuous monitoring of the health care system, organization, and program line performance is another reason for the use of epidemiology in management practice. The impetus for monitoring performance has been stimulated by the total quality management/continuous quality improvement movement and is formalized as part of various accreditation standards. The quality principles are espoused under the assumption that performance monitoring is one type of quality initiative and, as such, may be a means of improving organizational effectiveness and efficiency in the use of resources (e.g., personnel, supplies, equipment, etc.). For health care managers, the impact of these initiatives upon patients is the ultimate concern. Performance can be assessed through the use of epidemiologic measures or by means of analytic studies. (Subsequent chapters by Clement *et al.* and Sinioris and Najafi provide further discussion of these topics.)

Modifying Structure and Processes to Respond to Environmental Change

In addition to considering the internal environment of an organization, epidemiology enables managers to understand how forces external to the organization can affect the organization and delivery of care. A classic example of how hospitals were compelled to change their processes occurred with the introduction of the Prospective Payment System (PPS) in 1983 (Svahn and Ross, 1983). The PPS introduced reimbursement for treating Medicare patients on the basis of a single price per patient. The price was determined by the diagnostic-related group (DRG) in which the patient fell. The DRG is based upon the patient's clinical diagnosis, surgical procedures performed, age, and comorbidities present. The new method of payment stimulated the restructuring of hospital processes. Some of the changes included the introduction of utilization review programs and more prehospitalization (outpatient) testing. The major response by hospitals to the introduction of PPS was to reduce the length of stay as a means or providing services within a fixed price per case. Cases with lengths of stay longer than what could be accommodated by a fixed price created losses for the institution. Epidemiology provides a framework for examining excess variability and causes of variability that could create losses to a health care system receiving capitated payment for the provision of services to a population. For example, an epidemiologic investigation of delays in a teaching hospital found that the most frequent cause of an extended length of stay was difficulty in scheduling tests (Selker *et al.*, 1989). At the service delivery level, epidemiology can also be used to assess the effects of restructuring. For example, with the increasing shortages in allied health professions, particularly in rural areas of the country, cross-training of health care workers will become more common. The impact of this upon patient health status can be assessed with epidemiologic methods.

Formulation and Evaluation of Public Policy Affecting the Delivery of Health Care Services

Epidemiologic data and methods are also critical for the development and assessment of public policy affecting the delivery of health care services. Epidemiologic data consisting of cancer incidence, mortality, and survival rates are collected by the Surveillance, Epidemiology, and End Results (SEER) Program of the National Cancer Institute to assess the impact of cancer in the general population. Specifically, these data provide information on changes over time in the extent of disease at diagnosis and survival associated with various forms of therapy.

The SEER data are useful as well for developing studies to identify factors amenable to cancer control intervention (Gloeckler-Ries *et al.*, 1991). Extensive use of epidemiologic data has been incorporated into defining priorities and directions for national injury control efforts, in particular data from death certificates, hospital discharge abstracts, and from special surveys of emergency departments (U.S. Department of Health and Human Services, 1991b; McCaig, 1994; Fingerhut, 1993). These data have also been used to evaluate the impact of policies such as mandatory seat belt usage and minimum-drinking-age laws (Campbell and Campbell, 1988; Zador *et al.*, 1989). The End-Stage Renal Disease (ESRD) Program is an example of a public policy that did not utilize epidemiologic data in planning. Prior to the implementation of ESRD, estimates of future utilization of dialysis and transplant services were based upon current recipients of those services. Those individuals were predominantly white, males, educated, and employed. When the ESRD Program extended Medicare coverage to all persons under age 65 with end-stage renal disease, the demographic characteristics of the recipients paralleled that of the general population. And, the incidence of those on treatment doubled within a few years. The result was an extraordinary expenditure of resources, with ESRD patients representing 0.25% of the Medicare patients and approximately 10% of the Medicare Part B budget (Rubin, 1984). This could have been anticipated, and perhaps the extent and nature of coverage modified if population-based data had been used in planning prior to the implementation of the program. As new national efforts are introduced, epidemiologic methods can also be used to assess some of the other impending changes in health care delivery that would influence organizational restructuring. Epidemiology will be used to determine if the health status of populations served will improve in a new configuration of health care delivery. As local and national health care systems change in response to external pressures, epidemiologic methods will be employed to assess the responsiveness of organizations to those changes in terms of meeting the needs of populations served.

Feasibility of Using Epidemiology in Planning and Evaluating Health Care Services

The use of epidemiology in management decision making associated with the provision of therapeutic services is in its infancy, and many challenges are inherent in this situation. The major challenges are how to classify components of the health system and how to obtain relevant information in a timely manner.

Classification is particularly a problem in evaluating the impact of components of a health care system or organization. Problems arise in classifying service units and service systems. An example of difficulties associated with classification of service units is the case of intensive care units (ICUs): ICUs can be classified according to service area (e.g., medical, surgical), specialty (e.g., cardiac, burn unit), intensity of services (e.g., high dependency, subacute, step-down), or age group of patient (e.g., neonatal, pediatric, adult). The issue of classification of health service systems will become more important as a greater understanding is gained of how organizations could be reconfigured to serve larger populations more efficiently and effectively. For example, growing concern over the effect on the health status of populations in managed-care systems is emerging. Studies currently show no difference in outcomes between managed care and fee-for-service care for different patient populations (Carlisle *et al.*, 1992; Goldfarb *et al.*, 1991). However, differences in the definition of managed care render this body of research difficult to interpret. Managed care can be an organization such as a health maintenance organization, a group of providers providing discounted services as necessary to persons from a group (a PPO) or individual providers responsible for all the nonspecialty care of a defined population for a capitated annual amount.

Lack of uniformity in classifying health service units gives rise to difficulty in the precise evaluation of the outcome of patients served. For example, the admission of less acutely ill patients to an ICU could result in more favorable patient outcomes in implying that treatment at a particular health care provider is more advantageous when in fact the outcomes may largely result from differing patient characteristics (Dragsted and Qvist, 1992). With a more precise definition of health service units, a more precise estimate of organizational "risk factors" can be made. Without more precise classification of service units, it is difficult for a manager to interpret the effectiveness of the units of an organization and to understand the biases associated with selection into one health service unit versus another.

A second challenge lies in determining the epidemiologic measures that most appropriately represent the health status. In community-dwelling persons, mortality rates are a common surrogate measure of health status. Mortality rates are also used as measures of effectiveness of some health service units where the mortality is expected to be high, for example, in ICUs. The measures of mortality typically used to assess the immediate effect of health services are called "in-hospital mortality" or "case-fatality" rates. However, mortality rates alone may be insufficient as measures of provider impact on health status as smaller volume service units may have fewer deaths, thereby rendering the mortality rates unreliable. Patient surveys are also used to evaluate health status as a result of health care services, but the logistics of administering these may be problematic and may not be appropriate for certain populations.

Summary

To improve health status, an understanding of the population characteristics is essential. Through an epidemiologic framework, we can assess how and why health care needs are distributed throughout a population and evaluate the use and efficacy of interventions. Thus, to improve the health status of a population, one needs to understand the population characteristics, the distribution and level of need, factors affecting the use of health care services, and the implications upon the system if the desired level of health status is not achieved. In Chapters 2 and 3, issues and methods for measuring need and health are discussed. Subsequent chapters illustrate how analytic studies can be used to evaluate health care programs and policies.

Case Studies

Case Study No. 1
Service Population of an Urban Public Hospital

Cook County Hospital (CCH) is a large tertiary-care public hospital with medical school affiliations located on the near west side of the city of Chicago. It has 918 licensed beds. The inpatient population is 72% African-American, and 82% of patients are either covered by Medicaid or have no insurance. The average total number of patient days is 246,000, with an average length of stay of 6.9 days. The national average length of hospital stay for a comparable period was 6.2 days. Of approximately 35,000 discharges per year, an assessment of the reasons for hospitalization at CCH found that many of them might have been avoided if adequate primary care were available in the community. The top ten preventable types of hospitalization found were for: asthma, bacterial pneumonia, angina, kidney/urinary

infection, congestive heart failure, dehydration, gastroenteritis, diabetic complications, grand mal epi-
lepsy, and chronic lung disease. On a given day, 435 patients present to the emergency room for care.
According to triage figures from the emergency room, 14% of the patients are nonurgent, and 0.04% are
dead on arrival. The County Board began discussions regarding two issues. The first concerned how to
reduce the use of CCH for episodes of care that could be better handled in other than a tertiary-care
facility. The second issue was whether the average length of stay could be reduced if adequate patient
follow-up was provided. One of the solutions implemented was the purchase of a satellite community
hospital with a large primary-care outpatient clinic four miles south of CCH. After 1 year of operation of
the satellite community hospital, neither the emergency room volume nor the rates of potentially
avoidable hospitalization at CCH had decreased. The average length of hospital stay remained the same.

Q.1. Why did the opening of the new facility not have an impact on the patient volume at CCH?

Q.2. Why was there no reduction in the hospital length of stay at CCH?

Case Study No. 2
Rural Populations and Public Health Services

Alexander County is located in southern Illinois. During the period 1920 to 1950, the coal-mining
industry prospered in its hilly terrain. Since that time, the mines have closed, and a few small farms are
the mainstay of agricultural activity, the only remaining industry of any size. Local taxes are insufficient
to support a county health department. No new industry growth is expected. Thus, the State Health
Department must subsidize public health activities in that area. Due to budget cuts in the State Health
Department, the nature and amount of public health activities are being reexamined. Data from the Office
of Vital Statistics for Coles County are as follows:

Total population: 1950, 20,316; 1970, 11,977; 1980, 12,264; 1990, 11,272
Projected population: 2010, 11,126; 2020, 11,894
Number of births: 1984, 227; 1986, 204; 1988, 175
Number of deaths: 1984, 165; 1986, 160; 1988, 172

Q.1. Based upon this preliminary assessment, what initial course of action should the state consider?

Q.2. What other data should be compiled?

Case Study No. 3
Effectiveness of Comprehensive-Care Programs in Preventing Rheumatic Fever

Four comprehensive-care programs were introduced in Baltimore, Maryland. Three were Children
and Youth programs, two of which were operated by a medical school and one a community hospital. The
other was sponsored by the Office of Economic Opportunity and operated by a community hospital. The
census tract defined the eligibility for a particular program. The populations served by these programs
were located in the inner city and were predominantly black. To measure the effectiveness of the
programs, the change in the incidence rates of hospitalizations for first attacks of rheumatic fever was
evaluated by Gordis (1973). Three populations were selected as comparison groups: Group 1—adjacent
census tracts, Group 2—black populations in nonadjacent tracts, and Group 3—all census tracts not
eligible for comprehensive care whose population were over 90% black in 1970. Only data for black

children ages 5 to 14 were considered in the evaluation. The evaluation compared the annual incidence of hospitalizations for first attacks of rheumatic fever in the study areas prior to the inception of the programs and after they were fully operational. The incidence rate declined 60.4% in the census tracts in which the population was eligible for the comprehensive-care programs and increased by 27.0% in the combined noneligible tracts that had populations more than 90% black.

Q.1. Why were comparison populations selected on the basis of census tracts?

Q.2. Why was hospitalization for first attacks of rheumatic fever chosen as the measure of health status by which to evaluate program effectiveness in this population?

Q.3. What alternative reasons could explain why the incidence rate of hospitalized cases of rheumatic fever decreased in the census tracts served by the comprehensive care programs?

References

Alexander, B. H., Rivara, F. P., and Wolf, M. E., 1992, The cost and frequency of hospitalization for fall-related injuries in older adults, *Am. J. Public Health* **82:**1020–1023.

Becker, M. H., Haefner, D. P., Kasl, S. V., Kirscht, J. P., Maiman, L. A., and Rosenstock, I. M., 1977, Selected psychosocial models and correlates of individual health-related behaviors, *Med. Care* **15:**27–46.

Blackburn, H., Grimm, R., Luepker, R. V., and Mittelmark, M., 1985, The primary prevention of high blood pressure: A population approach, *Prev. Med.* **14:**466–481.

Branch, L. G., 1984, Relative risk rates of nonmedical predictors of institutional care among elderly persons, *Compr. Ther.* **10:**33–40.

Branch, L. G., and Jette, A. M., 1982, A prospective study of long-term care institutionalization among the aged, *Am. J. Public Health* **72:**1373–1379.

Brook, R. H., Ware, J. E., and Rogers, W. H., 1983, Does free care improve adults' health? *N. Engl. J. Med.* **309:**1426–1434.

Bureau of the Census, 1993, *Population Profile of the U.S. Current Population Reports, Series P-23 185*, Washington, U.S. Government Printing Office, Washington, DC.

Campbell, B. J., and Campbell, F. A., 1988, Injury reduction and belt use associated with occupant restraint laws, in *Preventing Automobile Injury: New Findings from Evaluation Research* (J. D. Graham, ed.), pp. 24–50, Dover, MA.

Carlisle, D. M., Siu, A. L., Keeler, E. B., McGlynn, E. A., Kahn, K. L., Rubenstein, L. V., and Brook, R. H., 1992, HMO vs. fee-for-service care of older persons with acute myocardial infarction, *Am. J. Public Health* **82:**1626–1630.

Donabedian, A., 1973, *Aspects of Medical Care Administration: Specifying Requirements for Health Care*, Harvard University Press, Cambridge.

Drafsted, L., and Qvist, J., 1992, Epidemiology of intensive care, *Int. J. Technol. Assess. Health Care* **8:**395–407.

Every, N. R., Larson, E. B., Litwin, P. E., Maynard, C., Fihn, S. D., Eisenberg, M. S., Hallstrom, A. P., Martin, J. S., and Weaver, W. D., for the Myocardial Infarction Triage and Intervention Project Investigators, 1993, The association between on-site cardiac catheterization facilities and the use of coronary angiography after acute myocardial infarction, *N. Engl. J. Med.* **329:**546–551.

Farquhar, J. W., Fortmann, S. P., Maccoby, N., Haskell, W. L., Williams, P. T., Flora, J. A., Taylor, C. B., Brown, B. W. Jr., Solomon, D. S., and Halley, S. B., 1985, The Stanford Five-City Project: Design and Methods, *Am. J. Epidemiol.* **122:**323–334.

Fingerhut, L. A., 1993, *Firearm Mortality among Children, Youth, and Young Adults 1–34 Years of Age, Trends and Current Status: United States, 1985–90. Advance Data from Vital and Health Statistics*, No. 231, National Center for Health Statistics, Hyattsville, MD.

Gloeckler-Ries, L. A., Hankey, B. F., Miller, B. A., Hartman, A. M., and Edwards, B. K., 1991, *Cancer Statistics Review, 1973–1988*, NIH Pub. No. 91-2789, National Institutes of Health, Bethesda, MD.

Goldfarb, N., Hillman, A. L., Eisenberg, J., Kelley, J., Cohen, A., and Dellheim, M., 1991, Impact of a mandatory medicaid care management program on prenatal care and birth outcomes, *Med. Care* **29:**64–71.

Gordis, L., 1973, Effectiveness of comprehensive-care programs in preventing rheumatic fever, *N. Engl. J. Med.* **289:**331–335.

Greenfield, S., Nelson, E., Zubkoff, M., Manning, W., Rogers, W., Kravitz, R. L., Keller, A., Tarlor, A. R., and Ware, J. E. Jr., 1993, Variations in resource utilization among medical specialties and systems of care. Results from the medical outcomes study, *JAMA* **267:**1624–1630.

Group Health Association of America, 1991, *Patterns in HMO Enrollment*, GHAA, Washington, DC.

Group Health Association of America, 1993, *Patterns in HMO Enrollment*, GHAA, Washington, DC.

Hulka, B. S., and Wheat, J. R., 1985, Patterns of utilization: The patient perspective, *Med. Care* **23:**438–460.

Hartz, A. J., Krakauer, H., Kuhn, E. M., Young, M., Jacobsen, S. J., Gay, G., Muenz, L., Katzoff, M., Bailey, R. C., and Rimm, A. A., 1989, Hospital characteristics and mortality rates, *N. Engl. J. Med.* **321:**1720–1725.

Institute of Medicine (U.S.), Committee for the Study of the Future of Public Health, 1992, *The Future of Public Health*, National Academy Press, Washington, DC.

Last, J. M., 1988, *A Dictionary of Epidemiology*, Oxford University Press, New York.

Lauderdale, D. S., Furner, S. E., Miles, T. P., and Goldberg, J., 1993, Epidemiologic uses of Medicare data, *Epidemiol. Rev.* **15:**319–327.

Leape, L. L., Park, R. E., Solomon, D. H., Chassin, M. R., Kosecoff, J., and Brook, R. H., 1990, Does inappropriate use explain small-area variations in the use of health care services? *JAMA* **263:**669–672.

Lembcke, P. A., 1952, Measuring the quality of medical care through vital statistics based on hospital services areas: 1. comparative study of appendectomy rates, *Am. J. Public Health* **42:**276–286.

Luft, H. S., Garnick, D. W., Mark, D. H., and McPhee, S. J., 1990, *Hospital Volume, Physician Volume, and Patient Outcomes*, Health Administration Press Perspectives, Ann Arbor, MI.

Maccoby, N., Farquhar, J. W., Wood, P. D., and Alexander, J., 1977, Reducing the risk of cardiovascular disease: Effects of a community-based campaign on knowledge and behavior, *J. Commun. Health* **3:**100–114.

McCraig, L. F., 1994, *National Hospital Ambulatory Medical Care Survey: 1992 Emergency Department Summary, Advance Data from Vital and Health Statistics*, No. 245, National Center for Health Statistics, Hyattsville, MD.

Mechanic, D., 1982, The epidemiology of illness behavior and its relationship to physical and psychological distress, in *Symptoms, Illness Behavior, and Help-Seeking* (D. Mechanic, ed.), pp. 1–24, Prodist, New York, NY.

Myers, A. H., Robinson, E. G., Van Natta, M. L., Michelson, J. D., Collins, K., and Baker, S. P., 1991, Hip fractures among the elderly: Factors associated with in-hospital mortality, *Am. J. Epidemiol.* **143:**1128–1137.

Myers, S. A., and Gleicher, N., 1988, A successful program to lower cesarean-section rates, *N. Engl. J. Med.* **319:**1511–1516.

National Committee for Quality Assurance, 1993, *Health Plan Employer Data and Information Set and Users Manual, Version 2.0.* NCQA, Washington, DC.

Oleske, D. M., Glandon, G. L., Giacomelli, G., and Hohmann, S., 1991, The cesarean birth rate: Influence of hospital teaching status, *Health Serv. Res.* **23:**325–337.

Ries, P., and Brown, S., 1991, *Disability and Health: Characteristics of Persons by Limitation of Activity and Assessed Health Status, United States, 1984–88. Advance Data from Vital and Health Statistics*, No. 197, National Center for Health Statistics, Hyattsville, MD.

Rubenstein, L. Z., Josephson, K. R., Wieland, G, D., English, P. A., Sayre, J. A., and Kane, R. L., 1984, Effectiveness of a geriatric evaluation unit, *N. Engl. J. Med.* **311:**1664–1670.

Rubin, R. J., 1984, Epidemiology of end stage renal disease and implications for public policy, *Public Health Rep.* **99:**492–498.

Selker, H. P., Beshansky, J. R., Pauker, S. G., and Kassirer, J. P., 1989, The epidemiology of delays in a teaching hospital, *Med. Care.* **27:**112–129.

Shapiro, S., 1977, Evidence on screening for breast cancer from a randomized trial, *Cancer* **39**(Suppl. 6):2772–2782.

Spector, W. D., and Takada, H., 1991, Characteristics of nursing homes that affect resident outcomes, *J. Aging and Health* **30:**427–454

Stamler, J., Wentworth, D., and Neaton, J. D., 1986, Is relationship between serum cholesterol and risk of premature death from coronary heart disease continuous and graded? *JAMA* **256:**2823–2828.

Steinwachs, D. M., 1989, Application of health status assessment measures in policy research, *Med. Care* **27:** S12–S26.

Svan J. A., and Ross, M., 1983, Social Security amendments of 1983: Legislative history and summary of provisions, *Soc. Sec. Bull.* **7:**3–48.

Svennignsen, N. W., 1992, Neonatal intensive care, *Int. J. Technol. Assess. Health Care* **8:**457–468.

U.S. Department of Health and Human Services, 1991a, *Healthy People 2000: National Health Promotion and Disease Prevention Objectives—Full Report, with Commentary*, U.S. Government Printing Office, Washington, DC.

U.S. Department of Health and Human Services, 1991b, *Injury Mortality Atlas of the United States, 1979–1987*, Centers for Disease Control, Atlanta, GA.

U. S. Department of Health and Human Services, 1993, *Monitoring Health Reform*, National Center for Health Statistics, Hyattsville, MD.

Vogt, T. and Schweitzer, S., 1985, Medical costs of cigarette smoking in a health maintenance organization, *Am. J. Epidemiol.* **122:**1060–1066.

Wennberg, J. E., and Gittelsohn, A., 1973, Small area variations in health care delivery, *Science* **183:**1102–1108.

Wetterhall, S. F., Olson, D. R., DeStafano, F., Stevenson, J. M., Ford, E. S., German, R. R., Will, J. C., Newman, J. M., Sepe, S. J., and Vinicor, F., 1992, Trends in diabetes and diabetic complications, *Diabetes Care* **12:**960–967.

Winslow, C. E. A., 1934, *A City Set on a Hill*, Doubleday, Doran, Garden City, NY.

Wissow, L., Gittelsohn, A., Szklo, M., Starfield, B., and Mussman, M. O., 1988, Poverty, race, and hospitalization for childhood asthma, *Am. J. Pub. Health* **78:**777–782.

World Health Organization, 1948, Test of the constitution of World Health Organization, *Official Rec. WHO* **2:**100.

Zador, P. L., Lund, A. K., Fields, M., and Weinberg, K., 1989, Fatal crash involvement and laws against alcohol-impaired driving, *J. Public Health Policy* **10:**467–485.

2

Measurement Issues in the Use of Epidemiologic Data

Denise M. Oleske

Health services, regardless of their purpose (e.g., health promotion, disease prevention, screening and diagnosis, treatment, or rehabilitation) are designed to improve the health of populations. It is the health care manager's responsibility to monitor these services continuously, to assess their efficacy, and to determine the most appropriate allocation of resources for achieving desired health status goals. These tasks require managers to measure the exposure factors that influence health as well as health itself accurately. Exposure factors are associated with the health services themselves, life-style, heredity, or the environment. Because factors other than health services affect a population's health, accurate measurement of both exposure and health status is fundamental and necessarily precedes any attempt to analyze relationships that may exist between variables.

Health care managers must decide what data should be collected on a routine or periodic basis and select an appropriate measurement approach. The trade-offs in terms of costs and time must be considered as decisions are made about the amount of information that should be collected. This chapter discusses the major issues pertinent to the measurement of exposure and the outcomes of health service delivery, including the methods and logistics of measurement, reliability and validity, the classification of results, and reduction of measurement error. A focus of the chapter will be the survey method of measurement.

Methods of Measurement

Numerous methods exist for measuring exposure factors and health status including: surveys, imaging techniques, laboratory tests, and physical measurements. Regardless of measurement method(s), the key question is: "Does it obtain the information needed?"

The most widely used method for obtaining information about both exposure factors and

Denise M. Oleske   Departments of Health Systems Management and Preventive Medicine, Rush University, Chicago, Illinois 60612.

Epidemiology and the Delivery of Health Care Services: Methods and Applications, edited by Denise M. Oleske. Plenum Press, New York, 1995.

health status is a survey or the use of forms to collect information. Survey forms may be designed to collect information from personal and telephone interviews, self-administered questionnaires, or medical or administrative records. The advantages and disadvantages of each of these approaches are contrasted in Table 2.1. Survey information may be recorded onto hard copy or onto a computer screen linked to a database software package. In practice, a combination of these approaches may be used.

A survey form, regardless of the medium on which it resides, consists of three elements: (1) any special instructions to the participant (or to the data collector), (2) the questions (or items) themselves, and (3) the scaling of each item.

The survey instrument should begin with instructions that contain the title of the study, a brief statement of its purpose, and instructions for completing the form. Instructions direct the respondent to provide or select one or more answers for each item, indicate how the choice(s) or answers should be provided (circled, checked), and specify how to proceed through the form when an item does not apply.

The content of the items depends on whether or not they concern exposure or outcomes. If one is measuring exposure, information should be sought on the exposure itself, periods of exposure, sources, intensity, frequency, and duration. If one is measuring outcomes, evidence is sought to enable classification based upon specified criteria (additional discussion on this follows). Whether measuring exposure or outcomes, the survey tool should contain cues to facilitate the retrieval of information. Cues may be provided relevant to the timing of the occurrence of the event or the degree of exposure. For example, in a study investigating the impact of the level of patient participation in treatment decisions (exposure) on health outcomes, the first item or question (intended as a cue) could be: "When was your most recent hospitalization?" A questionnaire concerning physical activity described in Paffenbarger *et al.*

Table 2.1. Advantages and Disadvantages of Various Types of Surveys

	Advantages	Disadvantages
Administrative/ medical/vital records	Often readily available Rules for coding in place May be available in computer files Nonreactive Clinical data available	Different persons complete May take long to obtain if personal identifiers are required Coding errors and missing data may not be corrected A fee may be required Different lab standards
Telephone surveys	Quick to obtain Less costly than personal interviews Can administer a lengthy form with branching questions Wide geographic coverage possible Can maintain tight quality control	Physical measures not obtainable Some persons do not have phones Confused with sales calls Behavioral cues missed Choices not able to be presented visually
Self-administered	Anonymous Inexpensive No interviewer effects	Low response rate Recording errors and missing data may not be corrected
Personal interviews	Can obtain physical measurements Can administer a lengthy form Allows impressions to be recorded	Responses may be modified by interviewer's characteristics Expensive and time-consuming

(1994) utilized different body figures to stimulate the recall of the past weight changes (exposure) that could affect current health status.

The level of measurement desired and the past use of a measure determine the use of scaling techniques. Levels of measurement may be **nominal** (exposed, not exposed; diseased, not diseased), **ordinal** (e.g., <$10,000, $10,000–11,999, etc.), or **interval** (e.g., blood pressure). For nominal and ordinal scales, the categories should be mutually exclusive. Responses for ordinal scales should reflect the most usual options. A common ordinal scale is called Likert-type, whereby a response with varying degree of intensity is represented between two extremes. For example:

	None	Very little	Some	Quite a bit	Very much
Q.1. I have pain.	0	1	2	3	4

When values are recorded for an interval level item, the units desired and the maximum number of integers should be indicated. For example:

Q.2. On the average, about how many cigarettes a day do you now smoke?

(1 pack = 20 cigarettes)	a. Number of cigarettes	—	—
	b. Don't smoke regularly	8	8
	c. Refused	9	9

Coding conventions for a scale include the use of 8 for responses not applicable and 9 for unknown, refused, or missing responses.

In deciding the particular scale to be used or cut-points for the scale, it may be helpful to review previous studies on the same topic. For example, the actual form used for the National Health Interview Survey is contained within each volume of the summary results from the Survey (NCHS, 1992). If nominal or ordinal scales are desired, cut-points may be determined by clinical significance or data-based rules such as quartiles of a distribution or tree-based models (recursive partitioning analysis) (Clark and Pregibon, 1991).

Logistics of Measurement

Regardless of the measurement method selected, the logistics for the collection of information should be determined. The logistics encompasses administration of the survey, supervision of the data collection, and data processing. The questions in Table 2.2 must be addressed to determine if the measurement process is feasible.

Information concerning potential influences on the measurement method applied should also be collected. For example, when data are obtained in a person-to-person process, the following information should be recorded: the level of compliance or effort, whether or not the data were collected from the index individual or an informant, and the relationship of an informant or proxy to the respondent to the index person, and the topic's apparent importance to the respondent.

Reliability and Validity of a Measure

A measure should be both reliable and valid. Therefore, in selecting or interpreting a measure, **validity** and **reliability** should be assessed. Many studies now report the level of reliability and validity for the measures used.

Table 2.2. Questions for Evaluating the Logistics of Measurement

1. How is the measure administered?
2. Has it been used in other similar situations, and to what degree of success?
3. Is the measure understandable by the study sample? by those who administer it?
4. Will the sample (patients, records, specimens) be accessible and identifiable?
5. Are there any risks associated with its administration?
6. What are the potential restrictions of its use (e.g., cost, copyright, patent)?
7. Are special training and equipment required?
8. What is the length of time involved in measurement?
9. How is it scored?
10. Will the results of the measurement be available in a timely manner?
11. Are normative data and interpretation guidelines available? If so, what is the cost?

Reliability

Reliability represents the extent to which a measurement instrument has consistency over time (stability), among various versions or applications (equivalence), and within the instrument itself (homogeneity). Various means can be employed to assess reliability, depending upon the level of measurement and the aspect of reliability being assessed. Three common statistical techniques used for assessing reliability are **correlation coefficients**, the *kappa* **statistic**, and the **coefficient of variation**.

Reliability may be determined from the product-moment (Pearson) correlation coefficient when the independent and dependent variables are continuous and bivariate normal. When the independent or dependent variables are at least ordinal or when the sample is less than 30, a rank-difference correlation coefficient (Spearman's ρ) may be utilized. The valid values for both correlation coefficients range from -1 to $+1$. The larger the value of the correlation coefficient, the greater the reliability, with values of at least 0.70 being important. The correlation coefficients can be computed from formulas found elsewhere (Rosner, 1990). Many statistical software and spreadsheet packages are capable of generating these coefficients.

The *kappa* statistic (κ) represents the extent to which agreement exists beyond that expected on the basis of chance (Maclure and Willett, 1987). It is represented as follows:

$$\kappa = (P_o - P_e)/(1 - P_e)$$

where P_o is the proportion of observations for which there is agreement, and P_e is the proportion of observations for which agreement is expected by chance alone. The *kappa* statistic is used to assess reliability when the ratings from two measures being compared are both nominal levels of measurement. Fleiss (1981) proposed the following scheme for assessing the strength of agreement of the *kappa* statistic: 0 to less than 4, poor; 4 to less than 7.5, fair to good; above 7.5, excellent. If the measures compared are ordinal (i.e., level of agreement), a weighted κ should be used. The reader is advised to consult Soeken and Prescott (1986) for a discussion and advice on the use of weights.

The coefficient of variation is used to compare the dispersion or variability of two measures whose order of magnitude of values are very disparate. The coefficient of variation (CV) is represented as

$$CV = sd/\bar{x}$$

where: sd is the standard deviation of x_i observations, and $\bar{x}$ is the mean of x observations. For example, the results of high-density lipoprotein (HDL, "good lipoproteins") and low-density lipoproteins (LDL, "bad lipoproteins") are often used to determine an individual's risk of cardiovascular disease. But because the average values for LDL are higher (mean 177, sd 34 mg/dl) than the values of HDL (mean 17, sd 4), does this mean that one test result is more reliable than the other? Substituting the values for LDL and HDL and computing the coefficient of variation for each reveals not only comparable measures of dispersion (CV_{HDL} = 21.9%; CV_{LDL} = 19.2%) but also that the two tests are reliable measures. A coefficient of variation over 50% indicates poor reliability.

Validity

Validity represents the precision to which the measure truly characterizes the phenomenon being studied. A measure must be reliable in order for it to be valid. Validity can be assessed through qualitative and quantitative means.

Qualitatively, the validity of a measure is influenced by its inherent quality and the method by which it is administered. In judging the quality of a survey instrument, Aday (1989) proposes that the following criteria be considered:

1. Clarity (items understood and concepts of interest adequately captured).
2. Balance (avoid weighting questions to a direction; provide equivalent alternative responses, e.g., "agree or disagree").
3. Length of questions and questionnaire (increased length may promote fatigue and inaccurate responses).
4. Order and context (a logical order facilitates data abstraction and participant recall).
5. Utility (instructions clear on how to proceed).
6. Comprehensiveness (ability of an open-ended question to evoke consistently what first comes to mind).
7. Constraints (provisions for neutral, don't know/don't recall responses, and missing data).

The process of obtaining information is influenced by the environmental conditions in which the measurement takes place, transitory personal factors of the participant (e.g., illness), effects of participant–technician interaction, and participant cooperation and recall. Inaccurate reporting, underreporting, or overreporting of exposures or outcomes biases the interpretation of cause–outcome relationships. Thus, to ensure the quality of information obtained, a protocol for collecting the information should be formulated. The elements of the protocol should include: an operations manual, provisions for training the data collectors, specification of rules for handling conflicting or missing data, pilot testing of the instrument, a definition of a standard environment in which the data are collected, routine checks of the accuracy of the data collected, and periodic retraining of the data collectors. The quality of the instrument is also assessed in terms of **content validity** (or **face validity**). The determination of content validity is based upon the degree to which experts, usually at least three, make a subjective determination that the measure represents the full domain of the concept or condition. Content validation is typically the first step in the validation process.

Quantitatively, the most commonly used methods for evaluating validity are **criterion validity** and **construct validity**. **Criterion validity** is assessed by comparing the test measure to known measure of the phenomenon. When a measurement contains interval level values, validity can be assessed by comparing the mean and standard deviation of the difference between the test measure and the valid reference mean. When measures are at the nominal level (e.g., tests to identify diseased from disease-free persons), validity is assessed through the construction of a 2×2 table that determines the sensitivity (the proportion of those who test positive for the trait and have the trait), the specificity (the proportion of those who test negative for the trait and do not have the trait), and the positive predictive value (the proportion of those testing positive who have the trait (Table 2.3). The values from criterion validity can help predict traits at a later time. From information on the sensitivity and specificity of a diagnostic test applied to a population to detect disease before its signs and symptoms occur (a process called screening), estimates can be made of the number of diseased persons who will require referral for treatment. Ideally, a measure should be 100% sensitive and 100% specific and have a 100% positive predictive value. **Construct validity** is the use of two or more measures yielding similar results to account for a phenomenon. Construct validity is used when multiple criteria are thought to measure a concept such as severity of illness. Thus, if one wanted to evaluate the validity of a new severity of illness measure, the measure could be compared against length of hospital stay or mortality. A correlation coefficient can be used to statistically assess this relationship.

Measures should be both reliable and valid in order to classify exposure to a causative factor accurately or to determine the presence or absence of an outcome. Reliability and validity assessments should not be considered absolute, as what is reliable and valid in one setting or among a certain type of patient population, may not be so for another.

Classification of Health Status

Decisions about initiating efforts to improve the health status of populations may be aided with the use of an appropriate system for classification of health status. Health status may be measured as single indicators such as diseases, injuries, death, or self-report of health. Health status may be represented as an index that is a score derived from a series of observations such

Table 2.3. Evaluation of the Criterion Validity of a Measure[a]

	Disease		
Measure results	Present	Absent	Total
Positive	True positive	False positive	
	A	B	A + B
Negative	False negative	True negative	
	C	D	C + D
Totals	A + C	B + D	A+C + B+D

[a]Sensitivity (those who have the disease and are so classified by the test) = $A/(A + C) \times 100\% = A$/all those with disease. Specificity (those who do not have the disease and are so classified by the test) = $D/(B + D) \times 100\% = D$/all those without the disease. False-negative rate (those with the disease not identified by the test) = $C/(A + C) \times 100\%$. False-positive rate (those without the disease wrongly identified by the test) = $B/(B + D) \times 100\%$. Proportion of the population with the disease (disease prevalence rate) = $[(A + C)/(A + B + C + D)] \times 100\%$. Positive predictive value (those with the disease who test positive) = $A/(A + B)$. Diagnostic accuracy = $[(A + D)/\text{total evaluated}] \times 100\%$. Sensitivity, specificity, and false-positive and false-negative rates can also be expressed as probabilities.

as functional ability or cognitive function. Health status may be represented as a profile that is a measurement of multiple concepts, such as a quality-of-life instrument. A **classification system** is a method for assigning individuals evaluated into one of k mutually exclusive categories or units representing a degree of pathology or manifestation of a condition. Classification aids in the precision of measurement, as it provides for a way of structuring information. Classification is essential for health planning—for characterizing health problems in the potential service population, for conducting etiologic studies, for devising and evaluating patient-intervention strategies, for monitoring organizational effectiveness, and for projecting resource utilization. Prior to measuring health status, it is essential to know the schema for classifying the intended results. Common classification systems for health status are discussed below.

Diseases

Disease refers to a state of dysfunction of the normal physiological processes manifested as signs, symptoms and abnormal physical or social function. The most commonly used schema for classifying disease is the *International Classification of Diseases*, ninth revision, *Clinical Modifications* (ICD-9-CM) (USDHHS, 1989). Currently in its ninth revision, this system was developed by medical and coding experts. It provides a method for classifying diseases and injuries as well as procedures and reasons for utilizing health care. Although the ICD-9-CM was originally designed to serve as a template for the uniform coding of death, it may also be used to classify symptoms, physical findings, severity, pathological processes, and etiologic factors. Codes are assigned to states on a nominal scale. The major limitation of the ICD is its clinical vagueness; that is, several codes could be used to represent the same trait (Iezzoni, 1990).

Injuries

Injuries are physical manifestations of bodily harm resulting from contact with temperature extremes, objects, or substances, or from bodily motion. In the United States, approximately 25% of the population is injured each year. Nonfatal injuries account for 10% of all hospital discharges and 1 in 6 hospital days (Rice and MacKenzie, 1989). Injuries are coded at the nominal level by anatomic site affected using ICD-9-CM. In addition, coding of the external cause of injury using E-codes in the ICD is required whenever an injury is the principal diagnosis or directly related to the principal diagnosis. The classification of fall injuries illustrates the cause and intent:

Accidental falls	E880–E888
Suicide and self-inflicted injuries by jumping from a high place	E957
Assault by pushing from a high place	E968.1
Falling from a high place, undetermined whether accidentally or purposely inflicted	E987

Space is provided for E-coding on the hospital discharge abstract (UB-92 form). When new coding demands are placed upon an institution, such as the introduction of the E-coding for emergencies, an administrator must consider how to include the process efficiently into the patient care flow. Otherwise, additional manpower may have to be acquired to handle the increased coding responsibility.

Functional Ability

The intent of classifying **functional ability** is to represent how independently an individual can perform or fulfill expected social roles. Function may be either directly assessed by a physician or other trained practitioner or be self-reported (Katz *et al.*, 1963, 1970; Jette and Branch, 1981; Lawton and Brody, 1969; Kuriansky and Gurland, 1976; Tinetti *et al.*, 1986; Guralnick *et al.*, 1989). Independence is the highest achievable outcome level of functioning in these scales. An aberration in functioning is termed **disability**; it can be physical or social. Physical disability is manifest by aberrations in an individual's sensory and motor performance. Social disability is characterized by an inability to interact with persons or handle problems in the course of performance of expected social roles and responsibilities. The measures of function selected to measure disability depend upon the degree of localization required to assess the problem (e.g., assessment of return to work functional ability after an acute episode of cumulative trauma disorder of the back), the expected degree of impairment, and the population being assessed (inpatient, community dwelling). The Rowland–Morris (1983) scale is an example of a condition-specific scale (back pain) that considers both physical and social functioning and is appropriate for measuring the effectiveness of product line services, namely orthopedics or rehabilitation services. Measures of functional ability are widely used in assessment and longitudinal follow-up of the health status of elderly, disabled, and chronically ill persons. They are also utilized to measure the response to intervention (e.g., rehabilitation services).

Quality of Life

Quality of life (QL) is multidimensional concept consisting of measures covering symptoms/problem complexes, mobility, physical activity, emotional well-being, and social functioning. Quality of life represents the perceived relationship of preferred states. There are both general and disease-specific measures. Examples of general quality-of-life instruments are the Sickness Impact Profile, the Psychological General Well-Being Index, and the Short Form 36 Health Survey (SF-36 form) (Bergner *et al.*, 1981; Dupuy 1984; Stewart *et al.*, 1989). Condition-specific measures of QL include the Functional Assessment of Cancer Therapy Scale for cancer patients and the Arthritis Impact Measurement Scales (Cella *et al.*, 1993; Meenan *et al.*, 1982). Qualify-of-life measures will also be used to measure the impact of health policy changes on the status of potential populations (Owen *et al.*, 1994). Quality-of-life measures do not require any assumptions about the intensity or duration of symptoms or about the existence of any underlying pathology. A limitation of most QL instruments is that they only measure perceptions at the present moment in time.

Control of Measurement Error

Measurement error is not perfectly capturing what is intended. Inherent in every measure is the possibility for error. The strategy for control of error, assuming the validity of the measure is acceptable, should be aimed at reducing variation in measurement. Variability of response can emanate from the individuals tested, the administrators of the test, or the measurement itself. Sources of measurement error include: transitory personal factors (e.g., technician or participant illness), measurement format (e.g., letters too small), technician/

interviewer effects (e.g., differences in response because of gender; technician not reading color accurately), variations in the administration environment (e.g., noise, temperature). Prior to initiation of the measurement process, a plan should be in place for the control of error. The aspects that should be considered in this plan are displayed in Table 2.4. Once the measurement is developed and is available for routine use, a manual should be prepared that contains the following information: the development of the instrument, procedures used for the administration, methods for assessing the quality of information for individual items, and the results of the reliability and validity testing of the instrument.

Summary

Because of the complexity associated with the emergence of health problems, precision in measuring both exposure and health status is essential for precision in the decision-making process. The more precise the ability to quantify exposure and outcome, the less likely a manager is to make a false claim about a relationship and the more likely are the chances of accurately evaluating the impacts of intervention. The soundness of the measurement should always be considered when interpreting the epidemiologic measures of effect and association and the results of analytic studies that are discussed in the next chapters.

Case Studies

Case Study No. 1
Measuring Quality of Life

The measurement of quality of life of patient populations is an important component of determining the impact of health care services. Purchasers of health services use information concerning a provider's success in favorably impacting the QL prior to entering into an agreement for services with that provider. The measurement of QL is becoming particularly important because of the increasing number of persons with chronic conditions and the possibility of delayed side effects of some treatments. Part of the controversy is whether or not it is necessary to have a condition-specific measure or a more global measure of QL.

Table 2.4. Strategies for the Control of Measurement Error

Have a written protocol for measurement.
Develop a standard procedure for training study staff.
Conduct a pilot study to determine the feasibility of administering the measure, its acceptability, and the time required for its administration.
Institute procedures to ensure the completeness and accuracy of recording measurements.
Monitor data collection staff's adherence to data collection protocol.
Use an outside referent (person or lab standard) to compare interviewer (or technician) staff findings.
Ensure that data are collected (or are available) from all eligible records or persons.
Perform reliability checks among those performing measurements.
Review data collected (in raw form and summary statistics) on a regular basis.

Q.1. Select a measure of the quality of life appropriate for the population of care patients served by a health care system in consideration of the guidelines in Table 2.1. Describe the measure and its use.

Q.2. Discuss its reliability and validity.

Case Study No. 2
Measuring Restoration of Function from a Work-Related Low-Back Disorder

Low-back disorders are a major source of disability and pain. The cause of these disorders may be frequent bending, twisting, or lifting, forceful movements, a static work environment, or vibrations. Some studies indicate it may also be related to work-related stress. After an acute episode suffered, the course of recovery may be long, as long as 45 days. Treatment may involve activity restriction, pain medication, muscle relaxants, physiotherapy, back support, athletic conditioning, counseling on life-style management, or surgery. Individuals with uncomplicated mechanical low-back disorders (e.g., not caused by cancer, fracture) can initially be treated in an ambulatory setting. The Center for Comprehensive Back care is a free-standing midwestern facility that contracts with a large automotive manufacturing company to provide rehabilitation service as necessary to its 30,000 employees. The Center utilizes exercise equipment, biofeedback, occupational therapy, and classroom education in the rehabilitation process. Company benefits executives carefully monitor employee progress in rehabilitation in determining whether or not a contract for services should be renewed.

Q.1. Choose measures for functional restoration that could be used to evaluate the efficacy of rehabilitation interventions by the Center for work-related low-back disorders.

Q.2. Discuss the reliability and validity of the measure(s).

Case Study No. 3
Inappropriate Emergency Department Visits
by Members of a Health Maintenance Organization

Studies indicate that 15 to 53% of all Emergency Department (ED) utilization is inappropriate. Since ED charges are expensive, health maintenance organizations (HMOs) should analyze inappropriate utilization of EDs by its members. A study by Freeway Medical Center's Health Plan (FMCHP) was conducted to determine how many inappropriate visits to a specific ED were made by its members. Freeway Medical Center Health Plan is a large urban HMO with 18 offices located throughout the metropolitan area, each of which is open daily from 8 A.M. to 10 P.M. The ED studied was located within two blocks of FMCHP's Central Office. Despite this, there were 6819 visits to the ED from the 39,000 enrollees of FMCHP served by its Central Office location. The first phase of the study was to obtain agreement on what constituted an "inappropriate" visit. Two lists were generated to represent if "inappropriate" care had been given (i.e., care could have been rendered in a primary-care setting). One was a list of services that were considered primary care and inappropriate for receiving treatment in the ED (e.g., urine culture, immunization, redressing of a wound). The other was a list of medical conditions that were appropriate for an ED (e.g., myocardial infarction, poisoning, fractured ankle). The next step was to determine if physicians agreed on what constituted "inappropriate." One physician from the ED and one physician from FMCHP conducted a retrospective chart review of 1745 cases from FMCHP who visited the ED in a 3-month time period. The results of their review is displayed in Table 2.5.

Table 2.5. Evaluation of Agreement
between Two Physicians regarding the
Appropriateness of Emergency Department Care

	Emergency department physician		
	Appropriate	Inappropriate	Total
Health plan physician			
Appropriate	257	57	314
Inappropriate	20	1411	1431
Total	277	1468	1745

Q.1. Compute the *kappa* statistic to determine the level of agreement between the two physicians and provide an interpretation of it.

Q.2. Why was the *kappa* statistic used?

Case Study No. 4
A Breast Cancer Screening Program

Westchester is a city of approximately 500,000 persons over 21 years of age, about half of whom are female. The number of deaths among women from breast cancer is high. To address the problem, the local health department decided to initiate a breast cancer screening program. In this program, mammography would be used to screen for the presence of breast cancer. Mammography has a 99% sensitivity and 99% specificity. About 0.3% of women in the community are estimated to have breast cancer.

Q.1. Approximately how many cases of breast cancer would you expect to find from screening?

Q.2. How many women testing false positive would be found?

Q.3. Is mammography a good test to use for screening? Why?

Q.4. Any concerns about the screening test?

References

Aday, L., 1989, *Designing and Conducting Health Surveys: A Comprehensive Guide*, Jossey-Bass, San Francisco.

Bergner, M., Bobitt, R. A., Carter, W. B., and Gilson, B. S., 1981, The sickness impact profile: Development and final revision of a health status measure, *Med. Care* **19**:787–805.

Cella, D. F., Tulsky, D. S., Gray, G., Sarafin, B., Linn, E., Bonomi, A., Silberman, M., Uellen, S. B., Winicour, P., Brannon, J., Eckberg, K., Lloyd, S., Purl, S., Blendowski, C., Goodman, M., Baricle, M., Stewart, I., McHale, M., Bonomi, P., Kaplan, E., Taylor, S. IV., Thomas, C. R. Jr., and Harris, J., 1993, The Functional Assessment of Cancer Therapy Scale: Development and validation of the general measure, *J. Clin. Oncol.* **11**:570–579.

Clark L. A., and Pregibon, D., 1991, Tree-based models, in *Statistical Models* (J. M. Chambers and T. J. Hastie, eds.), Wadsworth & Brooks/Cole Advanced Books and Software, Pacific Grove, CA.

Dupuy, H. J., 1984, The psychological general well-being (PGWB) index, in *Assessment of Quality of Life in Clinical Trials of Cardiovascular Therapies* (N. K. Wenger, M. E. Mattson, C. D. Furberg, and J. Elinson, eds.), pp. 170–183, Le Jacq Publishers, New York.

Fleiss, J. L., 1981, *Statistical Methods for Rates and Proportions*, second edition, John Wiley & Sons, New York.

Guralnick, J. M., Branch, L. G., Cummings, S. R., and Curb, J. D., 1989, Physical performance measures in aging research, *J. Gerontol.* **44:**M141–M146.

Iezzoni, L. I., 1990, Using administrative diagnostic data to assess the quality of hospital care, *Int. J. Technol. Assess. Health Care* **6:**272–281.

Jette, A. M., and Branch, L. G., 1981, The Framingham Disability Study: II. Physical disability among the aging, *Am. J. Pub. Health* **71:**1211–1216.

Katz, S., Ford, A., and Moskowitz, R., 1963, Studies of illness in the aged. The index of ADL: A standardized measure of biological and psycho-social function, *JAMA* **185:**914–919.

Katz, S., Downs, T. D., and Cash, H. R., 1970, Progress in the development of an index of ADL, *Gerontologist* **10:** 20–30.

Lawton, M. P., and Brody, E. M., 1969, Assessment of older people: Self-maintaining and instrumental activities of daily living, *Gerontologist* **9:**179–186.

Maclure, M., and Willett, W. C., 1987, Misinterpretation and misuse of the *kappa* statistic, *Am. J. Epidemiol.* **126:** 161–269.

Meenan, R. F., Gertman, P. M., Mason, J. M., and Dunaif, R., 1982, The arthritis impact measurement scales: Further investigations of a health status measure, *Arthritis Rheum.* **25:**1048–1053.

National Center for Health Statistics, 1992, *Current Estimates from the National Health Interview Survey, 1991. Vital and Health Statistics.* Series 10, no. 184, NCHS, Hyattsville, MD.

Owen, P., Senner, J., Leff, M., Bruekelman, J., Pledger, E., Louis, G., Steiner, B., Bramblett, K., Lederman, R., Salem, N., Smith, P., Huffman, S., Hann, N., Becker, C., Lane, M., Ridings, D., Giles, R., Brozicevic, P.,Schaeffer, R., Jennings, T., and King, F., 1993, Quality of life as a new public health measure—Behavioral Risk Factor Surveillance System, *Morbid. Mortal. Weekly Rev.* **43:**375–379.

Paffenbarger, R. S., Jr., Blair, S. N., Lee, I., and Hyde, R. T., 1993, Measurement of physical activity to assess health effects in free-living populations, *Med. Sci. Sports Exercise* **25:**60–70.

Rice, D., and MacKenzie, E. J., 1989, *Cost of Injury in the United States: A Report to Congress*, University of California, Institute for Health and Aging, and Johns Hopkins University, Injury Prevention Center, San Francisco.

Rosner, B., 1990, *Fundamentals of Biostatistics*, Duxbury Press, Belmont, CA.

Rowland, M., and Morris, R., 1983, A study of the natural history of back pain. Part I: Development of a reliable and sensitive measure of disability in low-back pain, *Spine* **8:**141–144.

Schipper, H., Clinch, J., McMurray, A., and Levitt, M. 1984, Measuring the quality of life of cancer patients: The Functional Living Index–Cancer: Development and validation, *J. Clin. Oncol.* **2:**472–483.

Soeken, K. L., and Prescott, P. A., 1986, Issues in the use of *kappa* to estimate reliability, *Med. Care* **24:**733–741.

Stewart, A. L., Hays, R. D., and Ware, J. E., 1989, The MOS short-form general health survey: Reliability and validity in a patient population, *Med. Care* **26:**724–735.

Tinetti, M. E., Williams, T. F., and Mayewski, R., 1986, Fall risk index for elderly patients based on number of chronic disabilities, *Am. J. Med.* **80:**429–434.

U.S. Department of Health and Human Services, Public Health Service and Health Care Financing Administration, 1989, *The International Classification of Diseases*, ninth revision, *Clinical Modifications*, U.S. Government Printing Office, Washington, DC.

3

Descriptive Epidemiologic Measures

Denise M. Oleske

Suppose you were responsible for drafting legislation for a new state-wide public health initiative aimed at preventing unnecessary death from cancer of the uterine cervix. How would you present evidence to show this is a problem? Suppose you were charged with evaluating a new health service provided by a health care system. How would you represent the magnitude of the health problem now and over time during the course of your program? In either scenario, your first step would be to measure the frequency of health events in the population for which services, programs, or policies are planned. In addition, the relationship of the health event to factors that might account for its occurrence and distribution should be described. This chapter presents common descriptive epidemiologic measures and sources of information concerning these. It also discusses how the measures are constructed and interpreted as well as how they are applied in the delivery of health care services.

Measuring the Frequency of Health Events in Populations

In order to quantify the magnitude of a health problem, it must be measured. In epidemiology, the measurement of events is expressed in terms of a referent population instead of raw numbers. Epidemiologic measures of the frequency of health events in populations may be quantified as **rates**.

Incidence Rate

An **incidence rate** is a descriptive measure in which the numerator consists of *new* or *incident* cases of a health event occurring in a population at risk for the event. A rate is computed as follows:

$$\text{Rate per } 10^k = E(t)/P(t) \times 10^k$$

Denise M. Oleske   Departments of Health Systems Management and Preventive Medicine, Rush University, Chicago, Illinois 60612.

Epidemiology and the Delivery of Health Care Services: Methods and Applications, edited by Denise M. Oleske. Plenum Press, New York, 1995.

where E is the number of events occurring in the population during a specified period of time (t), P is the population in the same area at the same time (t) in which the events were expected to occur, and 10^k is a unit of population to which the rate applies, expressed as a power of 10. Thus, the incidence rate of breast cancer per 100,000 women given 500 new cases of breast cancer in a population of 500,000 women would be computed as follows:

$$500 \text{ cases}/500,000 \text{ women} \times 100,000 = 100 \text{ per } 100,000$$

This is the same as:

$$500 \text{ cases} = 500,000 \text{ women} \times 100/100,000$$

The events in the numerator must be derived from a defined referent population, and both the event and the population should be related to the same time period and the same geographic area. In most circumstances, an individual hospital or provider cannot be a singular source of information for the construction of rates for a community unless all cases of the event occurring within a population in a well-defined geographic area come to the attention of the hospital or provider. In reality, many populations are served by multiple health care facilities and providers, and hence, data from only one source would yield an underestimate of the true rate of the event within a population.

The denominator should not include those who already have the condition or who are not susceptible to it by virtue of immunity, immunization, surgery, or some other factor that excludes the potential for being exposed. For example, a study of the incidence rate of uterine cancer among menopausal women using estrogen supplements should exclude from the denominator women who have had a hysterectomy. The choice of a denominator for a rate measure depends on the manner in which time is represented. The denominator used to construct rate measures for community populations is derived from the decennial census or interim population projections based upon census data. In this circumstance, the identification of persons who are truly at risk for the health event is not feasible. Thus, the average population at risk, the population at midyear (July 1), is used in computing the rate. The denominator for the rate may consist of the total population who develop the health event over a specified period of time. This is called the **cumulative incidence rate**. The denominator may consist of the number of persons who could develop the event in consideration of how long each person was observed. This measure is called the **incidence density**. The denominator for this measure expressed in terms of person-time units, is illustrated below.

Given a group of four persons: person A is observed for 5 days; person B is observed for 1 day; person C is observed for 1 week; and person D is observed for 1 month.* The total is 43.5 person-days of observation. If *Salmonella* infection developed in one of the four persons on a skilled-care nursing unit, the incidence density rate (IDR) would be:

$$\text{IDR} = [\text{No. of new events/person-time units of observation}] \times 10^k$$

$$= 1/43.5 \times 100 = 2.3 \text{ infections per 100 person-days}$$

The incidence density rate measure is used when persons at risk for an event are observed for different lengths of time as in a longitudinal study in a randomized clinical trial where the outcome is not immediately ascertainable, and in survival analysis. Incidence density rates that are averaged over a period of time to represent the instantaneous occurrence of an event are called **hazard rates**.

---

*Assumes the average month is 30.5 days.

The factor of 10 is used in the computation of a rate to make the relationship between events and the population more meaningful by removing the decimal fraction created by dividing a small number of events relative to a large population. The particular power of 10 used depends on convention (e.g., per 100,000 population for disease-specific rates in a community, per 1000 population when representing the total death rate in a community) or on convenience. Generally, a power of 10 is used such that the lowest level of the variable for which the rate is calculated is one digit to the right of the decimal. The same factor of 10 must apply to all levels within a variable.

Incidence rates may refer to the onset of an illness or condition (morbidity) or death (mortality). In order to identify a new case of an illness or condition, knowledge of the time of onset of the event is essential. This can only be achieved if the population is already under surveillance for changes in health status or will be involved in such monitoring. For acute onset conditions such as gastroenteritis, myocardial infarction, and nonfatal trauma, the identification of a "new" case can be pinpointed. When the onset is not readily apparent, as is the case with chronic conditions, mental disorders and sociobehavioral problems (e.g., substance abuse), surrogate measures are used. For defining an incident cancer case, the date of histological confirmation of the malignancy is used as the date of onset. The date of first use of an intravenous, nonprescription drug may be considered in defining the onset of drug addiction. In defining incident events, the numerator should specify whether events or persons are being counted. In some circumstances, multiple new events may occur within the same population. This is exemplified in the calculation of nonfatal injury rates. The numerator in the computation of the **injured persons rate** consists of the number of persons who experienced an injury, whereas, the numerator of the **injury rate** represents the number of episodes of injury in persons at risk during a specific time period.

The period of time identified for the observation of incident cases must be clearly defined. Incidence rates can be computed for short time periods, hours, days, and weeks as for epidemics, or over longer periods of time. Examples of incidence rates referring to short time intervals are attack rates and case-fatality rates. An **attack rate** is the number of persons experiencing illness during a specified time period, usually the same time interval for all persons, in relationship to a defined set of conditions. The **case-fatality rate** is the number of persons dying from a specific condition that was diagnosed within a short period of time, usually a year or less. It is also a measure of disease severity. Rare or infrequent events in a population may yield unstable rate estimates even if calculated on an annual basis. In such circumstances, incident cases may be pooled over a few years (3–5) with the denominator consisting of the population from the previous census year or at a midpoint of the interval being averaged. Because the incidence rate describes the likelihood of an event occurring in a population susceptible to its occurrence, the incidence rate is synonymous with the term **risk**.

Prevalence Rate

A **prevalence rate** is a measure of event frequency that represents the total number of persons with a health event (or other characteristic) divided by the total number of persons at a specific point in time (t) multiplied by a power of 10, as with incidence rates. The individuals with the health event examined who constitute the numerator must also be included in the denominator; that is, they both come from the same geographic area and in the same time period. The prevalence rate is represented as follows:

Prevalence rate = total number of persons with characteristic(t) $\times$ 10^k/total population(t)

The prevalence rate is influenced by how many individuals develop the condition in a particular time frame (incidence rate) and how long it lasts (duration). Thus, factors that influence the development of an incident case (e.g., changes in exposures that result in a disease, changes in the way the delivery system accesses new cases, or changes in diagnostic methods) also affect the prevalence. Intervention programs for the prevention or treatment of cases, changes in the physical manifestation of the incident case (e.g., increased virulence of an organism), or selective in- or outmigration of susceptible or immune persons for treatment may also affect the prevalence rate. Thus, if a community has an unexpected low prevalence of a health problem, this may be explained by a low disease incidence, a disease that is selectively more serious or fatal in that community (e.g., from lack of access to health care), or a disease that is very curable (e.g., high access to effective care). The selection of the time period for the computation of the prevalence rate is discretionary and may reflect cases existing over an interval of time such as 1 year (annual prevalence) or a specific moment in time, such as 1 day (point prevalence).

The prevalence rate reflects the total burden of a condition within a population. As such, it is useful for estimating the level and intensity of health care services required within a population. For example, the prevalence rates of hypertension in a community would be useful in determining if the initiation of a screening program would be worthwhile.

In addition to quantifying the proportion of persons in which an outcome has occurred (e.g., disease prevalence), the proportion of persons who have a characteristic that may be a determinant of a health outcome (exposure prevalence) may also be useful. For example, knowing that an HMO has a high prevalence of smokers, an administrator may consider initiating educational and smoking-cessation clinics for its service population in order to prevent premature births, chronic obstructive pulmonary disease, heart disease, and various forms of cancer such as cancer of the lung, larynx, and bladder, which are all associated with smoking.

Sources of Information for Incidence Rate Measures

The source of incidence information about the onset of illnesses or conditions varies according to the event studied. Physicians are responsible for defining most incident health events through laboratory, radiologic, or pathological means. However, all health professionals have responsibility for reporting certain events to the local health authority as required by state law (e.g., selected communicable diseases) or to the designated supervisor as required by the policies of a health care facility (e.g., patient falls). The list of health-related events to be reported by law varies somewhat from state to state, but selected infectious diseases must be reported in all jurisdictions of the United States (see Chapter 6). In addition to communicable diseases, malignant neoplasms, selected occupational diseases, and other health problems such as lead poisoning, may be required by law to be reported. Reportable morbidity data are available through local health departments, and the Centers for Disease Control provides regular national summaries for transmissable diseases in its periodical, *Morbidity and Mortality Weekly Review*. The incidence of some conditions requiring hospitalization, such as hip fracture, may be available from data files of hospital claims (Lauderdale *et al.*, 1993).

The primary source of information about deaths is the death certificate, one of the items of vital data required by law in each of the United States, in all industrialized, and many developing nations throughout the world. The death on the certificate is described in terms of an immediate cause (the mode of dying) and underlying causes (the injury or disease that initiated the chain of events that led directly to the death). In addition, the death certificate contains demographic information about the decedent including gender, race, birth date, social security number, residence, usual occupation, manner of death, and other significant conditions (that contributed to death and not listed in the chain of events), and information about next of kin (Figure 3.1). All states also require filing of a fetal death certificate if the fetus is determined to be a product of 20 or more completed weeks of gestation and not born alive. On the death certificate, a physician, medical examiner, or coroner provide information on the cause of death. The funeral director records the demographic information and files the certificate with the state vital registration office. The deaths listed on the certificate are classified by a nosologist at the state vital statistics office according to the most recent edition of the *International Classification of Diseases (ICD)*. All states and the District of Columbia periodically submit death certificate information on computer tape to the National Center for Health Statistics (NCHS), where data are coded and quality-control checked (CDC, 1989). The NCHS then disseminates the mortality data as annual volumes of *Vital Statistics of the United States*. The World Health Organization (WHO) collects, classifies, and tabulates mortality statistics from the United States and other countries. When using death certificates, caution must be employed. First, the assignment of the primary cause of death may not be accurate because the physician may be unfamiliar with the case or lack autopsy information. One must be wary in using mortality data to describe trends for several reasons including: the classification of diseases may change somewhat with each revision of the *International Classification of Disease*, definitions of diseases change over time, and new conditions may emerge. For example, although human immunodeficiency virus (HIV) infection was recognized in 1981, the ICD-9-CM code until 1986 was 279.19, "other deficiency of cell-mediated immunity." During 1986, the codes for AIDS were changed to 042.0, 042.1, 042.2, and 042.9. More recently the classification system has been expanded to include more diagnostic entities for AIDS (ICD-9-CM codes 042-044).

Incidence data are used for studies of the etiology of diseases, the evaluation of program or treatment outcomes (e.g., effectiveness of a vaccine program for reducing measles in a community), disease surveillance (e.g., cases of repetitive motion disorder caused by workplace exposures), and monitoring the quality of health care provided (e.g., nosocomial infection rate). Because recording of deaths is widely practiced, mortality rates represent the most universal method for prioritizing health problems within a population and for comparing the health status of populations across geographic areas.

Sources of Information on Prevalence

Population surveys provide information on prevalence, exposure, or disease. Two agencies are primary sources of health-related prevalence data for the United States population. One is the National Center for Health Statistics, which collects health-related data from self-reports of conditions, physical examination, and laboratory evaluation of individuals surveyed. Individuals are selected based upon probability selection of the population. Other surveys conducted by the NCHS useful for prevalence information are the National Health Interview Survey (NHIS) (NCHS, 1992) and the National Health Examination Survey (NCHS, 1993a). Data from the NHIS pertaining to chronic conditions are displayed in Figure 3.2. The prevalence rate of diabetes of 29.0 per 1000 persons means that among every thousand persons in the general population, 29 have reported being diabetic. The disadvantage of these data is that the precision of the survey provides estimates only reliable for large geographic regions of

U.S. STANDARD
CERTIFICATE OF DEATH

TYPE/PRINT IN PERMANENT BLACK INK — FOR INSTRUCTIONS SEE OTHER SIDE AND HANDBOOK

LOCAL FILE NUMBER   STATE FILE NUMBER

DECEDENT

1. DECEDENT'S NAME (First, Middle, Last) | 2. SEX | 3. DATE OF DEATH (Month, Day, Year)

4. SOCIAL SECURITY NUMBER | 5a. AGE—Last Birthday (Years) | 5b. UNDER 1 YEAR (Months / Days) | 5c. UNDER 1 DAY (Hours / Minutes) | 6. DATE OF BIRTH (Month, Day, Year) | 7. BIRTHPLACE (City and State or Foreign Country)

8. WAS DECEDENT EVER IN U.S. ARMED FORCES? (Yes or no) | 9a. PLACE OF DEATH (Check only one; see instructions on other side) HOSPITAL: ☐ Inpatient ☐ ER/Outpatient ☐ DOA OTHER: ☐ Nursing Home ☐ Residence ☐ Other (Specify)

9b. FACILITY NAME (If not institution, give street and number) | 9c. CITY, TOWN, OR LOCATION OF DEATH | 9d. COUNTY OF DEATH

10. MARITAL STATUS—Married, Never Married, Widowed, Divorced (Specify) | 11. SURVIVING SPOUSE (If wife, give maiden name) | 12a. DECEDENT'S USUAL OCCUPATION (Give kind of work done during most of working life. Do not use retired.) | 12b. KIND OF BUSINESS/INDUSTRY

13a. RESIDENCE—STATE | 13b. COUNTY | 13c. CITY, TOWN, OR LOCATION | 13d. STREET AND NUMBER

13e. INSIDE CITY LIMITS? (Yes or no) | 13f. ZIP CODE | 14. WAS DECEDENT OF HISPANIC ORIGIN? (Specify No or Yes—If yes, specify Cuban, Mexican, Puerto Rican, etc.) ☐ No ☐ Yes Specify: | 15. RACE—American Indian, Black, White, etc. (Specify) | 16. DECEDENT'S EDUCATION (Specify only highest grade completed) Elementary/Secondary (0-12) | College (1-4 or 5+)

PARENTS

17. FATHER'S NAME (First, Middle, Last) | 18. MOTHER'S NAME (First, Middle, Maiden Surname)

INFORMANT

19a. INFORMANT'S NAME (Type/Print) | 19b. MAILING ADDRESS (Street and Number or Rural Route Number, City or Town, State, Zip Code)

DISPOSITION

20a. METHOD OF DISPOSITION ☐ Burial ☐ Cremation ☐ Removal from State ☐ Donation ☐ Other (Specify) | 20b. PLACE OF DISPOSITION (Name of cemetery, crematory, or other place) | 20c. LOCATION—City or Town, State

21a. SIGNATURE OF FUNERAL SERVICE LICENSEE OR PERSON ACTING AS SUCH | 21b. LICENSE NUMBER (of Licensee) | 22. NAME AND ADDRESS OF FACILITY

(SEE DEFINITION ON OTHER SIDE)

PRONOUNCING PHYSICIAN ONLY — ITEMS 24-26 MUST BE COMPLETED BY PERSON WHO PRONOUNCES DEATH

Complete items 23a-c only when certifying physician is not available at time of death to certify cause of death. | 23a. To the best of my knowledge, death occurred at the time, date, and place stated. Signature and Title ▶ | 23b. LICENSE NUMBER | 23c. DATE SIGNED (Month, Day, Year)

24. TIME OF DEATH ___ M | 25. DATE PRONOUNCED DEAD (Month, Day, Year) | 26. WAS CASE REFERRED TO MEDICAL EXAMINER/CORONER? (Yes or no)

CAUSE OF DEATH (SEE INSTRUCTIONS ON OTHER SIDE)

27. PART I. Enter the diseases, injuries, or complications that caused the death. Do not enter the mode of dying, such as cardiac or respiratory arrest, shock, or heart failure. List only one cause on each line. | Approximate Interval Between Onset and Death

IMMEDIATE CAUSE (Final disease or condition resulting in death) ▶ a. _____ DUE TO (OR AS A CONSEQUENCE OF):

Sequentially list conditions, if any, leading to immediate cause. Enter UNDERLYING CAUSE (Disease or injury that initiated events resulting in death) LAST — b. _____ DUE TO (OR AS A CONSEQUENCE OF):

c. _____ DUE TO (OR AS A CONSEQUENCE OF):

d. _____

PART II. Other significant conditions contributing to death but not resulting in the underlying cause given in Part I. | 28a. WAS AN AUTOPSY PERFORMED? (Yes or no) | 28b. WERE AUTOPSY FINDINGS AVAILABLE PRIOR TO COMPLETION OF CAUSE OF DEATH? (Yes or no)

29. MANNER OF DEATH ☐ Natural ☐ Accident ☐ Suicide ☐ Homicide ☐ Pending Investigation ☐ Could not be Determined | 30a. DATE OF INJURY (Month, Day, Year) | 30b. TIME OF INJURY ___ M | 30c. INJURY AT WORK? (Yes or no) | 30d. DESCRIBE HOW INJURY OCCURRED

30e. PLACE OF INJURY—At home, farm, street, factory, office building, etc. (Specify) | 30f. LOCATION (Street and Number or Rural Route Number, City or Town, State)

CERTIFIER (SEE DEFINITION ON OTHER SIDE)

31a. CERTIFIER (Check only one)
☐ CERTIFYING PHYSICIAN (Physician certifying cause of death when another physician has pronounced death and completed Item 23) To the best of my knowledge, death occurred due to the cause(s) and manner as stated.
☐ PRONOUNCING AND CERTIFYING PHYSICIAN (Physician both pronouncing death and certifying to cause of death) To the best of my knowledge, death occurred at the time, date, and place, and due to the cause(s) and manner as stated.
☐ MEDICAL EXAMINER/CORONER On the basis of examination and/or investigation, in my opinion, death occurred at the time, date, and place, and due to the cause(s) and manner as stated.

31b. SIGNATURE AND TITLE OF CERTIFIER ▶ | 31c. LICENSE NUMBER | 31d. DATE SIGNED (Month, Day, Year)

32. NAME AND ADDRESS OF PERSON WHO COMPLETED CAUSE OF DEATH (ITEM 27) (Type/Print)

REGISTRAR

33. REGISTRAR'S SIGNATURE | 34. DATE FILED (Month, Day, Year)

PHS-T-003 REV. 1/89

(Left margin: NAME OF DECEDENT: For use by physician or institution — SEE INSTRUCTIONS ON OTHER SIDE — DEPARTMENT OF HEALTH AND HUMAN SERVICES – PUBLIC HEALTH SERVICE – NATIONAL CENTER FOR HEALTH STATISTICS – 1989 REVISION)

Figure 3.1. Sample death certificate.

the United States. The estimates are not generalizable to smaller population subgroups. The Centers for Disease Control and Prevention (CDC) are another major source of prevalence data, providing information on exposure to factors known to be associated with the major causes of death through the Behavioral Risk Factor Surveillance System (BRFSS). The BRFSS is a state-based, random-digit-dialing telephone survey of noninstitutionalized adults

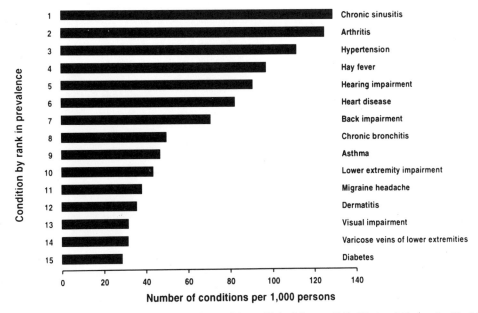

Figure 3.2. Prevalence of selected chronic conditions, United States, 1991 (National Center for Health Statistics, 1992).

developed by the Centers for Disease Control (Siegel *et al.*, 1993). Examples of the information collected in the BRFSS include the prevalence of certain high-risk behaviors (smoking, chronic or binge alcohol consumption, overweight, physical inactivity, and safety belt nonuse) and the use of selected medical screening tests (blood cholesterol screening, mammography, clinical breast examination, and Papanicolaou or "Pap" smear). Because the survey is operational in 47 states and the District of Columbia, trends at the national as well as the state level can be monitored.

Format of Descriptive Epidemiologic Measures

Descriptive epidemiologic measures can be represented as **specific measures, summary measures**, or **relative measures**.

Specific Measures

Specific measures pertain to a subgroup of the population and the number of events that occur in that subgroup. Specific rates assist in identifying population subgroups (i.e., by age group, gender, race) at risk for an event. Common specific rates are listed in Table 3.1. Through an examination of specific rates, unique patterns are observed for all health problems, regardless of whether the event is infectious, chronic, or resulting from injury (Fig. 3.3a–c).

Summary Measures

Summary measures represent the total events occurring in a population. Depending on the specific measure utilized, it may or may not take into account information from population

Table 3.1. Common Specific Rates

$$\text{Gender-specific death rate} = \left[\frac{\text{No. of deaths for gender during specified period}}{\text{Population (for the gender) in the middle of the period}} \right] \times 100,000$$

$$\text{Race-specific death rate} = \left[\frac{\text{No. of deaths for the race during a specified period}}{\text{Population (for the race) in the middle of the period}} \right] \times 100,000$$

$$\text{Age-specific death rate} = \left[\frac{\text{No. of deaths for the age group during a specified period}}{\text{Population in the middle of the period}} \right] \times 100,000$$

$$\text{Infant mortality rate} = \left[\frac{\text{No. of deaths} <1 \text{ year of age}}{\text{No. of live births}} \right] \times 1000$$

$$\text{Neonatal mortality rate} = \left[\frac{\text{No. of deaths} < \text{age 28 days}}{\text{No. of live births}} \right] \times 1000$$

$$\text{Perinatal mortality rate} = \left[\frac{\text{No. late fetal deaths plus deaths} < \text{age 7 days}}{\text{No. of live births plus late fetal deaths}} \right] \times 1000$$

$$\text{Fertility rate} = \left[\frac{\text{No. of live births}}{\text{No. of women 15--44 years of age}} \right] \times 1000$$

$$\text{Case fatality rate} = \left[\frac{\text{No. of deaths from a disease (in a specified time)}}{\text{No. diagnosed with that disease (in same time)}} \right] \times 100$$

subgroups. Summary measures include **crude rates, standardized rates**, and **potential life years lost**.

Crude (or **total**) **rates** relate the total number of events in a population. Crude death rates, for example, are used to rank deaths in a population in a specific time period. Overall, heart disease is the major cause of death in the United States, comprising 33.2% of all deaths (Table 3.2).

A **standardized rate** is a summary rate for a total population in which the frequency of events is weighted by the population demographic characteristics whose effect we wish to control (or remove). A standardized rate is used when it is necessary to compare population rates across geographic areas or time periods, because demographic characteristics that strongly influence the emergence of a condition vary greatly over these. Summary measures are also useful when cause-specific information is not comparable, and comparisons are likely to be unreliable. Such is often the case in making comparisons of health status using mortality data across nations. The most profound variations in disease are attributable to age; as a result, standardization is most often concerned with removing the effects of age as a confounding variable in order to characterize more accurately the magnitude of disease frequency in a population. This type of standardization is referred to as **age adjustment**. The principle behind standardization is to compute rates for the populations being compared that take into account possible differences in demographic characteristics that could influence the disease frequency. In order to do this, standardization takes into account the disease frequency in the study populations in the context of some "normative" or standard population. There are two approaches for standardization of rates, **direct** and **indirect**.

Direct adjustment is performed to enable comparison of disease frequency in a population over time periods or geographic areas. In this method, the category-specific rates in a comparison population are weighted according to the proportion of those in the category in the standard or reference population. The process is summarized below:

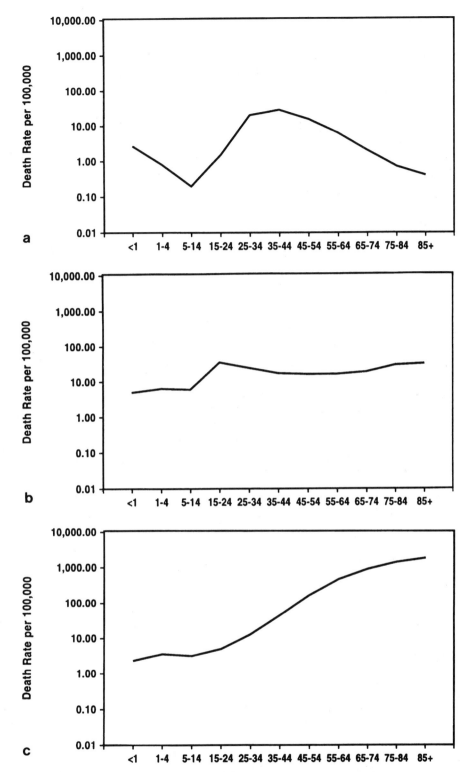

Figure 3.3. (a) Age-specific mortality rates for human immunodeficiency virus (HIV) infection, all races, both genders, United States, 1990. (b) Age-specific mortality rates for motor vehicle accidents, all races, both genders, United States, 1990. (c) Age-specific mortality rates for malignant neoplasms, all races, both genders, United States, 1990. Source for all data: National Center for Health Statistics (1993b).

**Table 3.2. Death Rates and Percentage of Total Deaths
for the Ten Leading Causes of Death, United States, 1991[a]**

Rank order	Cause of death (Ninth revision, *International Classification of Diseases*, 1975)	Rate per 100,000 population	Percentage of total deaths
	All causes	860.3	100.0
1	Diseases of heart	285.9	33.2
2	Malignant neoplasms, including neoplasms of lymphatic and		
	hematopoietic tissue	204.1	23.7
3	Cerebrovascular diseases	56.9	6.6
4	Chronic obstructive pulmonary diseases and allied conditions	35.9	4.2
5	Accidents and adverse effects	35.4	4.1
	Motor vehicle accidents	17.3	2.0
	All other accidents and adverse effects	18.2	2.1
6	Pneumonia and influenza	30.9	3.6
7	Diabetes mellitus	19.4	2.3
8	Suicide	12.2	1.4
9	Human immunodeficiency virus infection	11.7	1.4
10	Homicide and legal intervention	10.5	1.2

[a]Source: National Center for Health Statistics (1993b).

1. Compute the rate of the event of interest for each level of the variable using data from the standard population.
2. Compute the proportion of the standard population for each level of the variable whose effect is to be removed.
3. Multiply each level-specific rate by the proportion of the standard population in that level.
4. Sum the product obtained in each level from number 3 above to obtain the adjusted rate.

Table 3.3 illustrates the application of direct age adjustment to enable the comparison of the breast cancer incidence between white and black females. The conclusion suggested by directly standardized rates is that the age-adjusted incidence of breast cancer is higher among white females (179.3 per 100,000 women) than among black females (149.8 per 100,000 women) once adjustment is done for differences in the age distribution of the two populations. Another way of saying this is that white females have a higher overall incidence rate of breast cancer when the age distribution of the two groups is the same. The major disadvantage of direct rate adjustment is that it occludes the specific rate differences that may be important in identifying high-risk population subgroups. In the example presented, if one were to examine only the adjusted rate, one would not be aware of the higher incidence among black females compared to white females less than 45 years of age. Whether or not this indicates the beginning of a trend or that the risk is confined to that age group remain questions that require further study. The variance and standard error of the rate adjusted by the direct method may be obtained, and the reader is advised to consult Chiang (1961) or Kahn and Sempos (1989) for details about these computations. The major challenge in direct adjustment is the choice of the standard population. The larger population of several to be compared or the combined population of the populations being studied may be used.

Table 3.3. Calculation of Directly Standardized Incidence Rates per 100,000 Population for Breast Cancer, Females, 1984–1988[a]

Age group	White females: incidence rate (r) per 100,000 pop.	$r \times P$	Black females: incidence rate (r) per 100,000 pop.	$r \times P$	Proportion (P) of standard population
20–24	0.0	0.0	1.2	0.2	0.1294
25–29	7.3	0.9	10.2	1.2	0.1189
30–34	26.1	2.8	34.2	3.7	0.1079
35–39	65.2	5.7	79.9	6.9	0.0868
40–44	129.7	9.5	141.5	10.3	0.0730
45–49	190.8	13.4	173.6	12.2	0.0703
50–54	228.9	17.3	186.0	14.1	0.0757
55–59	277.9	21.3	226.1	17.4	0.0768
60–64	352.4	24.0	279.0	19.0	0.0682
65–69	408.4	25.2	287.8	17.7	0.0616
70–74	437.4	21.9	327.3	16.4	0.0500
75–79	475.8	17.7	368.8	13.8	0.0373
80–84	460.7	11.2	406.3	9.9	0.0243
85+	422.2	8.4	356.0	7.0	0.0198
Age-adjusted rate per 100,000 population $\Sigma (r \times P)$		179.3		149.8	

[a]Standard population is the number of white females plus the number of black females, $n = 68,808,029$.
Sources: rate measures, Ries, *et al.* (1991); population data, National Center for Health Statistics (1993c).

Indirect adjustment is performed when the number of events for each level of the variable whose effect is to be removed is either unknown or too small. This limitation is often present when one is attempting to make between-institution comparisons or comparisons over time or between small geographic areas for uncommon events. For example, an administrator may wish to determine if the mortality rate from acute myocardial infarction (AMI) is higher at one hospital than at other hospitals in the system. The distribution of deaths from AMI according to age group may not be known, or even if known, the number of deaths according to age group may be small. Thus, indirect standardization should be performed in order to make the desired comparisons. The process of indirect rate standardization is as follows:

1. Compute the crude rate (C) of the event in the standard population.
2. Using data from the standard population, compute the rate of the event (r) for each level of the event whose effect is to be removed.
3. Obtain the number (n) in the comparison population according to each level for which rates were computed.
4. Obtain the total number of events (O) that occurred in the comparison population.
5. Multiply the number in each level in the comparison population by the rate from the respective level in the standard population.
6. Divide the number of observed events by the sum of the expected number of events. This will yield a standardized mortality ratio (SMR).
7. Multiply the standardized ratio by the crude rate of the event in the standard population. This yields an indirectly adjusted rate.

**Table 3.4. Calculation of Indirectly Standardized Rates
Utilizing Hypothetical Data on Acute Myocardial Infarction
(AMI) Fatality Rates, 30 Days Posthospitalization**

Age	All hospitals AMI death rate per 100 AMI cases $(r)^a$	Hospital A[b]		
		No. AMI cases	AMI deaths (O)	Expected AMI deaths (E)
65–69	22.7	17	*	3.9
70–74	24.5	15	*	3.7
75–79	22.3	10	*	2.2
80+	30.5	29	*	8.8
Total	24.5	71	11	18.6

[a]Crude mortality rate (C) all hospitals = 24.2 per 100 AMI cases.
[b]Standardized mortality ratio (SMR) for Hospital A = O/E = 11/18.6 = 0.59. Indirectly adjusted rate
   = $C \times$ SMR = 24.2 deaths per 100 AMI cases $\times$ 0.59 = 14.3 deaths per 100 AMI cases.

Table 3.4 illustrates the application of this procedure. It may be concluded that the observed number of deaths is lower for AMI cases at Hospital A than the rate in the system hospitals even when the differences in age are accounted for.

Various other methods exist for performing standardization of rates, depending upon how many variables need to be controlled, the size of the comparison population, and the number of events in each of the various levels of the confounding variable(s) whose effect it to be removed. **Regression-based standardization** is another approach to standardization when the sample size of the comparison populations is small and large numbers of confounding variables need be considered (Rothberg, 1982). For other advanced methods, the reader is advised to consult Fleiss (1981).

The **years of potential life lost (YPLL)** is a summary measure of premature mortality. To compute the YPLL, the number of deaths in each age group is multiplied by the difference between the midpoint of the age group and 65 years. The difference represents the potential years of life lost for each age group and, when summed up over all age groups examined, becomes the YPLL (CDC, 1986). This process is repeated for each cause of death examined. The number of years of life lost may be expressed as a rate using the number of persons less than 65 years of age per 100,000 in the denominator.

The YPLL is useful for summarizing the frequency of events that disproportionately affect younger persons or for assessing the impact of community-based interventions in geographic areas with a large minority or immigrant population who are typically younger than the population of the larger community. Mortality data, represented as crude or adjusted rates, are weighted by the disease processes common to the elderly. The largest increases in YPLL from 1987 to 1990 are noted for conditions related to human immunodeficiency virus infection, homicide, and diabetes (Table 3.5). To stem the increases, intervention may include promoting increased use and availability of preventive health services and extensive community education on healthy behaviors among young persons. The success of these efforts could be measured if significant reduction in the YPLL were achieved.

Relative Measures

In addition to measuring the occurrence of health events in populations, it is often necessary to describe the presence of these relative to some characteristic. When this charac-

**Table 3.5. Years of Potential Life Lost (YPLL) Before Age 65
by Cause of Death, United States, 1987 and 1990[a]**

Cause of death (ICD-9 code)	YPLL per 100,000 persons under 65		Percentage change from 1987 to 1990
	1987	1990	
All causes (total)	5677.6	5623.0	−1.0
Unintentional injuries (E800–E949)	1084.1	984.7	−9.2
Malignant neoplasms (140–208)	854.4	848.6	−0.7
Suicide (E950–E959)	315.5	312.0	−1.1
Homicide (E960–E978)	308.5	374.3	21.3
Diseases of the heart (390–398, 402, 404–429)	403.2	350.0	−13.2
Human immunodeficiency virus infection (042–044)	170.9	303.4	77.5
Cerebrovascular disease (430–438)	116.6	110.7	−5.1
Chronic liver disease and cirrhosis (571)	110.6	103.1	−6.8
Pneumonia/influenza (480–487)	80.9	81.2	0.4
Diabetes mellitus (250)	57.8	67.0	15.9
Chronic obstructive pulmonary disease (490–496)	62.0	61.0	−1.6

[a]Source: National Center for Health Statistics (1993b).

teristic is thought to be associated with an increased probability of a specific outcome, the characteristic is referred to as a **risk factor**. The common approaches for descriptively representing the relationship between exposure and outcome are through the calculation of the **odds ratio**, the **relative risk**, and the **population attributable risk**.

The ratio of two rates representing risk (e.g., incidence or mortality rates) is termed the **risk ratio** or **relative risk (RR)**. Generally, the group with the higher risk or the group in whom exposure to the risk factor is the greatest is placed in the numerator. The rate of the lower risk group or the group with little or no exposure is in the denominator. For example, the male–female risk ratio for mortality from heart disease is computed as:

RR = incidence rate exposed/incidence rate nonexposed

= 201.0 per 100,000 among males/106.3 per 100,000 among females

= 1.89

The RR in this example means that males are 1.89 times more likely to die from heart disease than females. Because this ratio compares two adjusted rates, the conclusion can be extended to state that the elevated risk of death from heart disease in males is higher than that for females even after consideration of the differences in age distribution.

Ratios of adjusted rates can be utilized to identify health problems in certain population subgroups. An examination of the male-to-female ratios of the age-adjusted death rates reveals a two-fold greater risk of death among males for accidents, suicide, and homicide, with the largest male–female difference observed for death from human immunodeficiency virus infection (HIV). The ratio of black-to-white age-adjusted mortality rates indicates over a twofold greater risk of death among blacks for diabetes mellitus, nephritis, homicide, septicemia, perinatal conditions, and HIV (Table 3.6).

In addition to computing risk ratios from vital data, the concept of the risk ratio can be extended to examine the relationship between exposure and event from an analytic study (Chapter 5 provides additional discussion of study designs). Table 3.7 presents data from a

**Table 3.6. Ratio of Age-Adjusted Rates per 100,000 Population
for the Ten Leading Causes of Death by Gender and Race, United States, 1991[a]**

Rank order	Cause of death (ninth revision, *International Classification of Diseases*, 1975)	Ratio of Male to female	Ratio of Black to white
	All causes	1.73	1.60
1	Diseases of heart	1.89	1.47
2	Malignant neoplasms, including neoplasms of lymphatic and hematopoietic tissue	1.47	1.37
3	Cerebrovascular diseases	1.19	1.89
4	Chronic obstructive pulmonary diseases and allied conditions	1.74	0.83
5	Accidents and adverse effects	2.63	1.28
	Motor vehicle accidents	2.39	0.98
	All other accidents and adverse effects	2.94	1.69
6	Pneumonia and influenza	1.65	1.46
7	Diabetes mellitus	1.14	2.42
8	Suicide	4.37	0.57
9	Human immunodeficiency virus infection	7.44	3.42
10	Homicide and legal intervention	3.84	6.76

[a]Source: National Center for Health Statistics (1993a).

study in which elderly patients with repetitive chest pain were compared for fee-for-service (FFS) and health maintenance organization (HMO) systems of care. "Exposure" in this case is associated with the system of care; "referral to physician specialist" is the event of interest. The RR of referral to a physician specialist is the incidence rate of referral to physician specialist in the FFS group divided by the incidence rate of referral to physician specialist in the HMO group. From the data in this example, the RR is interpreted to mean that those in FFS plans are 1.21 times more likely to be referred to a physician specialist for repetitive chest pains than elderly persons in an HMO. A useful source of information to investigate the relationship between clinical, nutritional, and behavioral factors and morbidity, mortality, and hospital

**Table 3.7. Calculation of the Relative Risk (RR)[a]
and Odds Ratio (OR)[b] of the Relationship between
Referral to a Specialist and Type of Health Plan
among Enrollees with Repetitive Chest Pain,
65 Years of Age and Older[c]**

Plan type	Referral to specialist Yes	Referral to specialist No	Total
Fee for service	293 (*a*)	213 (*b*)	524
Health maintenance organization	256 (*c*)	200 (*d*)	556

[a]RR = $[a/(a+b)]/[c/(c+d)] = 1.21$
[b]OR = $(a/b)/(c/d) = 1.08$
[c]Data from Clement *et al.* (1994).

utilization is the National Health and Nutrition Examination Survey I Epidemiologic Follow-up Study (Finucane *et al.*, 1992).

Because true measures of risk cannot always be readily derived, some method for estimating chances of events occurring relative to exposure is required. For this reason, the odds ratio, which is an approximation of the relative risk, is used. The **odds** of an event is the ratio of the occurrence of some exposure that exists relative to it not existing. Thus, in 100 persons with lung cancer, if 80% of them were smokers, the odds in favor of being a smoker would be 80:20 or 4:1. The **odds ratio** (OR) is the ratio of one odds to another. The representation and interpretation of the OR depends upon whether or not the odds of exposure or the odds of an event is being compared between two groups (Table 3.8). The OR in Table 3.7 is computed as an event odds ratio, since the data are derived from a quasiexperimental design. Thus, the odds of referral to a specialist (event) is 1.08 times more likely for patients with repetitive chest pain in the FFS group than for those who were in a managed care group (exposure).

It must be kept in mind that both the OR and the RR are descriptive measures used to appraise the strength of an association. When data are presented in the format as in the 2×2 table arrangement found in Table 3.8, an OR or RR greater than 1 means that the exposure increases the likelihood of the event. An RR or OR less than 1 means that exposure decreases the likelihood of the event. An RR or OR equal to 1 means that the chances of the event occurring in the exposed and unexposed is equal. A statistical test, such as χ^2 or Fisher's exact test, must be applied to the data to determine if the association represented by the RR or OR is statistically significant.

To assess the proportion of the risk of exposure from a particular factor, the **population attributable risk** (PAR) percent may be computed. This measure has importance, as it assesses the theoretically achievable reduction in risk if the risk factor were entirely removed from a population. The PAR percentage is calculated as follows:

$$PAR\% = [P_e (RR - 1)]/[1 + P_e (RR - 1)] \times 100\%$$

where PAR% is the population attributable risk percentage, P_e is the proportion of the population exposed, and RR is the ratio of the incidence rate among the exposed to the incidence rate among the nonexposed. The PAR percentage can also be estimated from the OR (Cole and MacMahon, 1971).

When confronted with a variety of risk factors for a disease and limited resources, the PAR percentage can help determine which interventions may have the greatest impact for a

Table 3.8. Computation of Odds Ratios[a]

	Event	
	Yes	No
Exposure		
Yes	*a*	*b*
No	*c*	*d*

[a]Odds ratio of exposure = $(a/c)/(b/d)$.
Odds ratio of event = $(a/b)/(c/d)$.

Table 3.9. Prevalence of Risk Factors for Stroke and Population Attributable Risk Percentage[a]

Risk factors	Percentage of population exposed	Relative risk	Population attributable risk %
Hypertension	56.2	2.73	49.3
Cigarette smoking	27.0	1.52	12.3
Atrial fibrillation	4.0	3.60	9.4
Heavy alcohol consumption	7.2	1.68	4.7

[a]Data from Gorelick (1994).

population. Table 3.9 displays modifiable risk factors for stroke. The PAR percentage for hypertension was derived as follows:

$$PAR\% = [0.562 (2.73 - 1)]/[1 + 0.562 (2.73 - 1)] \times 100\% = 49.3\%$$

Thus, of the risk factors displayed, interventions aimed at preventing stroke through hypertension control would have the greatest impact on the health status of the population, potentially eliminating 49.3% of strokes.

Summary

This chapter has presented common descriptive measures useful in planning and evaluating health care services. Rates are used to identify and prioritize health problems with a population, assess variability of the utilization of health care resources, evaluate progress toward achieving health goals, and propose hypotheses regarding the etiology and control of health problems. Descriptive measures are also used to assess the relationship between exposure and outcome (relative risk, odds ratio, and population attributable risk). These measures are useful in identifying the components of the health care system that could be modified to improve the health status of populations. The type of epidemiologic measure used depends upon the objective of the assessment, the nature of the health problem being evaluated, and the type of data available.

Case Studies

Case Study No. 1
In-Hospital Mortality from Hip Fractures in the Elderly

Hip fractures are an important cause of mortality and morbidity in the elderly population. The incidence rate of hip fractures rises with increasing age, with the highest rates being among white females followed by white males, black females, and black males. Following hip fracture, persons are at greater risk of death than the general population. In addition, marked differences in survival following a hip fracture are noted according to gender and race. Differences in survival have been hypothesized to result from concomitant medical conditions, differences in medical care utilization and the delivery of services provided during hospitalization or subsequent to discharge. Since virtually all patients with hip fractures are likely to be hospitalized, the examination of factors contributing to mortality during hospitalization may suggest areas where measures could be implemented to improve survival for these persons. Myers *et al.* (1991) examined factors contributing to inpatient mortality. Hospital discharge abstracts provided information on patient demographics, clinical characteristics, and vital status at discharge. Selected data from this study are displayed in Table 3.10.

Q.1. Compute the age-specific and race- and gender-specific mortality rates for hip fracture per 100 persons admitted using data from the above table. Which population subgroups are at highest risk of death?

Q.2. Although women have a higher incidence of hip fractures than men, why would the mortality rate for men be higher?

Q.3. Why were data pooled over 10 years?

Q.4. What other source of mortality data could have been used in this study?

Q.5. What measurement errors could enter into the computation of the inpatient mortality rates using hospital discharge abstract data? How would these affect the estimate of the rate?

Case Study No. 2
Medicaid Prenatal Care: Fee for Service versus Managed Care

The move to a managed-care system for coverage of Medicaid recipients is being extensively adopted by states. Most studies show no difference between fee-for-service and managed-care (MC) arrangements. However, most of these studies have focused on outcomes of care for elderly persons. Little is known about outcomes of care under MC in low-income younger populations. Krieger *et al.* (1992) compared the outcomes of care for pregnant Medicaid recipients who were enrolled in either FFS or MC. Data from Medicaid eligibility files, managed care enrollment files, claims files, and birth certificates were merged to provide information on characteristics of the women and outcomes of care.

Table 3.10. In-Hospital Deaths among Admissions for Hip Fractures by Age, Race, and Gender, Maryland, 1979–1988[a]

Characteristic	Number of admissions for hip fractures	Number of deaths
Age		
65–69	2,542	68
70–74	3,842	140
75–79	5,374	216
80–84	6,541	297
≥85	9,071	618
Race and gender		
White males	4,980	392
White females	20,675	847
Black males	506	38
Black females	1,209	62
Total	27,370	1,339

[a]Data from Myers *et al.* (1991).

In the FFS plan examined, there were 4770 eligible enrollees; in the MC plans, there were 111 eligible enrollees. In the FFS plan, 7.1% had low-birth-weight (LBW) babies; in the MC plan, 5.8% had low-birth-weight babies.

Q.1. What is the odds ratio (OR) of a low-birth-weight baby in managed care versus fee for service?

Q.2. What would the OR be if the incidence of LBW babies in the managed-care group were twice that of the FFS?

Q.3. How could the sources of data used affect the OR calculated in Q.1?

Case Study No. 3
Rick Factors for Coronary Artery Disease

One of the leading causes of death in the United States is coronary artery disease (CAD). The Framingham Heart Study has provided a wealth of information on risk factors for CAD to guide the development of health promotion programs. From longitudinal studies, such as the Framingham Study, various epidemiologic measures are possible to compute including incidence, relative risk, and population attributable risk. Each measure of risk has its own meaning and utility in planning health services and health policy. Wilson and Evans (1993) report the following data from the Framingham Study: prevalence of smokers, 42%, nonsmokers, 58%; rate of CAD in smokers, 12.6 per 100 population, in nonsmokers, 7.7 per 100 population.

Q.1. What is the relative risk (RR) of CAD for smoking?

Q.2. What does an RR of 1.64 mean?

Q.3. What is the risk of CAD attributable to smoking?

Q.4. If you were planning to introduce health promotion services on an individual level, which epidemiologic measure would be most useful?

Case Study No. 4
Violence in the Workplace

Health professionals have, heretofore, accepted that assault by a patient was part of the "hazards" associated with the job. In May, 1993, the Occupational Health and Safety Administration (OSHA) laid out its policy on workplace violence. The implications of this policy were that suffering attacks by patients was no longer acceptable. In September, 1993, an employee of a midwestern psychiatric hospital reported to OSHA excessive exposure to patients' violent behavior. The hospital was cited for failing to protect hospital employees from patients' violent behavior. This was the first OSHA citation for an employer failing to deal with workplace violence. Violent behavior is common among patients in a psychiatric hospital. Patients who exhibit violent behavior are some elderly who may be cognitively impaired, individuals undergoing detoxification from a chemical dependency, those with psychiatric problems, and adolescents with behavioral disorders. The hospital did not contest the citation and provided a detailed description of how it analyzed its problem and would modify policies and procedures based upon the data. Epidemiologic measures were used in the analysis to develop strategies for prevention.

Q.1. The first thing the hospital did was establish a system to monitor the incidence rate of violence. Propose what events should be included in the numerator and how the denominator should be constructed.

Q.2. Describe how epidemiologic rate measures could be used to identify which patients pose the highest risk of violence to hospital personnel and when and where this occurs.

References

Centers for Disease Control, 1986, Premature mortality in the United States: Public health issues in the use of years of potential life lost, *Morbid. Mortal. Weekly Rev.* **35**:1S–11S.

Centers for Disease Control, 1989, Mortality data from the national vital statistics system, *Morbid. Mortal. Weekly Rev.* **38**:118–123.

Chiang, C. L., 1961, Standard error of the age-adjusted death rate, *Vital Stat.* **47**:275–285.

Clement, D. G., Retchin, S. M., Brown, R. S., and Stegall, M. H., 1994, Access and outcomes of elderly patients enrolled in managed care, *JAMA* **271**:1487–1492.

Cole, P., and MacMahon, B., 1971, Attributable risk percent in case-control studies, *Br. J. Prev. Soc. Med.* **25**:242–244.

Finucane, F. F., Freid, V. M., Madans, J. H., Cox, C. S., Kleinman, J. C., Rothwell, S. T., Barbano, H., and Feldman, J. J., 1992, *Plan and operation of the NHANES I Epidemiologic Followup Study, 1987*, Vital Health Statistics 1, National Center for Health Statistics, Washington, DC.

Fleiss, J. L., 1981, *Statistical Methods for Rates and Proportions*, John Wiley & Sons, New York.

Gorelick, P. B., 1994, Stroke prevention: An opportunity for efficient utilization of health care resources during the coming decade, *Stroke* **25**:220–224.

Kahn, H. A., and Sempos, C. T., 1989, *Statistical Methods in Epidemiology*, Oxford University Press, New York.

Krieger, J. W., Connell, F. A., and LoGerfo, J. P., 1992, Medicaid prenatal care: A comparison of use and outcomes in fee-for-service and managed care, *Am. J. Public Health* **82**:185–190.

Lauderdale, D. S., Furner, S. E., Miles, T. P., and Goldberg, J., 1993, Epidemiologic uses of Medicare data, *Epidemiol. Rev.* **15**:319–327.

Myers, A. H., Robinson, E. G., Van Natta, M. L., Michelson, J. D., Collins, K., and Baker, S. P., 1991, Hip fractures among the elderly: Factors associated with in-hospital mortality, *Am. J. Epidemiol.* **134**:1128–1137.

National Center for Health Statistics, 1992, *Current Estimates from the National Health Interview Survey, 1991*. Vital and Health Statistics, Series 10, No. 184, Public Health Services, Hyattsville, MD.

National Center for Health Statistics, 1993a, *Sample design: Third National Health and Nutrition Examination Survey*, PHS 92-1387, U.S. Government Printing Office, Washington, DC.

National Center for Health Statistics, 1993b, *Advance Report of Final Mortality Statistics, 1991. Monthly Vital Statistics Report* 42, no. 2, Suppl, Public Health Service, Hyattsville, MD.

National Center for Health Statistics, 1993c, *Health, United States, 1992*, Public Health Service, Hyattsville, MD.

Ries, L. A. G., Hankey, B. F., Miller, B. A., Hartman, A. M., and Edwards, B. K., 1991, *Cancer Statistics Review 1973–88*, NIH Pub. No. 91-2789, National Cancer Institute, Bethesda, MD.

Rothberg, D. L., 1982, *Regional Variations in Hospital Use*, Lexington Books, Inc., Lexington, MA.

Siegel, P. Z., Wallter, M. N., Frazier, E. L., and Mariolis, P., 1993, Behavioral risk factor surveillance, 1991: Monitoring progress toward the nation's year 2000 health objectives, *Morbid. Mortal. Weekly Rev. Surv. Summ.* **42**:1–20.

Wilson, P. W. F., and Evans, J. C., 1993, Coronary artery disease prediction, *Am. J. Hypertens.* **6**:309S–313S.

4

Strategic Planning, an Essential Management Tool for Health Care Organizations, and Its Epidemiologic Basis

Frances J. Jaeger

Organizations charged with the delivery of health services exist in an environment in which no single organization can isolate itself from the change that surrounds it. Strategic planning offers organizations a tool for analyzing the impact of changing trends and environmental conditions. It equips health care managers with a systematic process for setting future direction, developing effective strategies, and ensuring that the organization's structure and systems are compatible with long-term survival and success. Through the use of strategic planning, organizations learn *to think* and *to act* strategically, thereby making better judgments about the future and becoming more proactive in shaping it.

Epidemiologic Basis of Strategic Planning

To influence health positively by anticipating and responding to changes in needs and health status among populations targeted for service is the epidemiologic basis of strategic planning for health care organizations. Typically, such organizations exist to deliver a service or set of related services in response to the health needs of defined populations. Thus, an appropriate measure of the effectiveness of health care organizations is the extent that they attain, through service delivery, specific outcomes that improve the health status of those served.

Over time, the characteristics and the health needs of populations change. Consequently, health care organizations (as well as larger health systems) must employ a process, such as

Frances J. Jaeger   University of Illinois Perinatal Center and Department of Health Systems Management, Rush University, Chicago, Illinois 60612.

Epidemiology and the Delivery of Health Care Services: Methods and Applications, edited by Denise M. Oleske. Plenum Press, New York, 1995.

strategic planning, to maintain awareness of demographic changes and altered disease patterns. Otherwise, they risk obsolescence by responding to old and irrelevant sets of health needs and service demands.

The size of a population is considered the most useful predictor of future needs and the utilization of health services (MacStravic, 1984). As a population increases or decreases in size, the demand for health services generally varies in the same direction. Thus, a country experiencing significant population growth will require expansion of its health system and mobilization of additional resources to satisfy health needs.

Other demographic variables, including age, race, ethnicity, sex, family structure, education, and income affect population transformations that also alter needs and demand for health care. In the United States, the changing age distribution and the *"graying"* of the population are among the most dramatic factors altering the needs of health care consumers.

Age trends associated with defined populations can be summarized visually by population pyramids, which utilize stacked bars to represent age and gender distribution. Pyramids can be constructed to reflect either actual counts of persons in each age–gender subgroup or the percentages that result when the number of persons in each group is divided by the total number of persons in the population at a specific time. When bars of a pyramid represent percentages, the total pyramid must equal 100%. The population pyramids displayed in Fig. 4.1 indicate the changing population structure of the United States between 1950 and 1990, reflecting an aging population. As the post-World War II "baby boomers" begin reaching 65 (around 2011), the country will experience a comparable *"senior boom."* If current life expectancy and fertility trends continue, those 65 and over will constitute one-fifth of the population in 2050 when the declining fertility rates of the 1960s and 1970s will effect a reversal of the growth in the elderly population (U.S. Dept. of Commerce, 1993).

As the absolute numbers and the relative size of age categories change, the characterization of disease within a population and the impact of illness are altered as well. With more people growing older in the United States, heart disease, cancer, and stroke—the causes of illness more common in old age and the leading causes of death in the United States

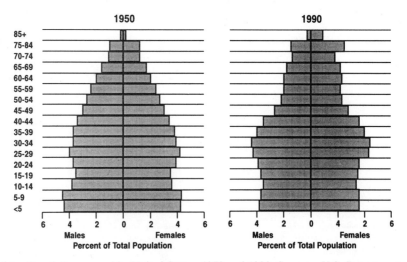

Figure 4.1. Population pyramids, United States, 1950 and 1990. Sources: U.S. Department of Commerce (1953, 1993).

population—are afflicting large numbers and consuming an ever-increasing share of the nation's health resources. The chronicity of these diseases influences the types and the quantity of services required to meet health needs. For instance, the demand for rehabilitative services is growing because more elderly patients need restorative services to improve functioning and to lessen the impact of the chronic conditions that have become prevalent among them (Fig. 4.2).

In the 1980s, notable declines occurred in death rates for several leading causes of death, including those for heart disease and stroke (U.S. Department of Health and Human Services, 1990). However, just when the country began to experience progress in the control of major chronic illness, it was confronted with acquired immune deficiency syndrome (AIDS), which was first identified in the United States in 1981. A disease that results from infection with the human immunodeficiency virus, AIDS, spread so rapidly that it soon reached epidemic proportions. Knowledge of the incidence of the disease, its natural history, and the frequency of comorbidities are essential to ensure the adequacy of health services for AIDS patients. For example, 60% of persons with AIDS have functional limitations at hospital discharge and may require rehabilitation intervention (O'Dell *et al.*, 1991). Since AIDS is a uniformly fatal disease, increasing the availability of resources such as hospices may be an appropriate focus of planning to enable a shift away from the hospital as a place to die. Such a shift would also imply a greater need for outpatient medical services.

Epidemiologic methods identify the variables that are associated with patterns of health problems, the need for care, and the utilization of services. What people do at work and during leisure hours, the level of attention given to good nutrition and exercise, and personal life-style behaviors can result in lesser or greater risks to health. Socioeconomic factors influence both disease patterns and the ability to access services to ameliorate health problems. Biological, hereditary, and genetic factors account for some differences in health status, and increasingly

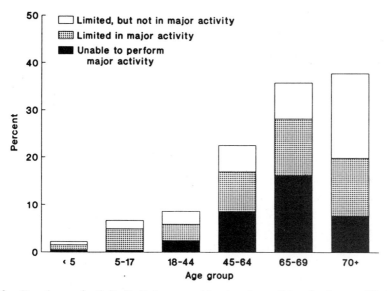

Figure 4.2. Prevalence of activity limitation caused by chronic conditions by degree of limitation and age, 1988. Reprinted with permission from Pope and Tarlov (1991). Copyright 1988 by the National Academy of Sciences. Courtesy of the National Academy Press, Washington, D.C.

the nation is gaining competence in controlling and altering the effects of these factors. Changing beliefs, values, perceptions of health status, and consumer expectations influence service utilization and judgments about the adequacy of available services.

An organization once effective in addressing traditional health problems may be unprepared to tackle the challenges that arise when a population is transformed or when new disease patterns emerge. Strategic planning is not the sole ingredient for success among health care organizations, but failure is almost guaranteed without an appropriate response to the demographic and epidemiologic changes that affect health care needs and demands.

The Theoretical Basis of Strategic Planning

Barry (1985) defines strategic planning as a process directed at finding the "*fit*" between the mission, purpose, and goals of an organization, the forces external to the organization (including the needs of the target population; competitors and allies; and social, political, economic, and technological forces), and the internal resources and capabilities under the organization's control. In the present age of "health care reform," an organization defining its mission as delivery of health care must be cognizant of altered health needs as well as changing organizational requirements that may be imposed from outside the organization. Payers, for example, may elect to do business only with providers organized into a health care alliance or community care network.

In the past, closed-system models were common among the theories proposed to explain organizational behavior. The classical works of Taylor (1947) and Weber (1964) presented closed-system views that were based upon the assumption that the internal structures and processes of an organization are its most important features. More recently, the analysis of organizations has moved toward an open-systems approach which recognizes the importance of the interface or optimum fit between an organization and its environment (Starkweather and Cook, 1983). According to open-systems theory, organizations are not self-contained units. They must relate to elements in their environments to acquire resources for organizational maintenance and for production of outputs associated with goals. They must also interact with their environments for disbursement of goods and services once these are produced (Shortell and Kaluzny, 1983).

Once it was realized that an organization's ability to thrive could be affected by other organizations in its environment, studies were initiated to test numerous hypotheses related to organizational success and interorganizational relationships. These studies led to the development of the tenets of **exchange theory**, which is the foundation of marketing. According to Day (1984), marketing is the primary means by which an organization looks outward and aligns itself with its environment. It is a tool for selecting customers to be served and competitors to be challenged, and it is a means for managing the exchange of valued resources among organizations.

Marketing is associated with the *voluntary* exchange of resources, and this implies that organizations exercise choice in marketing relationships. Organizations can generally select the parties and sometimes the values to be involved in transactions, but they must interact with other organizations if they are truly open systems. They cannot afford to direct all their energies to issues of internal control. An external orientation is critical to survival because the interconnections or resource dependencies that exist among organizations require them to replenish their resources by relinquishing the products or services they generate with the resources controlled by others (Pfeffer and Salancik, 1978). Health care organizations, which are designed primarily for the delivery of services rather than goods, can nevertheless benefit from the practice of good marketing, which is simply the effective management of the exchange process associated with providing services to selected beneficiaries and obtaining the resources for continued operations.

Strategic planning is generally considered essential for effective marketing because it facilitates an organization's understanding of its present and **probable future** environments and empowers the decisions associated with exchange interactions. An organization that successfully integrates strategic planning and marketing into its managerial functions will take advantage of environmental situations that improve relationships with other organizations, thereby satisfying its resource needs and strengthening its capabilities for achieving goals and objectives associated with its mission.

The strategic planning process requires the application of epidemiology to ensure that planning is market-based—that is, responsive to the needs, demands, and wants of targeted populations or the markets to be served. The use of epidemiology within the context of strategic planning has been limited in the past for two reasons. First, the market areas of health care organizations have been difficult to define because of problems in identifying the populations at risk who require specific health services and competing interests among providers. For example, a physician may staff more than one hospital, or multiple hospitals may provide the same service to the same geographic area or to areas that partially overlap. Second, disease and health status data have typically been reported only for large geographic areas or for civil units. With advances in small-area analysis (see Chapter 8) and automated management information systems that offer improved efficiency and expanded storage capabilities, it is possible to gain an increased level of confidence when constructing the probable future market of a health care organization based upon epidemiologic analysis.

Organizational theory and the principles related to the behavior of organizations in their environments provide the conceptual framework for strategic planning. Ideally, when an organization finds itself in a hostile environment or poorly aligned with opportunities as the result of changes in technology, unfavorable political circumstances, changing consumer needs and expectations, or any number of reasons, the organization will adjust its objectives and strategies accordingly. Unfortunately, this ideal scenario is not the reality for many health care organizations. Adjustments may be difficult because of inflexible organizational structures (which fail to alter personnel resources and relationships consistent with changing requirements), outdated management systems (or systems for information, planning, and control that are no longer workable under new conditions), or a general paralysis or inability to respond quickly enough when confronted with an accelerating rate of change. However, deliberative and conscientious application of the strategic planning process can minimize time lags between the recognition of changed environmental forces and the initiation of action to alter the organization's objectives, strategies, structure, and management systems (Kotler and Clarke, 1987). Additionally, when an organization realizes a need to identify new markets or otherwise redefine the population to be served, epidemiology can provide a framework for compiling and analyzing data for consideration during the strategic planning process.

The Strategic Planning Process

Strategic planning is a systematic process that involves a series of steps designed to define a situation or problem, develop strategies, and implement solutions. The process may be represented as six major steps formated around a circle to suggest that strategic planning is a

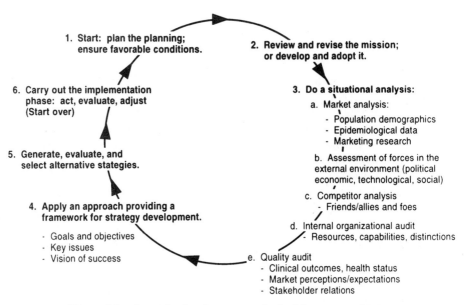

Figure 4.3. Strategic planning process for health care organizations.

cyclical and continuous process (Fig. 4.3). The steps and related tasks of this process are discussed below.

Step 1. Plan the Planning and Ensure Favorable Conditions for Effective Strategic Planning

There are certain conditions that are necessary for an organization to *think and act strategically*: a strategic orientation or ability to recognize the influence of the external environment and to sense significant changes in that environment; a commitment from top-level management to participate in the process and to implement the resulting recommendations; allocation of sufficient resources to carry out the process, including time and technical expertise (such as that required for market research and interpretation of data); consensus on the plan for planning with agreement on how planning participants will be selected, the timetable for initiation and completion of various phases of the process, the approaches and techniques to be employed, and the anticipated benefits or outcomes associated with the effort; and absence of barriers that could prevent completion of the process or interfere with strategic action. When the prerequisites for effective strategic planning are missing, the energy of the organization should be directed at establishing the necessary conditions *before* initiating the process.

Step 2. Review the Organization's Mission Statement and Revise It as Necessary to Ensure that It Remains Relevant to the Organization's Future. If No Written Statement of Mission Exists, Develop and Adopt One

Consideration of the organization's mission should occur early in the planning process because it is the mission that captures an organization's reason for being and defines its domain (or the territory in which the organization conducts its business). Later in the planning process (when an organization develops a better appreciation of its situation and unique capabilities), it may be necessary to refine the original mission statement or even replace it with one that is judged to be more appropriate for the present as well as the future.

The elements that Bryson (1988) recommends for inclusion in a well-defined mission statement, adapted for a health care organization, are presented in Table 4.1. Organizations that deliver health care should delineate the markets or populations that are targeted for service as well as the specific needs that will be addressed. Markets may be determined by geography or legal mandate, or other considerations (such as severity of need or purchasing power) may affect the selection and definition of the organization's customers.

Step 3. Do a Situational Analysis That Encompasses Assessments of Elements of the Organization's External and Internal Environments as Well as an Evaluation of the Impact of the Organization's Efforts

This step encompasses the *core* set of analytic activities that distinguish strategic planning from other types of planning. The five tasks associated with a situational analysis are: a market analysis, an assessment of forces in the external environment, a competitive analysis, an internal organizational audit, and a quality audit. Demographic and epidemiologic data are crucial to this step.

Task A: Market Analysis

A **market analysis** is a planning task initiated for the purpose of defining and characterizing the market and its health care needs and preferences. The term **market** usually refers to the constituency (of individuals, groups, or other organizations) that the focal organization actually serves or desires to serve through involvement in exchange transactions. A market analysis is essential for ensuring that health care organizations employ an approach for planning and delivering services that is **market-based**—that is, truly responsive to the needs and wants of current and prospective patients or customers. This market is what may be referred to in classical epidemiologic terms as the **population at risk** that a provider organization targets for the delivery of health care services.

To characterize both the current and future market, the analysis should include assess-

---

Table 4.1. Key Elements of a Mission Statement[a]

Identification of the organization

Specification of the population targeted for service (and the basis for selecting this "market," e.g., geography, disease category, other)

The health-related needs or problems the organization intends to address

In general terminology, what the organization will do to respond to specified needs or problems of the population targeted for service

How the organization will relate to key stakeholders, and the values to be promoted in stakeholder relationships

An indication of the organization's philosophy and values

Features that distinguish the organization

---

[a]Adapted from Bryson (1988).

ment of: the number of individuals constituting the actual or potential market; the numbers by sex and age associated with its subgroups (or market segments); fertility patterns and the life-cycle stage of the market; income, employment, and educational levels; racial, ethnic, and cultural characteristics; and the anticipated changes in the population over time. Data from the census of the population can be used for determining the numbers of persons in each of these market segments.

Relative to a defined market and within the context of strategic planning, epidemiology presents a conceptual framework and tools for describing the frequency of health problems in targeted populations. For organizations designed to serve market segments (such as specific diagnostic groups), epidemiologic methods can be used to provide estimates of the number of individuals currently affected by certain diseases and to project patterns of disease over time to facilitate a match between future needs and service availability. Table 4.2 illustrates an example of how an estimation can be done.

In planning services to address health problems using an epidemiologic framework, Baker and Reinke (1988) state the following questions should be answered: *What is the magnitude of the problem? What trends are evident? What populations and population subgroups are affected by the problem?* In order to address these questions, health status data may be presented for the market population of interest to the service provider. Data may consist of: population data related to health status and its determinants (e.g., the number and percentage of the population living below the poverty level or depending on public assistance, the proportion of pregnant women without a source of prenatal care, the percentage of unmarried mothers, vaccination levels of children); data that help to describe the intensity of a problem, such as incidence, mortality, and prevalence rates (of disease and of exposure); data for other rates, such as those related to fertility; and the results of epidemiologic studies pertinent to risk factors (person-related, life-style, or environmental). These data may be cross-tabulated based on selected demographic variables and contrasted with one or more sets of national, state, or local data. Such comparisons enable an understanding of differences in the distribution of diseases and determinants, and they provide guidance for development of actions. For a health care organization to address health needs, it is essential to perform a market analysis utilizing epidemiologic data.

The determination of appropriate measures of health status and the selection of formats for the presentation of data are among the most difficult tasks of a health planner charged with facilitating strategic planning. Crude death rates are easy to calculate and may suffice for

Table 4.2. Estimating Inpatient Cardiac Catheterization Volume in Decatur, Illinois

Age (a)	Number of persons[a] (b)	Rate of cardiac catheterization procedures in short-stay hospitals[b] (c)	Number expected to be hospitalized annually ($d = b \times c$)
<15	17,762	27.0 per 100,000 population	5
15–44	35,968	81.3 per 100,000 population	30
45–64	16,612	893.8 per 100,000 population	149
65+	13,543	1506.3 per 100,000 population	204
Total	83,885	462.5 per 100,000 population	388

[a]U.S. Department of Commerce, Bureau of the Census (1992a,b).
[b]Graves (1994).

purposes of a market analysis. However, when differences in needs among population segments are of concern, then specific rates may be preferred. When the rates of two or more populations are compared, it is usual to age-adjust rates in order to distinguish differences that result from better or poorer health from those that can be attributed to differences in the age composition of the groups (see Chapter 3 on how adjusted rates are computed).

Data on morbidity and disability may be obtained from a variety of sources in the United States, including the National Center for Health Statistics and the results of epidemiologic studies such as the *Established Populations for Epidemiologic Studies of the Elderly* (Cornoni-Huntley *et al.*, 1986). Most states mandate the reporting of certain communicable and noncommunicable diseases, and hence sources of these data are local or state health departments. The publication, *Morbidity and Mortality Weekly Report* (Centers for Disease Control), present disease data at the national level. Special surveys, such as those conducted by the National Center for Health Statistics, provide data on acute and chronic conditions (National Center for Health Statistics, 1992), and health care services utilization (of hospitals, ambulatory care, and long-term care) (Schappert, 1993; Graves, 1994; Strahan, 1993; McCaig, 1992). However, these data may not be generalizable to small geographic areas.

Market analysis facilitates assessment of psychographic variables of the targeted population such as values, attitudes, and belief systems that affect need, the perception of need, and the actual utilization of health services. Marketing can also identify the most favorable conditions for ensuring that exchanges occur and that mutually beneficial results are realized by the parties participating in exchange transactions—that the right clients or patients receive the right services, in a timely manner and in the right places, and that the organizations delivering the services are offered appropriate values in return.

Although many health care organizations define the market to be served on the basis of history and tradition (that is, the market remains the same population that was selected for service from the organization's very beginning), it is important to realize that an organization may find its chances of survival improved by a redefinition of its market—by expanding the traditional delineation, by selecting only specified segments or subsets of the market as originally defined, by turning to an entirely new market, or by applying these strategies in any of a number of combinations. A market audit may thus include the assessment of the various scenarios and consequences of altering the organization's current market. Will a change increase or decrease the types and level of resources available to an organization? What new needs must be addressed if the organization attempts to serve a new market? Which of several potential markets has the greatest needs, would generate the highest level of demand for a given service, or return the greatest benefit if selected for a new venture? These and other questions may require consideration to ensure that an organization and the market it elects to serve receive mutual benefit from the relationship so that it can be sustained over time.

Task B: Assessment of Forces in the External Environment

An **assessment of external trends and forces** is necessary to achieve a clear understanding of the opportunities and threats inherent in the present as well as the future environment of the organization. The assessment should consider factors that affect patterns of disease and disability, the health needs of the population or markets to be served, the actual expression of needs into service demand, and the capabilities of the organization to respond.

Bryson (1988) has used the acronym **PESTs** to refer to the *p*olitical, *e*conomic, *s*ocial, and *t*echnical forces in the external environment. Use of this device may serve as a memory aid, but the external trends and forces should not simply be considered nuisances (or pests). The challenge of strategic planning is to *think strategically* and thus to design strategies that interface with these forces and trends so that they represent opportunities, not annoyances or threats.

Task C: Competitive Analysis

A **competitive analysis** assesses an organization's position in the marketplace relative to other organizations, some of which may compete for the same customers or valued resources or otherwise interfere with an organization's ability to serve its selected markets. Porter (1980, 1985) argues that an organization should analyze key forces that shape its industry and identify strategic options for gaining competitive advantage through modification of variables under its control. If an organization performs a competitive analysis and judges itself weak in comparison to its competition, then it should seek strategies to improve its position. If the organization is already positioned well, a situational analysis can strengthen awareness of the elements of the organization's advantage and increase the probability of sustaining it.

The structure of the United States health system is becoming more complex and pluralistic every day. Despite the declining prominence of hospital care and a nearly a 14% decrease in inpatient admissions between 1980 and 1990, the health care system has expanded because of *"exploded"* demand for outpatient services and the growth of long-term care (American Hospital Association, 1991). Many different types of providers now function in a variety of settings under numerous organizational arrangements. In response to increasing competition, many health delivery organizations have become engaged in aggressive pursuit of competitive strategies to improve market share. In today's climate, competitive analysis must do more than identify competitors; it must also find those who could be allies or potential collaborators. Thus, joint ventures, mergers, and partnerships are among the cooperative relationships that could represent suitable strategies for ensuring the adequacy of resources for organizational maintenance and effectiveness. Coddington and Moore (1987) include a discussion of several noncompetitive strategies (e.g., physician bonding, networking, and development of multi-hospital systems) that should be evaluated as options for attaining competitive advantage.

Task D: Internal Organizational Audit

An **internal organizational audit** is an assessment of the resources under an organization's control. It encompasses current and projected staff resources and capabilities, financial assets and sources of reimbursement, facilities and equipment, planning and decision-making systems, and market assets (such as a favorable reputation in the community and good public relations). The purpose of this type of audit is to develop an understanding of the strengths and weaknesses of the organization so that it will balance what is needed and wanted by its markets against what it can feasibly do to respond to such needs and wants (Kotler and Clarke, 1987).

Since health care is a personnel-intensive field, it can be affected significantly by changes in the quantity and quality of the human resource pool that is prepared and available to deliver services. Ratios of major categories of health personnel to a specified population are useful indicators for assessing availability. Table 4.3 provides an example of such ratios. The table indicates that registered nurses will become less numerous among the U.S. population by 2020—although the projected 2020 ratio will be nearly equivalent to that for 1980. The primary reason for this projected decrease is declining enrollments in nursing educational programs. As a consequence, the production system is unable to replace members of the current pool as they reach retirement age.

Ratios alone are inadequate for assessing the adequacy of human resources. Personnel

**Table 4.3. Actual and Projected
Ratio of Registered Nurses
to the U.S. Population, 1970–2020**[a]

Year	Ratio per 100,000 population
1970	368.9
1980	560.0
1988	670.4
2000	713.0
2020	558.0

[a]Sources: National Center for Health Statistics
(1991); Bureau of Health Professions (1990).

requirements change over time and are influenced by such factors as changing needs and demands, structural changes in the health system, and changing productivity levels resulting from use of supportive personnel and technological advances (Baker, 1988). Therefore, the current and projected supply of any personnel category must be compared to the requirements for that category based upon a model that incorporates multiple factors for determination of need. This comparison is called **gap analysis**, and it results in the quantification of deficits or surpluses based upon a comparison of the actual or projected supply against numbers representing current or anticipated requirements. The *Seventh Report to the President and Congress on the Status of Health Personnel in the United States* (Bureau of Health Professions, 1990) provides several examples of gap analyses. The report supports its conclusion that the supply of registered nurses in 2000 will be deficient by 135,000 to 690,800 nurses according to a criteria-based model utilized by the Bureau of Health Professionals. This model projects future nursing requirements based upon the Bureau's judgment about the quantity of nursing personnel that will be required to achieve national health care goals.

Although national and regional manpower trends may have an impact on the capabilities of a health care organization, the internal audit should focus on resource variables that are subject to change through alteration of organizational strategies. If an organization is affected by constrained resources (personnel, financial, or otherwise) or resources that vary in availability, it may be difficult to provide health services consistent with the needs of its service population. The "resourceful" organization will recognize and evaluate several alternatives for adjusting to a troubling set of circumstances. Alternatives may include identifying and employing new resources to accomplish essentially the same mission, defining a new mission that can be accomplished with diminished resources, or determining how resources can be used more efficiently to achieve an equal effect with fewer resources.

Task E: Quality Audit

A quality audit is an assessment of how well the organization is meeting expectations. This audit should consider the objectives the organization has set for itself (as reflected in its mission, goals, and objectives) as well as the expectations that affect consumer judgment about quality. In addition, the audit should assess the ability of the organization to satisfy the expectations of stakeholders or constituencies that have an interest in or an influence on the organization (Table 4.4).

Within the context of strategic planning, quality audits should address the traditional elements of clinical outcomes (or effects that result from the application of medical science

**Table 4.4. Questions to Address in the Quality Audit Component
of the Situational Analysis (of the Strategic Planning Process)**[a]

What does quality mean to staff of the organization (at various levels) and to members of its governing or policy-making board? What does quality mean to those the organization seeks to serve?

What gaps in service quality do consumers experience in the use of our services?

Does the organization meet performance standards commonly utilized for measuring services like ours?

Is there evidence that the organization is achieving objectives pertinent to improving the health status of the population (by decreasing morbidity, mortality, disability, pain, or discomfort)?

What does the organization need to achieve desirable clinical outcomes and meet the expectations of consumers as well as the expectations set by organizations that monitor quality in health care (such as the Joint Commission on Accreditation of Healthcare Organizations)?

Does the organization have the capability to provide quality, and if not, what does it lack?

What specific mechanisms (such as committee structures and approaches for monitoring satisfaction) should be implemented to ensure that the organization meets quality expectations?

[a]Adapted from Baynham (1991).

and technology) and the processes of delivering care. However, it is not enough for a health care organization to decrease mortality, morbidity, disability, pain, and discomfort in the population served. It must also determine if consumers are satisfied with the behavior of caregivers and the attributes and conditions of service delivery (i.e., timeliness, price, convenience, and the attractiveness of surroundings). Based upon findings of a quality audit, the organization should position itself to promote its positive image or implement modifications to improve patient/customer satisfaction. In addition, the organization should strive to maintain productive and beneficial relationships with organizations with the potential for greatest impact (positive or negative) due to control of certain values—either concrete resources or the ability to grant or withhold approval or recognition. Third-party payers, licensing, and accrediting organizations are examples of such stakeholders. Since it is generally impossible to satisfy all stakeholders at once, it is important to concentrate on effective management of relationships with *key* stakeholders.

Step 4. Apply an Approach for Defining the Key Issues, Focusing the Attention of the Organization, and Establishing the Framework for the Next Step of Strategy Development

Generally, this step involves proposing and achieving consensus on goals and measurable objectives relating to an organization's desired future. A goal can be defined as a broad statement indicating general direction toward a desired future state. Objectives are more specific statements that indicate in measurable terms what is to be accomplished and when. Each objective should make a contribution toward achievement of a goal, but a single objective need not lead to full attainment of the goal. The situational analysis that precedes the formulation of goals should result in the generation of objectives that are meaningful and significant to the organization, realistic, sufficiently ambitious and yet attainable, consistent with the organization's responsibilities and authority, and compatible with its goals and values. When appropriate objectives are developed, they provide both a framework for designing strategies as well as one for measuring performance. Epidemiologic data are used in the formulation of the goals and objectives as well as in the formulation of strategies. For example, the *Epidemiologic Catchment Area Study* (discussed in Johnson *et al.*, 1992) has reported that

23% of the population has depressive symptoms. Depressive symptoms are associated with high population-attributable risk percentages of emergency department use, medical consultations for emotional problems, and suicide attempts (Johnson *et al.*, 1992). These data may prompt the organization to ensure the inclusion of mental health services in its future plans.

Step 5. Generate, Evaluate, and Select Alternative Strategies for Achieving Organizational Goals and Objectives or the Best Alignment of the Organization with the Opportunities in Its Environment

Characteristic of any true planning process is the systematic generation of potential strategies, or the means to achieve a defined end. Depending on the planning approach utilized, the strategies must also be evaluated to assess their potential for achieving objectives, addressing strategic issues, or moving the organization toward its vision of success.

Bandrowski (1985) recommends that strategies be developed through the use of a **sequential thought process** and "**creative planning**" techniques. The first step in the thought process (which is comparable to the situational analysis discussed in Step 3) is to gain an understanding of issues to be addressed, problems to be solved, or the future to be created. Next, an unconstrained thought process is employed for combining ideas and generating a sufficiently large number of potential strategies; this is to be done in a nonjudgmental manner to facilitate creative leaps in the design of new visions and innovations. Nutt (1984) provides a detailed description of useful creative thinking techniques, including brainstorming and synectics (or the combining of seemingly unrelated things), nominal groups, and Delphi surveys. Day (1984) elaborates five other approaches for generating creative strategy options: challenging present strategies, looking for strategic windows, playing on competitors' vulnerabilities, changing the rules of the competitive game, and enhancing customer value. Following the development of options, judgmental thinking should be utilized to narrow the field of potential strategies to those that can achieve the desired results and meet selection criteria such as technical and financial feasibility, acceptability to key decision-makers, consistency with objectives, adaptability, and cost-effectiveness. The number of strategies to be selected generally depends on the level of resources available for application during the implementation phase. When resources are plentiful, multiple strategies may be selected. In the more usual scenario of scarce resources, a limited number of alternatives can be selected, and some order of priority may be assigned.

Step 6. Carry Out the Implementation Phase of Strategic Planning, Detailing Operational Action Plans and Budgets, Monitoring Impact, and Making Midcourse Adjustments as Necessary

This step encompasses translating decisions about strategic directions into plans that specify the organization's programs, tactics for attracting customers and promoting the organization's products and services, and the application of resources to support implementation efforts. Generally, action plans contain a purpose or objective for each program (or set of related services), the steps or series of actions required to implement the program, a timetable, and identification of the individuals responsible for carrying out the actions. For complex organizations, strategic action plans may be developed for major programs or groupings of related services, on a departmental basis, or by functional areas. Budgets serve as a control and coordinating mechanism for integrating all aspects of strategy within available resources. Therefore, if implementation of the strategic plan requires organizational restructuring, modification of staff assignments, or redistribution of resources from one program or service to another, then these changes should be reflected in approved budgets.

Effective implementation requires a control system for monitoring organizational performance, assessing the impact of overall strategies and specific tactics, and providing feedback about adjustments that may be necessary to achieve desired outcomes. If specific and quantifiable objectives were delineated previously, then evaluation of effectiveness will focus on two questions:

Were the recommended tactics or actions carried out?
If yes, did they accomplish the stated objectives?

If an organization identified strategic issues or created a vision of success, then performance would be measured against key indicators of success. Epidemiologic data can provide measures of that success and answer such questions as:

Did the health status of the population improve as a result of the strategic initiative?

Performance of a quality audit (discussed previously as a component of the situational analysis) is another means of determining if the organization improved its ability to deliver health services in a manner consistent with quality expectations.

Data Resources for Strategic Planning

Each step of the planning process requires data. However, the analytic phase of the situational analysis (step 3) is especially dependent on the compilation of relevant and accurate data and the transmittal of information that will directly aid decision makers. Summarized in Table 4.5 are some useful resources for strategic planning.

Tools to Facilitate Strategic Planning

Decisions stemming from strategic planning are appropriately influenced by facts, the subjective interpretation of factual data as well as the attitudes, preferences, values, and beliefs that are held by planning participants. Various tools and group techniques have been utilized to summarize important facts and to build consensus around key issues and preferred strategies. One tool that has been recommended for strategic planning is a SWOT analysis (or an assessment of *s*trengths, *w*eaknesses, *o*pportunities, and *t*hreats). A **SWOT analysis** combines the systematic analysis of an organization's internal strengths and weaknesses with the externally oriented assessment of the opportunities and threats in the environment (Bryson, 1988). The same type of systematic analysis has been recommended (and named by various acronyms) by others who propose that such an analysis is a prerequisite for an organization to undertake conscientious action to improve its alignment with new opportunities in the environment.

Figures 4.4 and 4.5 provide examples of worksheets that can be utilized for purposes of obtaining input for a SWOT analysis. They are designed as tools to stimulate discussion among members of a planning group. Additional examples of tools that can be used during the strategic planning process can be found in the growing body of literature on this subject (Barry, 1985; Kotler and Clarke, 1987; Spiegel and Hyman, 1991).

Table 4.5. Examples of Useful References for
Strategic Planning for Health Care Organizations

Reference	Description
TrendWatch (AHSM)	Health care marketing experts rate the importance and significance of trends affecting the health care industry in quarterly newsletters
Environmental Assessment for Rural Hospitals (AHA, 1992a); *Environmental Assessment for Urban Hospitals* (AHA, 1992b)	External factors influencing urban and rural hospitals and their communities are discussed; strategies for addressing the future are presented
The Health Care Data Source Book (Fry and Young, 1992)	For each state, information is provided about organizations that publish inpatient, outpatient, and financial data; studies and reports of special interest to planners and managers are listed
Patterns in HMO Enrollment (GHAA, 1993)	HMO enrollment is described by various characteristics; inpatient and physician utilization patterns are presented
Market Research Handbook for Health Care Professionals (Keckley, 1988)	Various market research approaches and analytical tools are described; sample questionnaires are provided
National Health Interview Survey (NCHS, 1992)	Data are provided on incidence of acute conditions, prevalence of chronic conditions, restriction in activity for these conditions, and use of medical services
Health, United States, 1993 (NCHS, 1994b)	Data are provided on indicators and determinants of health status, utilization of health services, current health care resources, and health care expenditure patterns
HEDIS 2.0 (NCQA, 1993)	Information is provided about how to specify, calculate, and report information on quality, enrollee satisfaction, utilization, and financial data for health plans
Measuring and Managing Patient Satisfaction (Steiber and Krowinski, 1990)	Approaches for collecting and analyzing patient satisfaction with services are presented
Statistical Abstract of the United States (U.S. Dept. of Commerce, annually)	Population projections and data on various aspects of the nation's health and use of services are provided
1990 Census of the Population (U.S. Department of Commerce, 1992a,b)	Detailed characteristics of the population by geographic area, including age, gender, race, education, and income, are presented
Healthy People 2000 (USDHHS, 1990)	Health promotion and disease prevention objectives are presented for the nation with supporting data and references

Sample Opportunities and Threats Worksheet for a Health Care Organization

Instructions:

1. Utilize this worksheet to identify and describe: (a) the current and future market(s) targeted for service, (b) key stakeholders and their expectations, (c) current and potential competitors and allies, and (d) important environmental forces and trends.
2. After completing sections a–d, label each entity or force/trend as an opportunity (O) or a threat (T) or a combination of opportunity/threat (O/T).

A. **Current/Future Market(s):**   Clearly describe the current population (of patients/ customers) that the organization is serving as well as that it intends to serve in the future. Specify size, geographic base (if relevant), as well as *demographic and epidemiologic factors* that are relevant to the health needs of the market(s).

B. **Key Stakeholders:**   List the key stakeholders that influence your organization (such as accrediting bodies and funding sources); briefly summarize the expectations of these stakeholders relative to your organization.

C. **Competitors and Allies:**   Identify both current or potential competitors as well as current or potential allies; briefly indicate the factors that affect the nature of the relationship with these and rate the probability of a change (positive or negative).

D. **Environmental Forces and Trends:**   List the PESTs—political, economic, social, and technological—that will affect the market(s) and its health needs as well as the abilitiy of the organization to respond to needs. Examples: changing fertility patterns and family/ household structures, attitudes toward self vs. governmental responsibility for health care, probability of technological improvements and anticipated treatment break-throughs, passage of new health insurance provisions to cover indigent care.

Figure 4.4.

Sample Internal Organization Audit Worksheet to Identify Strengths and Weaknesses of a Health Care Organization

Instructions:

1. In column A, summarize the status or current level of each resource.
2. In column B, indicate the ideal current level and the level that will be required 3–5 years in the future.
3. In column C, summarize strengths related to each resource category as well as weaknesses. Be specific and identify what health outcome cannot be achieved or what quality expectation cannot be achieved at current or projected future resource levels.

	A. Current status/ level of resource	B. Desirable current and future status or level	C. Strengths and weaknesses (and associated problems related to poor health outcomes and quality expectations)
Staff:			
Financial resources:			
Reimbursement sources:			
Facilities:			
Systems for planning, information, and control:			
Market assets:			

Figure 4.5.

Applicability of the Strategic Planning Process

The strategic planning process is most often applied within a single organization. However, the techniques and steps of the process can be utilized across organizational boundaries to identify and address the health care needs of health systems, communities, regions, states, or even nations.

The Format and Content of the Strategic Plan

By definition, a strategic plan captures the organization's plans for the future and discusses how the organization intends to achieve its vision or desired future state. Strategic plans usually include a mission, broad goals, and specific objectives that are to be accomplished over a period of time, such as 5 years; for some organizations, these elements constitute the entirety of the document labeled "*Strategic Plan.*" A written plan, as opposed to one expressed verbally, provides a more effective tool for influencing budgeting and resource allocation decisions. It can also be a useful tool for gaining consensus during the strategic planning process and communicating the logic and the assumptions underlying strategy recommendations to those who will be responsible for implementation over time.

There is considerable variation in the format and content of strategic plans. They may be very short or detailed and complex. They may include the situational analysis with all data collected and analyzed to generate alternatives and recommendations; or this data may be compiled as an appendix or published as a separate document.

Organizations may publish their strategic plans together with their shorter-term, operational plans and budgets that are generally prepared on a yearly basis. It is not essential that the long-range, strategic plan and the operational plan be printed under one cover. However, it is important that an organization use its strategic plan as the framework for the design of its tactical or operational plan. The two plans must "hang together" or achieve consistency with each other. To ensure this, it is sound practice for an organization to review its strategic plan, assessing the need for changes, prior to preparation of the next operational plan. A sample outline of a strategic plan may be found in Table 4.6.

Conclusions

If an organization engages in effective strategic planning—performing an accurate situational assessment, developing a clear sense of direction, and achieving consensus on appropriate overall strategies—then it should produce a plan suitable for motivating and guiding its action for at least a few years into the future. Because many variables in the health care field are surrounded by uncertainty and defy precise prediction, strategic plans typically focus on a planning horizon of 3 to 5 years. It is appropriate for an organization to apply a mechanism for at least a cursory review, and revision as necessary, of its strategic plan on an annual or biannual basis.

Because planning is an adapting and ongoing activity, it can accurately be presented as a circular process—one that is never really finished because the end of one planning process signals the beginning of the next cycle (Day, 1984). During intervals when planning is not occurring on a formal or intensive basis, organizations must nevertheless maintain systems for

Table 4.6. Sample Outline, Strategic Plan for a Health Care Organization

Executive summary (brief statement of overall strategy)[a]

Mission and long-range perspective on where the organization or system should be 3, 5, or more years in the future[a]

Market(s) or population(s) targeted for service (includes demographic and epidemiologic descriptors)[a]

Products or program of services to be offered with volume projections[a]

Goals—what the organization or system hopes to accomplish as a result of the products and services to be offered[b]

Description of the organization's or system's structure with details pertinent to products, services, and resources (staff, facilities, etc.)[b]

Description of governance structure, including function, composition, and membership[b]

Staffing plans and identification of developmental needs; the quantity and quality of personnel required to implement selected strategies[a]

Description of facilities and plans for facility expansion, renovation, or closing[b]

Financial plans with revenue and expense projects; capital budgets if relevant; for an organization, cash flow or balance sheet projections; for a larger system, resources needs and sources of support for the system[a]

Implementation steps—what major tasks should be carried out over the next year and beyond[a]

Identification of obstacles and organizational or system constraints and contingency plans indicating what the organization or system will do under varying circumstances (recognizing that the future cannot be predicted precisely)[b]

Broad operating policies for the future and an overview of anticipated changes to maintain the organization's or system's viability[b]

[a]Sections generally included in strategic plans.
[b]Additional sections recommended for inclusion in strategic plans but not essential.

monitoring compliance with plans, assessing impact, and determining if the assumptions underlying strategies remain valid. Given the proposed changes in the delivery of health care at the national level, organizations must be prepared to change. Strategic planning must be used to determine what changes are required to promote organizational survival and to provide the organization with the benefits of functioning proactively, not simply reactively.

Case Studies

Case Study No. 1
Strategic Planning for a County Health Department

A County Health Department that serves a population of 358,000 in a collar county of a major metropolitan area was recently faced with the resignation of the Director of the Mental Health and Alcoholism Division. This Division is the Health Department's largest; five other divisions support traditional public health functions. Since the Board of Health gained recognition as a community mental health provider, the Division is operated with public funding from the state's Department of Mental Health and Developmental Disabilities (DMH-DD), the Department of Alcohol and Substance Abuse, and a local tax levy.

During the 20-year tenure of the Mental Health Director, change had been incremental and gradual. But at the time he retired, the Health Department was confronted with numerous changes both from within the department and external to it. Within a 6-month time frame, both state agencies funding the Mental Health and Alcoholism Division announced that new conditions on the receipt of funds (such as the implementation of new quality assurance measures) would become effective at the beginning of the next fiscal year. These agencies also offered financial incentives for increasing addiction services to the youth of the county. Medicaid reimbursement for mental health services was also expanded, and DMH-DD allocated new monies to provide mental health services to the homeless and to develop community residential programs for the mentally ill. Other providers in the county also expressed interest in applying for funds, since grant awards for these new initiatives were to be provided on a competitive basis.

The staff of the Division varied in their reactions to the prospects of new leadership. Some of the "old timers" were saddened by the Division Director's departure. Others, especially members of the staff who had been hired in recent years, felt that it was time for a change; they welcomed the beginning of a new era. They felt that the Division had been reactive, rather than proactive, in the face of changing needs and growing demands for services.

The Executive Director, who felt he had the responsibility of attending a range of community meetings and business affairs, sensed increasing discontent in the county with certain areas of health care—especially the availability of primary health care. He frequently heard suggestions that the Health Department should do more. Although the county had been gradually aging, there had been recent support of economic development. Many light manufacturing and service-oriented businesses were relocating to the area, and young adults were moving to the county to take advantage of new job opportunities. The number of births occurring in the county was increasing, as well as the demand for prenatal care and maternity services. One of the hospitals located in the county had almost discontinued its maternity service a few years ago due to poor occupancy of beds; now it was actively recruiting obstetricians and helping them establish their practices. (So far this effort has had limited success.) Families with young children were having difficulty in finding pediatricians who would accept new patients. Just before the opening of school in the fall, the Health Department was inundated with calls from parents who were seeking the location of clinics that would provide school physicals and immunizations.

The Executive Director of the Health Department was relatively new to the Department, having arrived only 6 months prior to the resignation of the Mental Health Director. Members of the Health Department's Board expressed various opinions to him about the hiring of a new Director. Some suggested that a young, ambitious, entrepreneurial individual with credentials in health care as well as business administration was needed to direct the Mental Health Division; such an individual could provide the leadership required for the Division to take advantage of the new opportunities in the field. Other Board members expressed concern that the Mental Health and Alcoholism Division had grown too big; they did not want the community to think only of mental health services when they thought of the Health Department. Some Board members felt more attention should be given to expanding the resources for primary care and to monitoring and improving the quality of the environment, especially since the county was experiencing so much industrial growth all at once.

Q.1. Is this a good time for the Board of Health to initiate strategic planning? Why or why not?

Q.2. Does the scenario, as described, suggest that those involved with the County Health Department share a sense of a common mission?

Q.3. Assuming that a decision is made to proceed with strategic planning, what types of data should be reviewed for the purpose of identifying the key issues?

Q.4. How could these data be used to make an epidemiologic assessment of the needs of the county's service population?

Q.5. Who should be involved in the strategic planning process? Why?

Q.6. Does the scenario suggest any pitfalls or problems that could be encountered during the strategic planning process? Can anything be done to avoid these?

Case Study No. 2
Strategic Planning for Inpatient Rehabilitation Services

In 1988, University Center (UC) Hospital realized that providing patients comprehensive, inpatient rehabilitation services had become a money-loosing endeavor, although other area hospitals had found these services to be among those most profitable. University Center Hospital is part of a major, state-supported university and academic medical center. Its problem seemed to be that it had failed to obtain exemption from the Medicare Prospective Payment System (PPS) for its inpatient rehabilitation program. The hospital therefore received reimbursement for older patients (who tended to utilize more rehabilitation services than other groups) on the basis of each patient's diagnosis-related group (DRG) classification. Since DRGs were designed as a payment mechanism for acute-care episodes, these payments were inadequate to reimburse fully the care of patients who stayed in the hospital beyond the acute phase to undergo rehabilitative therapy designed to improve physical and psychosocial functioning.

Under certain conditions, a hospital could obtain exemption from the Prospective Payment System, and this would result in more favorable cost-based reimbursement for Medicare patients served in the rehabilitation unit. One of the conditions associated with exemption was recognition from the appropriate state agency that the hospital operated a unit meeting state qualifications for a comprehensive rehabilitation service. The hospital was located in Illinois, which operated a Certificate-of-Need Program. The hospital had never sought recognition of beds for a distinct unit; the service utilized beds licensed as acute-care beds. Thus, the first condition for exemption did not exist.

The Hospital Director and other members of the management team, including several Associate Directors, the Chief of the Medical Staff, the Director of Nursing, the Chief Financial Officer, and the Dean of the Medical School met to address the question of whether a rehabilitation unit was really needed, since average daily census was only eight patients over the past year. The state mandated that a rehabilitation unit have at least 12 beds for approval. The first decision made by the Hospital Director and the management team was to hire a consulting firm specializing in development of rehabilitation services. No one on the management team had experience in preparing a Certificate-of-Need or addressing the host of legal and political issues surrounding the process of attaining exemption from PPS. In addition, the management team was concerned with so many other issues that it felt it was impossible to adequately solve the rehabilitation problem without additional personnel.

The consulting firm hired by the hospital was directed to undertake a preliminary feasibility study to assess the probability of gaining state approval through award of a Certificate-of-Need (CON) for a rehabilitation unit. The firm's consultants were also requested to determine if the hospital could demonstrate compliance with other exemption conditions. When the consultants completed this initial study and indicated that the hospital's chances of gaining both a CON and exemption were relatively good, the management team endorsed a more comprehensive feasibility study to assess other factors.

Q.1. Using an epidemiologic framework, what elements should be included in a more comprehensive feasibility study?

Q.2. Did hospital administration abdicate its role in providing leadership to a strategic planning process?

Q.3. Does the scenario describe the best approach for engaging in strategic planning around the issue of the hospital's future direction relative to the delivery of rehabilitation services consistent with epidemiologic trends?

Case Study No. 3
Strategic Planning for Health Professionals' Education

Illinois currently has only one pharmacy school, and it is located in Chicago on the campus of a state university. In 1990, the Metro Health System (MHS), a voluntary association of a medical college and several not-for-profit hospitals serving the Chicago area, began development of another pharmacy school that it planned to open in the fall of 1993. The new pharmacy school would be located in a suburb immediately west of the city, and it would offer a 5-year baccalaureate degree in contrast to the state university's program, which offers only a Doctor of Pharmacy degree requiring 6 years of full-time study. Since the state university attracts many students pursuing academic careers or planning to obtain positions in drug research and development, MHS has designed its program to attract students interested in a shorter program and a practice focus. However, just when student recruitment was to begin in anticipation of the school's opening, the accrediting organization (the American Association of Colleges of Pharmacy) began discussing a recommendation that would eliminate the baccalaureate degree by requiring that all students be educated at the doctoral level by the year 2000.

Currently, arguments are being presented both for and against maintaining the option of a 5-year baccalaureate degree. Some pharmacy schools have expressed fear that payrolls would skyrocket if it became necessary to recruit additional faculty to support a doctoral program. Additionally, there simply would not be enough doctoral-prepared faculty to accommodate all existing pharmacy schools. Drugstore chains and independent owners are opposing the recommendation, suggesting that pharmacists do not need preparation at the doctoral level to practice within their stores. Yet many educators in the pharmaceutical field are countering these arguments by stating that recent scientific advances, the complexity of practice, the changing relationship between the physician and the pharmacist, growing consumer demand for drug information, and many other factors provide a solid rationale for upgrading the education and clinical training of pharmacy students. In addition, many drug companies are expressing dissatisfaction with the supply of researchers and their preparation. They recommend that educational programs begin producing more pharmaceutical personnel with advanced degrees. Otherwise, pharmaceutical companies will be unable to meet the challenges presented by modern-day killers like cancer and AIDS.

Metro Health System is being urged by some of its trustees to reconsider its previous decision to offer a 5-year program. Since only 14 of the 74 pharmacy schools in the nation offer a doctoral degree, the Metro program could gain distinction in the national market despite the fact that the closest competitor already offers such a degree. Other trustees are not as confident that the system has adequate resources and capabilities to offer a doctoral degree at this time; they favor a "wait and see" approach and warn that the proposed recommendation may not have enough support for passage.

Q.1. Which entity or entities in this case could benefit from strategic planning?

Q.2. If you were hired as a consultant to provide guidance to MHS as it evaluates its options, what would you do?

Q.3. List epidemiologic data that would be helpful for performance of an adequate situational analysis.

Case Study No. 4
Strategic Planning for a Perinatal Center

For several decades, Illinois has maintained a state-funded system of perinatal care based on a model of a regional "network" of maternity and neonatal service providers. The leadership within each of the state's ten networks is provided by an officially designated perinatal center consisting of a medical school and its associated tertiary-care hospital. By law and regulation, every hospital licensed to provide maternity care must be affiliated with a perinatal center, and a letter of agreement must be written between a center and each hospital in its network. Although the service areas of downstate networks are geographically distinct, the six centers serving metropolitan Chicago attempt to coordinate care among hospitals and other service providers, which tend to be scattered throughout the metropolitan area.

When networks were initially organized in the late 1970s, public health officials provided guidelines for the structure of networks and supervised negotiations among representatives of Chicago area hospitals as they determined the membership of the various networks. At that time, it was determined that six centers were needed for the area and that the hospitals in a single network should account for approximately 20,000 deliveries. Primary consideration was given to maintenance of relationships that existed between medical schools and the community hospitals they utilized as clinical resources for medical education programs. Attention was also given to ensuring that each network had a fair distribution of facilities with high-risk, specialized resources.

Over the years, many changes have occurred, and the configuration of some of the Chicago area networks presents problems. For example, there is a wide range (from 3 to 20) in the number of hospitals affiliated with each center, and two networks have responsibility for deliveries far in excess of the recommended 20,000. More importantly, the distribution of specialized services and high-risk beds appears poorly matched to the needs of the populations served by the hospitals in each network. Too often, when an affiliated community-based hospital refers a high-risk maternal patient for delivery or tries to send a sick neonate to a perinatal center's intensive care unit, the center is unable to identify an available bed within its own hospital or another network facility providing high-level care. Center staff must then arrange for care within another network, but this often requires considerable time and effort and compromises the quality of care.

In addition to poorly distributed resources between networks, there are other reasons why membership in metropolitan networks no longer reflects the rationality that existed in the past. Some networks have a much higher percentage of low-income patients (and therefore a relatively sicker population) than other networks, but the state's formula for providing perinatal centers with funds to administer their networks does not adequately take this into account.

Medical school alignments have changed, and more and more hospitals are bonding together and forming multiinstitutional systems. Some hospitals have formally changed their perinatal network affiliations to achieve consistency with the pattern of new relationships, but others have not (and this sometimes results in weak linkage with a perinatal center and less-than-ideal relationships). Another factor confounding the situation is the growing importance of health maintenance organizations and other forms of managed care. Sometimes the gatekeepers associated with these programs will not approve the transfer of a high-risk patient to the specified perinatal center, in accordance with established referral provisions, because the center is not a recognized HMO or managed care provider.

Recently, the administrators of all six metropolitan networks forwarded a request to the Department of Public Health to provide staff assistance as they study the problems and explore a more rational approach to network configuration. The Department agrees that some restructuring of networks may be necessary, but it refuses to dictate the membership of each network, preferring that local providers assume responsibility for correcting deficiencies.

Q.1. Discuss how epidemiologic data could be used in strategic planning to resolve some of the problems suggested in this case.

Case Study No. 5
Strategic Planning for a University-Based Wellness Center

A comprehensive wellness center (CWC) associated with a major state university and academic medical center experienced great success and rapid growth during its initial years of operation. The CWC achieved designation as one of only seven health promotion and disease prevention centers recognized nationally by the Centers for Disease Control. It went from a program with three faculty and two staff working on four projects funded at less than $200,000 during the first year to a unit with over 60 people (approximately 35 FTEs) involved with projects worth over $4.4 million during its seventh year. The CWC, which was started in less than 700 square feet of office space, now is located on an entire floor of a large office building. In the next year, CWC will begin utilizing another floor, thus occupying nearly 23,000 square feet of office, computer, and general research space.

Since its inception, the CWC has received nearly $20.0 million to support three training programs and 50 research projects on a wide range of diseases, behaviors, and populations. It has attempted to maintain a good sense of its mission, described by its leadership as the following:

> To provide a multidisciplinary research focus for the study, analysis, and dissemination of information on health promotion and the prevention of the major causes of morbidity and mortality among the diverse population groups of the city [in which CWC is located] and the state.

The CWC has determined that its overall direction for the next 5 years will be to consolidate and build on strengths in ways that support the urban mission of the major university with which it is associated. It has also determined that its focus should be diverted from continuing expansion (since there is some sense that the CWC will soon be big enough) to assurance of high quality research and effectiveness of impact. The CWC has been able to involve faculty from 35 departments in eight colleges across the university campus. The benefits offered to participating faculty include collegial advice and review during grant proposal preparation, ongoing interaction with other prevention researchers, the services of its business office, computer facilities, research offices, and support of graduate students. The CWC's success and favorable reputation are responsible for attracting an ever-growing number of faculty who desire assistance with their research activities. Can the CWC continue to respond to anyone and everyone? Should it lend support to research on any topic related to the broad category of health promotion and disease prevention? How will the new era of "health care reform" affect the CWC's future? The CWC's leadership has begun asking these questions as they direct their attention to positioning CWC for success in the years to come.

Q.1. Discuss how strategic planning could be utilized by the CWC to address the questions raised in this case.

Q.2. Considering the mission of the CWC, how might epidemiologic and demographic data be utilized to assist it in becoming more focused?

Case Study No. 6
Strategic Planning for Professional Associations

Members of one of the largest state medical societies in the United States have expressed concern that the various models proposed for health care reform will have a detrimental impact on physicians, especially those engaged in subspecialties. Even as the debate rages over which reform plan will be implemented, the increasing popularity of managed care has already eroded the position of subspecialists. Concern over escalating costs has resulted in greater scrutiny of the need for referral to specialists, and increased emphasis is being placed on the role of the primary-care provider, who frequently is charged as gatekeeper to the larger system.

The Council on Graduate Medical Education, an advisory group to Congress, has estimated that the United States will have 115,000 too many medical specialists and 35,000 too few general practitioners by the year 2000 if current trends continue. This prediction has resulted in implementation of physician-retraining programs in a few areas of the country. Specialists are being retrained to ensure their competency in the delivery of primary care.

An *ad hoc* committee of the state medical society has been charged with assessing existing retraining programs and determining if sponsorship of such a program would be an appropriate activity for the society. If the committee recommends initiation of the retraining program, it is also charged with developing objectives and implementation procedures.

As the committee begins its work, it is aware that the society's membership could be split on the need for and the benefits of a retraining program. A southern California hospital that offered a retraining program experienced the resignation of many physicians from its medical group because of issues associated with retraining.

Q.1. What type of epidemiologic and demographic data could be used by the committee to assist it in assessing the need and feasibility of a training program?

Q.2. If the committee approaches its charge as undertaking strategic planning for the medical society, describe a process that may be employed in this situation. Because the medical society is a professional association, should the strategic planning process it utilizes differ from the process for an organization responsible for direct delivery of care?

References

Alliance for Healthcare Strategy and Marketing, *TrendWatch*, Alliance for Health Care Strategy and Marketing, Chicago (quarterly newsletter).

American Hospital Association, 1991, A decade of change: AHA's annual survey traces national trends, 1980–1990, *Hospitals* **December 20:**32–33.

American Hospital Association, 1992a, *Environmental Assessment for Rural Hospitals 1992*, American Hospital Association, Chicago.

American Hospital Association, 1992b, *Environmental Assessment for Urban Hospitals 1992*, American Hospital Association, Chicago.

Baker, T. D., 1988, Health personnel planning, in *Health Planning for Effective Management* (W. A. Reinke, ed.), pp. 131–146, Oxford University Press, New York.

Baker, T. D., and Reinke, W. A., 1988, Epidemiologic base for health planning, in *Health Planning for Effective Management* (W. A. Reinke, ed.), pp. 117–130, Oxford University Press, New York.

Bandrowski, J. F., 1985, *Creative Planning Throughout the Organization*, AMA Membership Publications Division, American Management Association, New York.

Barry, B. W., 1985, *Strategic Planning Workbook for Nonprofit Organizations*, Amherst H. Wilder Foundation, St. Paul, MN.

Baynham, B., 1991, Strategic planning and evaluation for QA, *Dimensions* **February:**21–24.

Bryson, J. M., 1988, *Strategic Planning for Public and Nonprofit Organizations*, Jossey-Bass, San Francisco.

Bureau of Health Professions, Health Resources and Services Administration, U. S. Department of Health and Human Services, 1990, *Seventh Report to the President and Congress on the Status of Health Personnel in the United States*, U.S. Department of Health and Human Services, Rockville, MD.

Coddington, D. C., and Moore, K. D., 1987, *Market-Driven Strategies in Health Care*, Jossey-Bass, San Francisco.

Cornoni-Huntley, J., Borck, D. B., Ostfield, A. M., Taylor, J. O., and Wallace, R. B., 1986, *Established Populations for Epidemiologic Studies of the Elderly*, NIH Pub. No. 86-2443, U.S. Government Printing Office, Washington, DC.

Day, G. S., 1984, *Strategic Marketing Planning*, West Publishing Company, St. Paul, MN.

Fry, J. D., and Young, R. W., 1992, *The Health Care Data Source Book*, American Hospital Publishing, Chicago.

Graves, E. J., 1994, *1992 Summary: National Hospital Discharge Survey. Advance Data from Vital and Health Statistics, No. 249*, National Center for Health Statistics, Hyattsville, MD.

Group Health Association of America, 1993, *Patterns in HMO Enrollment*, GHAA, Washington, DC.

Hospital Research and Educational Trust and Society for Healthcare Planning and Marketing, American Hospital Association, 1989, *Environmental Assessment Workbook*, American Hospital Publishing, Chicago.

Johnson, J., Weissman, M. M., and Klerman, G. L., 1992, Service utilization and social morbidity associated with depressive symptoms in the community, *JAMA* **267:**1478–1483.

Keckley, P. H., 1988, *Market Research Handbook for Health Care Professionals*, American Hospital Publishing, Chicago.

Kotler, P. and Clarke, R., 1987, *Marketing for Health Care Organizations*, Prentice-Hall, Englewood Cliffs, NJ.

MacStravic, R. S., 1984, *Forecasting Use of Health Services*, Aspen Systems Corporation, Rockville, MD.

McCaig, L. F., 1992, National hospital ambulatory medical care survey: 1992 outpatient department summary, *Adv. Data Vital Health Stat.* **248:**1.

National Center for Health Statistics, 1991, *Health, United States, 1990*, Public Health Service, Hyattsville, MD.

National Center for Health Statistics, 1992, *Current Estimates from the National Health Interview Survey, 1991*, Public Health Service, Hyattsville, MD.

National Center for Health Statistics, 1994, *Health, United States, 1993*, Public Health Service, Hyattsville, MD.

National Committee for Quality Assurance, 1993, *HEDIS 2.0 (Health Employer Data and Information Set)*, National Committee for Quality Assurance, Washington, DC.

Nutt, P. C., 1984, *Planning Methods for Health and Related Organizations*, John Wiley & Sons, New York.

O'Dell, M. W., Crawford, A., Bohi, E. S., and Bonner, F. J., Jr., 1991, Disability in persons hospitalized with AIDS, *Am. J. Phys. Med. Rehabil.* **70:**91–95.

Pfeffer, J., and Salancik, G. R., 1978, *The External Control of Organizations, A Resource Dependence Perspective*, Harper & Row, New York.

Pope, A. M., and Tarlov, A. R., 1991, *Disability in America*, National Academy Press, Washington, DC.

Porter, M., 1980, *Competitive Strategy*, Free Press, New York.

Porter, M., 1985, *Competitive Advantage: Creating and Sustaining Superior Performance*, Free Press, New York.

Shortell, S. M., and Kaluzny, A. D., 1983, Organization theory and health care management, in *Health Care Management: A Text in Organization Theory and Behavior* (S. M. Shortell and A. D. Kaluzny, eds.), pp. 5–37, John Wiley & Sons, New York.

Schappert, S. M., 1993, *National Ambulatory Medical Care Survey: 1991 Summary. Advance Data from Vital and Health Statistics. No. 230*, National Center for Health Statistics, Hyattsville, MD.

Society for Healthcare Planning and Marketing, American Hospital Association, 1990, *Planning for AIDS Cases*, American Hospital Association, Chicago.

Society for Healthcare Planning and Marketing, American Hospital Association, 1993, *Working Together to Shape the Future: Environmental Assessment 93/94*, American Hospital Association, Chicago.

Spiegel, A. D., and Hyman, H. H., 1991, *Strategic Health Planning*, Ablex Publishing Corporation, Norwood, NJ.

Starkweather, D., and Cook, K. S., 1983, Organization–environment relations, in *Health Care Management: A Text in Organization Theory and Behavior* (S. M. Shortell and A. D. Kaluzny, eds.), pp. 333–377, John Wiley & Sons, New York.

Steiber, S. R., and Krowinski, W. J., 1990, *Measuring and Managing Patient Satisfaction*, American Hospital Publishing, Chicago.

Strahan, G., 1993, *Overview of Home Health and Hospice Care Patients: Preliminary Data from the 1992 National Home and Hospice Care Survey. Advance Data from Vital and Health Statistics, No. 235*, National Center for Health Statistics, Hyattsville, MD.

Taylor, F., 1947, *Scientific Management*, Harper & Row, New York.

U.S. Department of Commerce, Bureau of the Census, 1953, *Census of Population: 1950, Vol. II. Characteristics of the Population*, U.S. Government Printing Office, Washington, DC.

U.S. Department of Commerce, Bureau of the Census, 1992a, *1990 Census of Population, General Population Characteristics: Illinois*, U.S. Government Printing Office, Washington, DC.

U.S. Department of Commerce, Bureau of the Census, 1992b, *1990 Census of the Population, General Population Characteristics, United States*, U.S. Government Printing Office, Washington, DC.

U.S. Department of Commerce, 1993, *Statistical Abstract of the United States, 1993*, U.S. Government Printing Office, Washington, DC.

U.S. Department of Health and Human Services, Public Health Service, 1990, *Healthy People 2000: National Health Promotion and Disease Prevention Objectives (with Full Commentary)*, U.S. Government Printing Office, Washington, DC.

Weber, M., 1964, *The Theory of Social and Economic Organization*, Free Press, Glencoe, IL.

5

Evaluating Health Care Programs and Systems

An Epidemiologic Perspective

Dolores Gurnick Clement, Thomas T. H. Wan,
and MeriBeth Herzberg Stegall

The evaluation of health care is vitally important to our efforts directed at reforming and improving the performance of our health care system. Evaluation is a means by which a program or a process is examined and an informed judgment is made concerning the extent of success in reaching predetermined goals. Evaluation plays two major roles in health care: (1) assuring the delivery of high quality care, and (2) providing a tool for controlling costs and promoting accountability for public program expenditures. Evaluation is not merely the application of methods; it involves managerial and political decision making pertinent to the allocation of resources to other functions such as program planning, design, implementation, and ongoing monitoring. Evaluations are done for a variety of purposes: to improve the delivery of care, to test an innovation, to determine the effectiveness of regulatory policy, or to assess the appropriateness of continuing or altering an intervention. The use of epidemiologic principles and methods in the evaluation process can clarify information required for program development or guide decisions relevant to continued operations. In addition, epidemiology provides measures, analytic study designs, and methods for investigating the effectiveness of programs in controlling disease, disability, and other health problems and for measuring their consequences in populations receiving health care services.

The purpose of this chapter is to present the conceptual dimensions of program evaluation, promote an understanding of study design, explain issues related to the introduction of interventions in populations, and describe specific statistical approaches for analyzing the impact of programs. The use of epidemiologic techniques is especially appropriate at this time

Dolores Gurnick Clement and **Thomas T. H. Wan**   Department of Health Administration, Virginia Commonwealth University, Medical College of Virginia, Richmond, Virginia 23298.   **MeriBeth Herzberg Stegall**   Program in Healthcare Administration, University of Osteopathic Medicine and Health Sciences, Des Moines, Iowa 50312.

Epidemiology and the Delivery of Health Care Services: Methods and Applications, edited by Denise M. Oleske. Plenum Press, New York, 1995.

as larger and more diverse populations are being targeted for services. As health care becomes increasingly customized to meet the needs of specific populations, particularly those vulnerable or at high risk for certain problems, program evaluation based upon epidemiologic principles becomes necessary to determine the most effective delivery strategies.

Conceptual Dimensions of Health System Evaluation

Program evaluation must address several conceptual issues in the design and conduct of analyses. These are summarized in Table 5.1 and described in this section.

Population Targeted for Intervention

The most important design consideration is determining the people, organizations, or communities to whom the intervention should be directed. Overinclusion, underinclusion, or exclusion of those who could benefit should be addressed during the design of an intervention and reexamined during the evaluation phase. Ethical considerations arise if a social program overlooks the population at risk, or benefits those with no need for the services encompassed by the program. Epidemiologic methods can determine a population's need, identify those who could benefit most from intervention, and determine if care is being provided at an acceptable level. For example, ongoing evaluation is performed to monitor the quality of care provided to the population covered by Medicare. One of the parameters used in the evaluation is hospital mortality rate categorized by diagnostic related groups (DRGs) (Health Care Financing Administration, 1992).

Aspects of Health Care to Be Evaluated

In evaluating health care, the major aspects to be considered are:

- The quality of care
- The accessibility and availability of resources
- The continuity of care
- The effectiveness of the care provided
- The efficiency involved in care delivery
- The acceptability of care provided through the program

Table 5.1. Summary of Conceptual Issues Addressed in Evaluation of Health Programs

Determine the population to whom the program applies
Identify aspect(s) of the health care system to be evaluated
Identify and develop evaluation criteria: standards and measures
Specify the design and analytic approaches appropriate to the evaluation
Identify who will conduct the evaluation and how it is to be financed
Assess the impact of the findings on cost, quality, and access to medical care
Identify limitations of findings and implications

Epidemiologic methods are appropriate for evaluation of each of these aspects, since the focus of evaluation is the impact of interventions within populations. Descriptive measures alone or in combination with analytic studies (which are discussed later in this chapter) can be used to assess each system aspect. Several examples follow.

Quality

In order to evaluate quality, the concept must first be defined. Donabedian (1980) states:

> Quality is a property of, and a judgment upon, some definable unit of care, and that care is divisible into at least two parts: technical and interpersonal. At the very least, the quality of technical care consists of the application of medical science and technology in a manner that maximizes its benefits to health without correspondingly increasing its risk.

Quality, in epidemiologic terms, examines variation in rates and the likelihood of both beneficial and adverse outcomes.

Retchin and Brown (1990) provide an example of the use of analytic epidemiologic methods to evaluate quality in a quasi-experimental study of the delivery of routine and preventive care. The likelihood of receiving various forms of preventive care was presented as an odds ratio with a specified confidence interval. This study suggests that routine and preventive advice is more likely to be offered to Medicare enrollees in staff/group model health maintenance organizations (HMOs) than in the traditional fee-for-service setting. In an experimental study, Wan et al. (1980) used a variety of patient outcomes measures, including mortality rates, to assess the impact of day-care and homemaker services. Significantly higher mortality was found in the control group relative to the intervention group that received both categories of service.

Accessibility

Donabedian (1980) defines accessibility of care as the ease with which care is initiated and maintained. Public and private programs are often designed to alleviate problems of access. Thus, the evaluation of these programs frequently focuses on changes in accessibility. Young and Cohen (1991) examined patient insurance status, a variable that affects access to care, in relationship to outcomes. Significantly greater mortality rates were observed among uninsured patients compared to rates for HMO and traditionally insured fee-for-service patients. Okada and Wan (1980), in their study of the impact of community health centers and Medicaid on the utilization of health services, found that health centers in low-income areas contributed to increased access to care among the disadvantaged. They also documented that the extensive Medicaid coverage of study populations was an indicator of increased access to care.

Accessibility in situations of restrictive benefit packages is an issue that requires further evaluation. Variation between plans can be compared, using epidemiologic techniques for monitoring prevention screening and treatment rates among different segments of the population, for example.

Continuity

Continuity can be defined as maintaining a relationship between successive episodes of health care. Evaluation of continuity generally focuses on interruptions in needed care.

Donabedian (1980) suggests that an important feature of continuity is the retention of past findings and the recording of decisions so that they may be used in the management of current problems in a manner reflecting constancy in the objectives and the methods of care. Continuous monitoring may be required in an evaluation, because reports at a single point in time only portray a segment of an ongoing intervention. Assessment of results that can improve or deteriorate should continue, unless a study is designed to be time-limited. When feasible, a longitudinal study should be conducted to monitor changes in care and outcomes over time and to evaluate the continuous effects of an intervention. For example, recidivism is an indicator of program outcome that is utilized to evaluate behavioral change associated with substance abuse and smoking-cessation programs. The effectiveness of such programs is most appropriately quantified several months after the intervention has taken place (Bibeau *et al.*, 1988).

Effectiveness

Effectiveness is the degree to which the health care system has succeeded in meeting stated or accepted goals in the ordinary setting in which the intervention will be conducted (Greenlick, 1981). In assessing effectiveness, two distinct variables should be evaluated: effectiveness of care and the psychosocial impact of the delivery of care on outcome. The evaluation of technical effectiveness is concerned with the degree to which a system can influence a favorable patient physiological or physical outcome (e.g., patient survival rates). The consideration of psychosocial dimensions is concerned with how the provider–patient relationship affects the outcomes of care (e.g., patient satisfaction rates). An example of evaluating technical effectiveness using epidemiologic methods was demonstrated in a study done by Lane *et al.* (1992). Breast cancer screening rates among the socioeconomically disadvantaged attending publicly funded health centers were found to be comparable to (or even higher than) screening rates for the general population.

Efficiency

Efficiency is the ability to produce a desired result using minimal resources. Cost is often the resource measure used to evaluate program efficiency, and efficiency evaluations are often concerned with whether the same end result can be achieved at lower cost. Knaus *et al.* (1983), using the Acute Physiological and Chronic Health Evaluation (APACHE) score, found that over 50% of the admissions monitored at the study hospital were at less than 10% risk of needing ICU therapy. Therefore, the researchers concluded that these patients should have been treated on a regular hospital unit, since the delivery of care appropriate to the level of need represents efficient use of ICU (program) resources.

Acceptability

Acceptability evaluations consider whether expectations of various persons within the health system are met. The expectations of planners, participants, providers, and patients should be reflected in the goals and outcomes to be achieved by a program. The manner in which a service is delivered and received determines the level of cooperation, compliance, and achievement of expected results. Health care might be deemed to be effective or efficient in its delivery, but if it is provided in an inappropriate setting or without respect and dignity, it may be unacceptable to intended beneficiaries.

Acceptability can be determined by using preestablished criteria or by surveying those involved with the program. A study assessing the acceptability of free-standing birth centers compared to hospital confinement for labor and delivery utilized the following criteria to assess program outcome: complication rates, intrapartum and neonatal mortality rates, and Apgar scores (Rooks *et al.*, 1989). It was concluded that free-standing centers represent an acceptable alternative to a hospital for selected women, particularly those who had had a prior delivery.

The Process of Evaluation

Evaluation is a dynamic process that is bounded by formal application to specific problems. There are four interrelated aspects of the evaluation process: planning, implementation, intervention, and monitoring/feedback. The evaluation process is iterative, continuous, and repetitive in nature (Fig. 5.1).

Planning

What is to be evaluated and accomplished by a health care system, or an organization or program, is determined in a planning stage as described in the previous chapter. Since a program or intervention is designed as a response to a recognized or perceived problem, the initial stage of program development should include assessment of the magnitude of the health problem and establishment of criteria for use during evaluation. Epidemiologic data may provide essential information supportive of need, and some of the same data may be applicable in the evaluation process. For example, Kotchen *et al.* (1986) cite the high cardiovascular disease death rate in the rural southeast as one reason for initiating a high-blood-pressure control program in two counties in southeastern Kentucky. The same rate became one of the epidemiologic measures used to monitor the impact of the program (Fig. 5.2).

The goals of the intervention, specific and measurable objectives, the processes by which the objectives can be accomplished, budgetary considerations, and the means of monitoring progress are all established through planning. Sufficient documentation of plans is required for inclusion of planning phase considerations into the overall evaluation of a program. The study design to be utilized to assess an intervention should be determined during the planning stage and included in the plans.

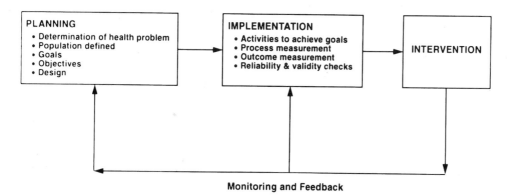

Figure 5.1.   The evaluation process: a reiterative model.

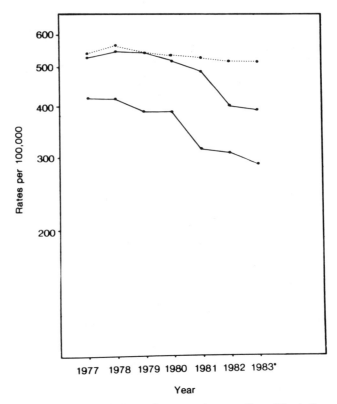

Figure 5.2. Cardiovascular disease death rates by year and county. Dotted line indicates control county; solid lines represent intervention counties. Reprinted from Kotchen *et al.* (1986) with permission from the American Medical Association. Copyright 1986.

Implementation

Implementation is the process of carrying out the activities planned to achieve goals and monitor an intervention. It involves not only doing what is needed but also measuring and documenting all the tasks of an evaluation or process. An ongoing evaluation process is needed from the beginning to ensure reliability, to safeguard the integrity of the program or intervention, and to ensure fiscal accountability.

Intervention

A well-planned program is established to effect change, and interventions are designed to modify expectations and actions. Evaluations of interventions measure change and enable modification in direction or the design of alternative, innovative programs. It is important to note that the design of an evaluation should be customized for the specific intervention used.

Monitoring and Feedback

Effective administration and coordination of tasks associated with evaluation are necessary for monitoring an intervention. Periodic reports may indicate interim trends, and concurrent monitoring can ensure accountability and the appropriate allocation of resources. An evaluation should include a system to relay information or feedback about a program or process so that planned change is achieved. Rosen and Feigin (1983) have suggested that feedback can lead to improved performance, and they stress three principles of feedback. First, the group that is most likely to be influenced by the feedback must participate in selecting what is to be measured. Second, the feedback must be relevant to that group's goals. Third, the feedback should be used in a positive and supportive manner, rather than in a negative or punitive way. Corrective mechanisms to address deficiencies in a program or process must also be incorporated into the evaluation process. The changes instituted as a result of feedback and implementation of corrective measures should then be monitored in this reiterative process.

Conceptual Framework for Specifying Evaluation Criteria

The delineation of clear objectives and evaluation criteria during a program's planning phase facilitates evaluation. Objectives for what will be accomplished, who will be affected, and the expected time frame should be explicitly stated and quantified. Evaluation criteria must be developed to assess a program's performance against the standards. Utilizing the conceptual framework of Donabedian (1980, 1981), evaluation criteria may be categorized into **structural, process** and **outcome measures**, which can be used to determine achievement of objectives.

Structural measures represent characteristics of the people performing or receiving an intervention, the location where service is given, and the resources needed and used, including the resources required to plan, perform, and monitor the intervention. Structural criteria are derived from the design and objectives of the intervention. Human, material, and capital resources expended on a program are all structural variables.

Process measures represent what you do to accomplish the objectives of an intervention. These measures have several advantages including the relative ease of specifying process criteria to characterize what occurs in the program and the availability of administrative documentation and other records containing information about the intervention. Specific responsibility for tasks associated with the process of care can be determined in evaluations using process measures; this, in turn allows for specific corrective action to be taken. Process criteria identify standards for assessing the means employed to achieve the purpose of the intervention. The disadvantages of process criteria are that they tend to overemphasize technical care at the expense of the interpersonal process.

An **outcome** is the change achieved through the intervention. Outcome criteria must relate to results specifically attributable to the intervention being evaluated. For example, an outcome criterion for a smoking-cessation program could be that 80% of those in the program will stop smoking for at least 2 years after program completion. The major difficulty in assessing outcome is determining how much of an outcome can be considered a direct result of the intervention. Therefore, it is necessary to monitor other factors that could contribute to the outcome. In the case of smoking-cessation programs, these factors could include illness or a large increase in cigarette taxes. Caution must also be used when assessing a program based on a singular outcome. The duration of the intended behavior change is an important outcome consideration for smoking-cessation programs; it would be inadequate to evaluate these programs only on the outcome achieved at a point in time (such as immediately after the conclusion of a program intervention).

A component of the process of evaluation includes the determination of goals and objectives to be accomplished through a program's intervention. Ideally, a variety of measures pertinent to the goals and objectives are used in an evaluation. Whether evaluation criteria represent structure, process or outcome, they must address the adequacy of the intervention. Ultimately the evaluation determines whether or not the goals and objectives are met by assessing the level of conformance to evaluation criteria.

Analytic Approaches to Evaluation: An Epidemiologic Perspective

Evaluation studies are an essential part of the assessment of health program performance. Since the success of a program in achieving its goals is influenced by the characteristics of the population served, an epidemiologic perspective is crucial in the evaluation process. Programs are instituted in defined populations; thus epidemiologic methods can be used to quantify the problem and measure and analyze program outcomes. Since epidemiologic research also focuses on defined populations, the study designs and statistical methods applicable for conducting program evaluations are often those used in epidemiologic research. A description of these designs and statistical methods follows.

Study Designs for Evaluating Interventions

Once it has been determined what aspect of the health care delivery system will be evaluated, the design of the evaluation can be developed. The initial and most crucial consideration in design selection is the timing for introduction of a program (or intervention) relative to the evaluation process. If the program has been ongoing when the evaluation is initiated, an observational study may be selected. If the program is introduced simultaneous with the evaluation process, an experimental design is more appropriate.

Observational Studies

The three common observational designs used in evaluation studies are: **cross-sectional**, **case-control**, and **longitudinal** (or **prospective**). These designs are termed observational as no manipulation occurs of the independent variable.

A **cross-sectional study** can be done to estimate population parameters (e.g., means, proportions, odds ratios, totals) that represent the magnitude of a risk factor, to determine the extent of a health problem in a population, and/or to test a hypothesis related to the degree of association between a causative factor and a health outcome in a defined population. The estimates provided by a cross-sectional study are static, representing the amount of the exposure, condition or association at one point in time or period. Seldom is an entire population studied; rather, a sample or a collection of individual or group members is selected in order to estimate the desired population parameters. The sample for a cross-sectional study is selected in a random manner to represent the population from which it came. The reader is advised to consult Levy and Lemeshow (1980) for a discussion of the various methods for selecting a random sample. The source of data used in cross-sectional studies is most often some form of survey methodology, namely telephone or personal interviews, self-administered questionnaires or record reviews. Some studies may also obtain information derived from clinical examinations and biological measurements.

An example of a cross-sectional analysis is a study by Bennett *et al.* (1989) that examines the relationship between hospital mortality of patients with AIDS-related pneumonia and the experience of hospitals with these patients. Findings indicated that regionalization of AIDS-related services may improve outcomes for this complication.

The cross-sectional study design provides a quick assessment of the strength of the relationship between a factor (experience in treatment in the above example) and a health outcome (e.g., mortality) associated with it. However, because the sample is cross-classified with respect to the attributes present at the time of sample selection, a cross-sectional study has limited use for determining causality because its design does not enable delineation of the timing of the onset of the putative cause relative to its hypothetical outcome.

The purpose of a **case-control study** is to compare the prevalence of exposure factors between two or more groups. One group possesses the outcome under investigation; the other group or groups, known as control or comparison groups, do not. Information pertaining to exposure is obtained after the outcome has occurred. When rapid assessment of the relationship between exposure and outcome is required, for example when an initial assessment of a new medical technology is required, a case-control study may be conducted. Ideally, such evaluations should be done with a randomized clinical trial. However, this may not be feasible or economical during initial assessment.

An example of an evaluation of the quality of care provided to Medicare patients is illustrated by Carlisle et al. (1992) in a study utilizing a case-control design. Two samples of persons with a diagnosis of recent acute myocardial infarction were drawn, one with HMO coverage and the other having traditional fee-for-service arrangements. The medical records of these persons were reviewed against 93 process-of-care criteria. Compliance with the criteria was found to be high among those covered by an HMO. This study suggested that health plans can enhance the quality of care by utilizing process criteria to monitor care and improving the process by which it is given.

How are controls selected for a case-control study? Controls may consist of the total population or a sample that is alike in every way to the cases except that they do not have the outcome under investigation. If a control sample is selected, it may be a random or a matched sample. Matching may be pairwise or nonpairwise. In pairwise matching, comparison members of a sample are selected when they have exactly the same value, or nearly the same within a given tolerance, of a confounding variable. Thus, if a case is a white male, 30 years of age, the control must be a white male, 30 plus or minus 1 to 5 years, depending on the desired matching tolerance for age. One of the most common approaches for nonpairwise matching is frequency matching. In frequency matching, cases are randomly selected and controls are selected in proportion equal to that of the cases. Thus, if the cases are 20% white, 40% male, and 10% over 65 years of age, controls must be selected to achieve a comparable distribution. Matching is recommended when the number of cases is small (<50) and when the available comparison or control pool is large. Matching must not be done on exposure. In numerous variables are required in order to control for the confounding variable, multivariable matching should be considered. The reader is advised to consult Anderson et al. (1980).

Case-control studies can be done relatively quickly and inexpensively, and they can be performed with a comparatively small sample size. The limitations of case-control studies arise from the manner in which the study sample was acquired (because of the possibility of missing incident cases due to high mortality or other types of losses) and from the retrospective measurement of exposure to the suspect causative factors. The limitations include participant definition bias, self-selection bias, and lead-time bias.

Relevant questions to ask to assess participant definition bias include: Do criteria accurately distinguish between cases and controls? Were the criteria uniformly applied? Questions relevant to self-selection bias are: Did the cases and controls arise from different service populations? Are the controls a "healthier" population? A question related to lead-time bias is: Did the cases come to diagnostic attention sooner?

A major disadvantage of a case-control study is the reliance upon the recall of past events or the abstraction of records that may have incomplete information on exposure to causative factors. Case-control studies cannot be used to establish cause and effect *per se*. However, historical sequencing of suspect causative events relative to the outcome under investigation can be preliminarily gleaned with careful structuring of interview questions and data abstraction forms. Sackett (1979) discusses in depth other potential biases of case-control studies.

The major purposes of a **longitudinal study** (or **prospective study**) are to observe and document the time between exposure to a factor and outcome as well as the amount of change in outcome relative to variation in exposure to a factor, or to measure change over time resulting from cohort, aging, or period effects. The sample for a longitudinal study consists of individuals who are free of the outcome variable(s) of interest at the time the study begins. The distinguishing feature of this study design is that information on exposure is collected before the outcome occurs.

The two types of longitudinal studies are **concurrent prospective** and **historical prospective**. A **concurrent prospective study** is usually conducted in two stages. The first stage consists of the recruitment of participants. The sample selected must be stable (i.e., unlikely to move away or drop out of the study) and representative of the demographic and health-status characteristics of the population from which it was drawn. In the second stage, participants are carefully evaluated to determine that they do not have the health outcome being examined. The individuals who are determined to be "outcome-free" are then followed and observed for a preestablished period of time to determine the occurrence of an outcome relative to exposure levels. A **historical prospective study** uses existing records from a cohort of persons thoroughly and uniformly characterized from a past time, such as persons receiving a comprehensive medical examination and history upon enrollment in an HMO. Although exposure data are assumed to be complete, information on outcome events of interest may have to be compiled.

When the sample of "outcome-free" individuals is selected for a longitudinal study on the basis of some common event, such as birth year or period of employment at a company, this type of longitudinal study is referred to as a **cohort study**. A sample may be selected to study **period effects** or the impact of some event on all groups over time. Changes in health service utilization rates during economic recessions or in the incidence of back injuries after introduction of a new process in the workplace are topics that could be examined for period effects using a longitudinal study design. A sample may also be selected to study **aging effects** whereby the context of the study is concerned with the changes occurring with the passage of time, regardless of cohort or period of measurement, that are physiological, cognitive, and functional in nature. This type of study could be important to a large employer attempting to project the demand for health care benefits among retirees.

Longitudinal studies offer both advantages and disadvantages. By following individuals over time, measurement of the causative factors as well as the outcome can be more precise. In addition, more than one outcome can be studied if the parameters for defining the outcomes are established at the onset of the study. The duration of observation of participants depends on the estimated average time between exposure to the causative factor(s) and the occurrence of the outcome of interest. Significant potential for selection bias may exist in a longitudinal study as a result of differential participation by age, gender, education, and health status. Other disadvantages include: the necessity of a long observation period to ascertain accurately the outcome in the sample, the potential for excessive attrition ($>20\%$) if sample members refuse continued participation, and loss in follow-up or death before the outcome is observed. As the trend toward contracted health care continues, longitudinal studies will become increasingly important because of the need to characterize the experience of population subgroups known to have high utilization rates such as older adults and cigarette smokers (Wolinsky and Johnson, 1991; Vogt and Schweitzer, 1985).

Observational studies often serve as precursors to experimental studies. When associations are detected that suggest that a program has impact upon health status and the intervention(s) can be well defined, the next step is to evaluate a program using an experimental study design.

Experimental Studies

In **experimental studies**, an outcome is measured after a program is introduced or an intervention has been applied. The measurement of the outcome can either be immediately after the intervention or at some designated time in the future. Interventional studies may be **experimental** or **quasiexperimental**. The elements of **experimental studies** in human populations are: (1) volunteerism, (2) randomization, (3) intervention, and (4) control. An experimental design is the preferred method for evaluating a program. A study by Wan *et al.* (1980) is an example of an experimental study with the objective of evaluating the impact of support services for elderly persons on their health status. Elderly persons were randomized to one of the following groups: those to receive day-care services, those to get homemaker services, those to receive both these services, and those to get neither service. When assignment to a group is not random, depending instead on current group assignment, then the study design would be quasiexperimental and less convincing in its conclusions.

When an experimental situation does not meet the full requirements of experimental control and randomization, evaluations of planned interventions in the field of health care can be carried out by a **quasiexperimental design**. One such design is a **time series design**, which utilizes multiple measurements before the intervention and multiple measurements after the intervention. This design can be schematically represented as:

$$O_1 \; O_2 \; O_3 \; O_4 \ldots O_i \; X \; O_{i+1} \; O_{i+2} \; O_{i+3} \ldots O_{i+n}$$

where O_i are measurements taken before and after the introduction of the intervention at time interval i, and X is the intervention. This design is most useful when no cyclical or seasonal shifts are expected in the occurrence of the dependent variables. An evaluation of the introduction of a driving-under-the-influence legislation was performed using this method (Fig. 5.3).

Although a randomized, controlled experiment is an ideal design for program evaluation, it is often difficult to meet the requirements of such an experiment in social research. Political and economic circumstances may occur during the course of an evaluation and render it difficult to determine if an intervention had the desired effects. For example, legislation may be passed that substantially changes eligibility to include higher income groups; characteristics of program participants may change, and this may affect the outcome, confounding the impact of the intervention. An ethical concern may be raised if randomization is seen as presenting some deprivation or harm to a set of participants. This could occur if study participants are randomized into groups provided different health insurance coverage. If one group has a high copayment, this could be perceived as adversely affecting health by restricting access to care. Since randomized trials rely on volunteers, the individuals comprising a study group may be different from the general population.

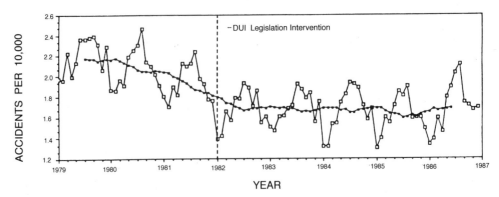

YEAR

Figure 5.3. Monthly distribution of nighttime fatal and injury accidents per 10,000 population with a 12-month moving average. Source: Rogers and Schoenig (1993). Copyright 1993 by Elsevier Science Ltd., The Boulevard, Langford Lane, Kidlington OX5 19B, United Kingdom, and reprinted with kind permission.

Analyzing Intervention Effects

The statistical methods selected to assess program impact depend on both the design and the level of measurement applied for evaluating outcome. A program intervention or independent variable is commonly represented as a discrete variable (presence or absence of an intervention). Outcome or dependent variables are commonly concerned with the presence or absence of a condition in the population served by the program being evaluated. Because the dependent variables are typically binary, **logistic regression**, **survival analysis**, or **Cox regression** are commonly used in program evaluation. A description of these methods follows.

Logistic regression is used when the outcome variable is a binary variable and the independent variables (risk factors or intervention) are continuous or discrete variables, or both. A logistic regression may be expressed in terms of the log of the odds ratio (OR), which is the proportion of those with the event divided by the proportion of those without the event. This can be represented as:

$$\log \text{OR} = b_0 + b_i X_i$$

where b_i is the value of a coefficient, and X_i is the value of an independent variable.

A multiple logistic regression model in which there is more than one independent variable (the variable representing the program and variables for attributes of the population served such as age, gender, and duration of exposure) and the log odds ratio is a linear combination of multiple predictor variables (X_i) can be specified as:

$$\log \text{OR} = b_0 + b_i X_i \ldots + b_n X_n$$

The log OR is assumed to be a linear function of the magnitude of intervention instituted by a program represented by a X_i where the coefficient b_i measures the change (multiplicative) in the odds associated with a one-unit change in the intervention magnitude on the log-odds scale.

The logistic regression equation can also be rewritten to represent the odds ratio as follows:

$$\text{odds ratio (OR)} = e^{b_i}$$

The change associated with a one-unit change in the intervention variable on the odds scale is represented by e^{b_i}.

An example of the results from a multiple logistic regression is presented in Table 5.2, which indicates the likelihood of an HMO failing:

$$OR = e^{2.974} = 19.57$$

The OR indicates that an HMO with less than 10,000 members is nearly 20 times more likely to fail than one with more than 100,000 members (the referent group). The significance of the OR can also be assessed using the Wald χ^2 statistic:

$$\text{Wald } \chi^2 = [b_i/SE(b_i)]^2 = (2.97/1.07)^2 = 7.69$$

The Wald χ^2 indicates that a statistically significant relationship exists between HMO size and likelihood of failure.

Because the OR, a descriptive parameter, is only an estimate, the 95% confidence interval (CI) containing the true OR can be estimated from computing the upper confidence limit (UCL) and lower confidence limit (LCL) as follows:

$$\text{UCL for ln OR} = b_1 + 1.96[SE(b_1)] = 2.97 + 1.96(1.07) = 5.07$$

$$\text{LCL for ln OR} = b_1 - 1.96[SE(b_1)] = 2.97 - 1.96(1.07) = 0.88$$

These values can be transformed:

$$\text{UCL for OR} = e^{b+1.96[SE(b)]} = e^{2.97+1.96(1.07)} = 158.72$$

$$\text{LCL for OR} = e^{b-1.96[SE(b)]} = e^{2.97-1.96(1.07)} = 2.39$$

This means that the true value for the odds of terminating lies somewhere between 2.39 and 158.72. Because the 95% CI does not contain unity, the OR of terminating is statistically significant. The conclusions reached from a two-sided test statistic will be identical to those

Table 5.2. Odds Ratio (OR) of HMO Failure by Various Characteristics Obtained from Multiple Logistic Regression[a]

Characteristic	β coefficient	SE	Wald statistic	OR	95% CI
<10,000 members	2.97*	1.07	7.69	19.57	2.39, 158.72
10–24,000 members	1.75	1.08	2.61	5.76	0.69, 48.10
25–99,999 members	1.34	1.12	1.43	3.82	0.42, 34.44
Profit status	−0.08	0.46	0.03	0.92	0.37, 2.25
Federal qualification	0.04	0.38	0.01	1.04	0.49, 2.18
IPA model	0.60	0.38	2.56	1.81	0.86, 2.81
Staff model	−0.66	0.51	1.76	0.52	0.19, 1.41
Network model	0.79	0.62	1.63	2.19	0.65, 7.47
Region 1	−1.43*	0.49	8.52	0.24	0.09, 0.62
Region 2	−1.15*	0.41	7.79	0.32	0.14, 0.71
Region 3	−0.86	0.53	2.56	0.43	0.15, 1.21

[a]SE, standard error of the β coefficient; CI, confidence interval for the odds ratio; * χ^2 significant at the 5% level. Note: The odds ratios are those derived from the simultaneous inclusion of all the characteristics in the model.

from an assessment of the CI. The wider the confidence interval, the less precise is the estimate of the OR. A small sample size and a limited number of events contribute to the imprecision.

Survival analysis examines the probability of an event (e.g., death, relapse) in relationship to the amount of time each member in the sample was observed. For program evaluation, the period of concern is the time from a group's exposure to an intervention to the occurrence of the outcome of interest. This requires that the members of the sample be routinely monitored to document when an outcome occurs. The most common method for computing survival estimates is the product-limit method (Kaplan and Meier, 1958). Table 5.3 displays survival estimates (expressed as percentages or probabilities) of patients in a rehabilitation program. These estimates were obtained by applying the Kaplan–Meier approach. The steps necessary to obtain survival estimates are: (1) compute the interval from the beginning of the observation to the date the subject was last seen or the date of occurrence of the outcome of interest for each member of the cohort (the survival time); (2) order the survival times; (3) compute the probability of surviving from the beginning to the end of an interval by dividing the number experiencing the outcome during the interval by those alive at the beginning of the interval (the conditional probability); (4) compute the probability of surviving beyond this point, $\hat{s}(t)$, by multiplying together previous conditional probabilities. Individuals not experiencing the event by the end of the study are "censored" in their contribution of time to the estimation of the survival experience. Individuals experiencing the event are "uncensored" observations. The validity of the survival estimate is enhanced by following the cohort long enough to enable documentation of all the events of interest (i.e., there are a large proportion of "uncensored observations"). A graph of these estimates (Fig. 5.4) illustrates that the 1-year survival of the group is 72.6%, and the median survival is 19 months.

If all events could not be observed by the end of a study period, it is desirable to have at least half of the events occur and to have the censored events distributed evenly throughout the study period. If the survival estimates of two or more groups are to be statistically compared, the log-rank test or the Mantel–Haenszel χ^2 test should be used. The reader should consult Kahn and Sempos (1989).

Unlike the log-rank or the Mantel-Haenszel test that divides variables into groups to test the equality of survival curves, the **Cox proportional hazards regression** can handle both continuous and discrete variables (e.g., gender, educational attainment) and time-varying

Table 5.3. Computation of Product-Limit Survival Estimates of a Hypothetical Cohort of Liver Transplant Patients in a Rehabilitation Program

Ordered survival time (t_x)	Number at risk[a]	Number censored	Number of deaths	Conditional probability of survival	Survival function $\hat{s}(t)$
2	15	0	1	1-1/15 = 1-0.067	14/15 = 0.933
3	14	0	1	1-1/14 = 1-0.071	0.933 × 13/14 = 0.866
6	13	1	1	1-1/13 = 1.-0.077	0.866 × 12/13 = 0.799
12	11	2	1	1-1/11 = 1-0.091	0.799 × 10/11 = 0.726
18	8	2	0	1-0/8 = 1.000	0.726 × 8/8 = 0.726
20	6	0	2	1-2/6 = 1-0.333	0.726 × 4/6 = 0.484
22	4	0	0	1-0/4 = 1.00	0.484 × 4/4 = 0.484

[a]Number at risk at time t_x is the number alive and under observation just before t_x who have the potential for experiencing the outcome.

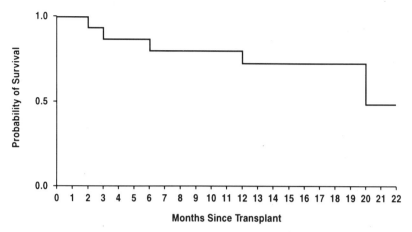

Figure 5.4. Plot of product-limit survival estimates of hypothetical liver transplant patients receiving rehabilitation intervention. Note that the plot of survival probabilities starts at 1.0 (100% of the sample is alive at the start of observation).

independent variables, such as those related to duration of a program (Cox, 1972). The formula below states that a hazard at time t, or $h(t)$, is the probability of an outcome m at time t, or $m(t)$, given that the population at risk $r(t)$, has survived to time t_{x+n}:

$$h(t) = m(t)/r(t)$$

In Cox regression, the comparison of two groups with respect to an outcome is expressed as an exponential set of independent variables (X_i), as in a regression equation with coefficients (b_i):

$$h_i(t)/h_0(t) = e^{b_i x_i}$$

The ratio of the hazards in the above equation represents a relative risk. A major assumption in Cox regression is that the effect of the relative risk associated with a variable does not change over time. This method should be considered for use only if a small proportion of the observations are censored.

Other Analytic Methods

In reality, many programs are simultaneously operating within a health care system. Administrators may wish to isolate the significance of the occurrence of multiple outcomes (e.g., those associated with complications, repeated hospitalization, and mortality) given multiple, ongoing programs. At times, these outcome variables may be correlated with each other and considered indicators of a single underlying latent construct (e.g., adverse patient outcomes). An administrator may also be interested in assessing the effect of an intervention on more than one outcome variable at a time for the purpose of assessing the relationships between the outcome variables as well as the relationship between the intervention and the outcomes. An analytic method called **structural equation modeling (SEM)** can be used in evaluating these relationships. An SEM consists of two parts: a confirmatory factor analysis to evaluate how one or more latent variables or hypothetical construct (e.g., adverse health care outcomes) may be formed from observable indicators (e.g., hospital mortality rate, complication rate), and a structural regression model that specifies regression relationships among latent constructs (Bollen, 1989). LISREL is a statistical software package that performs this analysis and also tests the fit of the model to the data by comparing the observed correlations with the predicted correlations among the study variables (Joreskog and Sorbom, 1993). For example, health system administrators who are concerned with controlling "adverse patient outcomes" may attempt to accomplish this by selective program introduction. The question is, "Which program should be chosen?" given the lack of time to conduct a formal program evaluation. Using the LISREL method, Wan (1992) examined 13 aspects of hospital structure and operations (e.g., market share, number of beds) and five observed epidemiologic measures (in-hospital trauma rate, rate of discharges with unstable medical conditions, rate of treatment problems, postoperative complication rate, and rate of unexpected deaths) representing the latent construct, adverse outcomes. The latent constructs were regressed on the hospital variables. The analysis indicated that the 13 aspects of hospital operations accounted for 39.8% of the total variance in the hospitals' adverse patient outcomes and identified those with the greatest influence on these outcomes such as the significant relationship between low technical efficiency and increasingly poor outcomes.

When the design calls for the measurement of multiple observations over a duration of time, such as in the case of a time series design, an analytic model called **autoregressive integrated moving average (ARIMA)** may be used (Box and Jenkins, 1976). This method uses a regression structure to predict future values from past values.

Because studies may not always support the same finding, even when the same design and analytic methods are used, **meta-analysis** may be appropriate. In the context of program evaluation, meta-analysis may be used to summarize the estimate of the size of the program's effect (commonly measured by the odds ratio and relative risk) on specific program outcomes across several studies. Hedrick *et al.* (1989) applied meta-analysis to assess the results of 13 studies of home care. When the data from these studies were pooled, the summary odds ratio of nursing home placement was significantly lower among those receiving home care services than those not receiving these services (OR = 0.77, 95% CI: 0.62, 0.95). Chapter 7 presents additional information on meta-analysis.

There are two major approaches to analyzing the costs and benefits of health care that are not within the scope of epidemiologic applications but are often used to supplement evaluations. These two approaches are **cost–benefit** and **cost-effectiveness analysis** (Warner and Luce, 1982). **Cost–benefit analysis** plots the dollars expended for each program against the monetary value of benefits represented as society's value of the outcome (e.g., how much is a life worth?). In **cost-effectiveness** analysis, costs are calculated and programs are compared based upon their achievement of a specific outcome expressed in terms of years of life saved or days of illness avoided. For both methods, the direct program costs (personnel, equipment, etc.) and indirect costs (e.g., caregiver time and time lost from work) are computed, with indirect costs being the most difficult to quantify. Benefits and costs should also be discounted as they are factored into the computations because their present values may not be the same as the future values.

Prospects of Health Services Evaluation

Who should evaluate health care, and how these evaluations should be financed are issues of increasing importance within our health care system. The answer to the first question is contingent upon what aspects of the health care system are being evaluated. If the technical quality of care is being assessed, then the medical profession has the knowledge required to evaluate this aspect capably (Greenlick, 1981). If the broader interrelationships of access, availability, effectiveness, efficiency, and acceptability are being evaluated, the competencies of a range of nonmedical professions and lay persons may be necessary to accomplish the assessment.

The answer to the question of financial responsibility for evaluations depends upon who mandates the implementation of a program. If it is initiated because of a governmental mandate, then the responsibility for financing the evaluation lies with the government. For example, programs implemented at a national level for hospitals or nursing homes should be evaluated by researchers funded by federal funds. Similarly, mandated state and local interventions should be financed through state/local initiatives. Alternately, if the focus of an evaluation is a program implemented by a single hospital or nursing home, a chain of one of these, or an individual group practice, then the responsibility for funding lies with that single entity responsible for implementation of the program, whether the funding comes from internal resources or an external source such as a private foundation.

Conclusion

Evaluation will continue to play an important role, irrespective of the type of reform that occurs within the U.S. health care system, for several reasons. First, the organization of formal and informal alliances in the health care industry and the competition among them will prompt managers on a continual basis to evaluate morbidity, mortality, and disability trends associated with service delivery and treatment of health problems in order to modify or discard services and treatments that are not efficient, effective, and of high quality. Second, the number and size of social programs have grown over time with the broadening scope of government involvement in health and social service issues. The application of epidemiologic methods is useful for monitoring the health of the population and identifying changes over time. Epidemiology is based upon the premise that health problems that can be identified can often be corrected. Finally, programs addressing the needs of an aging population will proliferate and necessitate evaluation to assess changing needs, assure that expectations are met, and promote achievement of the desired health outcomes. Epidemiologic methods can be used effectively to target identified needs and to assess the implications of programs or interventions for health care policy.

Case Studies

Case Study No. 1
Mandated Evaluation of the Elderly in Preferred Provider Organizations

The federal government mandates the evaluation of demonstration programs it extends to covered, eligible populations. The Health Care Financing Administration (HCFA) is particularly interested in assessing expanded coverage of the elderly and disabled under Title XVIII (Medicare) of the Social Security Act. A program extending Preferred Provider Organization (PPO) coverage to the Medicare population is being proposed. It must be evaluated and compared with traditional fee-for-service (FFS) arrangements and provisions for those who join health maintenance organizations (HMOs). Medicare recipients have a choice about which program they will enroll in. A particular concern is evaluating the access and quality of care across alternative ambulatory settings, i.e., PPOs, HMOs, and the traditional FFS setting.

Q.1. Propose a study design to evaluate access of the elderly to health care in this program.

Q.2. What outcome criteria are most important to a comparison of preventive maintenance approaches directed at the elderly population covered by each arrangement (PPO, HMO, FFS)?

Q.3. What process criteria can be measured to determine if preventive care practices are different among the three payment systems?

Q.4. What statistical methods can be utilized for comparing the quality of care in the three payment systems?

Q.5. How can one select a comparison group if no "no intervention" group is used?

Case Study No. 2
Impact of a Hospital-Based AIDS Program

Recent concern has been raised in a small, urban community (population approximately 250,000) because of an increasing number of inpatients testing HIV positive. You are asked to design a program that will include both hospital personnel and patients. In addition, because the hospital has a mandate to serve the community, your program must also be able to assess the magnitude of the problem in the community, provide appropriate outreach services, and project utilization of resources to address the projected increase in the number of HIV cases.

Q.1. What should be the first step to initiate the design for this intervention? What epidemiologic methods can be used at this stage?

Q.2. How could the level of awareness of AIDS risk factors among hospital personnel and among those persons in the community be determined?

Q.3. If the hospital received funding to do an evaluation of the impact of the introduction of a new AIDS prevention program in the community, how should you proceed?

Case Study No. 3
Planning and Evaluation of a Program for Maternal Cocaine Users and Their Babies

Cocaine abuse among women of childbearing age has increased substantially in recent years. According to estimates of the National Institute on Drug Abuse, there are between 15.5 million and 17.4 million female illicit drug users in the United States. Earlier, total cocaine use for the female population was estimated at 4.4 million (National Institute on Drug Abuse, 1985). The annual prevalence of substance abuse (including cocaine) during pregnancy is estimated to be approximately 11% nationally. However, the prevalence of cocaine use among pregnant women hospitalized for delivery can range as high as 27% in some urban hospitals. At least 375,000 babies are born annually to mothers who use drugs. Effects experienced by the neonate can be withdrawal and premature delivery.

An awareness of the increase of maternal cocaine abuse in metropolitan communities has aroused serious concern about the social and financial burden of caring for the victims. Little is known about the patterns and costs of services rendered to pregnant cocaine users, their infants and children. You have been appointed by the hospital director to a task force charged with designing an evaluation of this issue in your metropolitan area. The evaluation should enable an assessment of the availability of treatment and service modalities compared to what is needed.

Q.1. What epidemiologic measures can be used to define and analyze the problem of maternal cocaine abuse in the metropolitan area?

Q.2. How can the task force assess utilization of health care resources across the metropolitan area for both mothers and babies?

Q.3. What outcome measures could be used to compare the efficacy of services and treatment of maternal cocaine users? Of "crack babies"?

Q.4. Propose a study design to evaluate an outreach program intended to reduce the incidence of maternal substance abuse in your area.

Q.5. Discuss the advantages and disadvantages of this study design.

Case Study No. 4
Evaluating a Community-Based Hypertension Control Program

Hypertension is a major risk factor for cardiovascular disease. A decline in mortality for coronary heart disease has been observed since the late 1960s resulting from changes in life-style and the availability of antihypertensive drug therapy. This decline, however, has not been as pronounced in rural areas as it has been in urban areas, and cardiovascular mortality rates are especially high in the rural south. In response to this problem, a community-wide high-blood-pressure control program was introduced into two adjacent rural counties in Kentucky (Kotchen *et al.*, 1986). The program was multifaceted. One aspect of the program was a hypertension registry that included individuals having high blood pressure who would receive periodic mailings about cardiovascular disease risk reduction and a description of community resources to help them. A 4-H Club conducted educational programs and blood pressure screening for school-aged children. Blood pressure screening and monitoring sites were established in churches and businesses. Radio and television stations and newspapers were asked to provide information about cardiovascular disease risk factors and the importance of risk factor reduction. Educational programs were provided to nurses, physicians, community groups, and to participants in

Table 5.4. Hypertension Status at Baseline and Follow-up[a]

	Control County		Intervention Counties	
	Baseline	Follow-up	Baseline	Follow-up
% of population (No.) who are hypertensive (blood pressure ≥ 160 or ≥ 95 mm Hg) or receiving medication	22.7 (186/820)	22.4 (94/419)	27.7 (565/2,040)	26.5 (199/752)
% of all hypertensives (No.) who are controlled (blood pressure $<140/90$ mm Hg)	22.0 (41/186)	28.7 (27/94) (NS)	24.8 (140/565)	39.7* (79/199) ($P<.0001$)
% of hypertensives (No.) who are receiving medication and who were controlled (blood pressure $<140/90$ mm Hg)	36.6 (41/112)	39.7 (27/68) (NS)	36.8 (140/380)	53.4* (79/148) ($P<.0001$)

*$P<.04$, one-tailed test, compared with control county.

[a]Reprinted from Kotchen *et al.* (1986), with permission from the American Medical Association. Copyright 1986.

county and health fairs. The interventions lasted over a 5-year period. A county in geographic proximity to the intervention counties was selected as a control site. Before the inception of the program, a census of households in the three counties was performed, and a 15% random sample of household clusters was selected for a detailed baseline survey. The baseline survey consisted of social, demographic, medical history, and health attitudes and beliefs data as well as standardized measurements of blood pressure. After 5 years, a repeat survey of blood pressure was performed consisting of 25% of the original sample and newly surveyed households.

Q.1. What criteria should be used to monitor program effectiveness?

Q.2. What type of study design is this?

Q.3. Why was it necessary to have a comparison county?

Q.4. What may be concluded from Table 5.4 regarding the efficacy of the program?

Q.5. What could have been done to improve the evaluation?

References

Anderson, S., Auquier, A., Hauck, W. W., Oakes, D., Vandaele, W., and Wersberg, H. I., 1980, *Statistical Methods for Comparative Studies*, John Wiley & Sons, New York.

Bennett, C. L., Garfinkle, J. B., Greenfield, S., Draper, D., Rogers, W., Mathews, C., and Kanouse, D. E., 1989, The relation between hospital experience and in-hospital mortality for patients with AIDS-related PCP, *JAMA* **261**:2975–2979.

Bibeau, D., Mullen, K., McLeroy, K., Green, L., and Foshee, V., 1988, Evaluations of workplace smoking cessation programs: A critique, *Am. J. Prev. Med.* **4**:87–95.

Bollen, K., 1989, *Structural Equations with Latent Variables*, John Wiley & Sons, New York.

Box, G. E. P., and Jenkins, G. M., 1976, *Time Series Analysis: Forecasting and Control*, Holden-Day, San Francisco.

Carlisle, D. M., Siu, A., Keeler, E. B., McGlynn, E. A., Kahn, K. L., Rubenstein, L. V., and Brook, R. H., 1992, HMO vs. fee-for-service care of older persons with acute myocardial infarction, *Am. J. Public Health* **82**:1626–1630.

Cox, D. R., Regression models and life-tables, *J. R. Statist. Soc.* **B34**:187–220.

Donabedian, A., 1980, *Explorations in Quality Assessment and Monitoring, Vol. I: The Definition of Quality and Approaches to Its Assessment*, Health Administration Press, Ann Arbor, MI.

Donabedian, A., 1981, Advantages and limitations of explicit criteria for assessing the quality of health care, *Milbank Mem. Fund Q. Health Soc.* **59**:99–106.

Greenlick, M. R., 1981, Assessing clinical competence: A society view, *Eval. Health Professions* **4**:3–12.

Health Care Financing Administration, 1992, *Medicare Hospital Information*, U.S. Government Printing Office, Washington, DC.

Hedrick, S. C., Koepsell, T. D., and Inui, T., 1989, Meta-analysis of home-care effects on mortality and nursing-home placement, *Med. Care* **27**:1015–1026.

Joreskog, K. G., and Sorbom, D., 1993, *Lisrel 8 with Prelis 2*, Scientific Software International, Chicago.

Kahn, H. A., and Sempos, C. T., 1989, *Statistical Methods in Epidemiology*, Oxford University Press, New York.

Kaplan, E. L., and Meier, P., 1958, Nonparametric estimation from incomplete observations, *J. Am. Statist. Assoc.* **53**:457–481.

Knaus, W. A., Draper, E. A., and Wagner, D. P., 1983, Toward quality review in intensive care: The APACHE system, *Quality Rev. Bull.* **9**:(7):196–204.

Kotchen, J. M., McKean, H. E., Jackson-Thayer, S., Moore, R. W., Straus, R., and Kotchen, T., 1986, Impact of a rural high blood pressure control program on hypertension control and cardiovascular disease mortality, *JAMA* **255**:2177–2182.

Lane, D. S., Polednak, A. P., and Burg, M. A., 1992, Breast cancer screening practices among users of county-funded health centers vs. women in the entire community, *Am. J. Public Health* **82**:199–203.

Levy, P. S., and Lemeshow, S., 1980, *Sampling for Health Professionals*, Lifetime Learning, Belmont, CA.

National Institute on Drug Abuse, 1985, *National Household Survey on Drug Abuse: 1985 Population Estimates*, National Institute on Drug Abuse, Rockville, MD.

Okada, L. M., and Wan, T. T. H., 1980, Impact of community health centers and Medicaid on the use of health services, *Public Health Rep.* **95:**520–534.

Retchin, S. M., and Brown, B., 1990, The quality of ambulatory care in Medicare health maintenance organizations, *Am. J. Publ. Health* **80:**411–415.

Rogers, P. N., and Schoenig, S. E., 1993, A time series evaluation of California's 1982 driving-under-the-influence legislative reforms, *Accid. Anal. Prev.* **26:**63–78.

Rooks, J. P., Weatherby, N. L., Ernst, E., Stapleton, S., Rosen, D., and Rosenfield, A., 1989, Outcomes of care in birth centers, *N. Engl. J. Med.* **321:**1804–1811.

Rosen, H. M., and Feigin, W., Sr., 1983, Quality assurance and data feedback, *Health Care Manage. Rev.* **8:**67–74.

Sackett, D. L., 1979, Bias in analytic research, *J. Chron. Dis.* **32:**51–63.

Vogt, T. M., and Schweitzer, S. O., 1985, Medical costs of cigarette smoking in a health maintenance organization, *Am. J. Epidemiol.* **122:**1060–1066.

Wan, T. T. H., 1992, Hospital variations in adverse patient outcomes, *Qual. Assur. Util. Rev.* **7:**50–53.

Wan, T. T. H., Weissert, W. G., and Livieratos, B. B., 1980, Geriatric day care and homemaker services: An experimental study, *J. Gerontol.* **35:**256–274.

Warner, K., and Luce, B. R., 1982, *Cost–Benefit and Cost–Effectiveness Analysis in Health Care: Principles, Practice, and Potential*, Health Administration Press, Ann Arbor, MI.

Wolinsky, F. D., and Johnson, R. J., 1991, The use of health services by older adults, *J. Gerontol.* **46:**S345–357.

Young, G. J., and Cohen, B. B., 1991, Inequities in hospital care, the Massachusetts Experience, *Inquiry* **28:**255–262.

6

Control of Transmissible Diseases in Health Care Organizations

Andrew Kucharski and Robert Mittendorf

Epidemiology as a discipline had as its historical focus the investigation of epidemics. In the United States, the period between 1800 and 1875 was characterized by a number of great epidemics, in particular cholera, yellow fever, smallpox, and typhoid fever (Smillie, 1952). The epidemiologic thinking of that time was that an epidemic was the result of uncontrollable conditions, not spread from person to person. Several authors linked poverty, overcrowding, and bad social conditions to the great excess in mortality that occurred during the epidemics. Between the period of 1900 and 1980, a large decline in mortality from transmissible disease was observed. Improved nutrition, sanitation, and less crowded housing coupled with the advent of the use of antibiotics in 1940 contributed to this decline. However, since 1980, the incidence and mortality from transmissible diseases have been increasing for several reasons.

First, there has been an emergence of newly identified pathogens and syndromes. These include: hepatitis C virus, human immunodeficiency virus (HIV), Legionnaire's disease, and Lyme disease. Second, infectious diseases resistant to current antimicrobial drugs are becoming more prevalent. These diseases include: gonorrhea, malaria, pneumococcal disease, salmonellosis, shigellosis, tuberculosis, and staphylococcal infections. Third, more aggressive medical treatments, such as multidrug high-dose chemotherapy, have increased the number of immunocompromised patients. Last, changes in social behavior have promoted the transmission of infectious diseases. Increased use of illicit intravenous drugs, for example, has contributed to the spread of AIDS and hepatitis because of the use of contaminated needles. The behavior of exchanging sex for drugs has also been associated with an increase in the incidence of transmissible diseases, particularly for many sexually transmitted diseases, notably syphilis. The purpose of this chapter is to provide an introduction to the principles required to allow health care managers to make informed decisions in light of the challenges

Andrew Kucharski   Department of Clinical Development, Immunex Corporation, Seattle, Washington 98101. **Robert Mittendorf**   Department of Obstetrics and Gynecology, University of Chicago, Chicago, Illinois 60637.

Epidemiology and the Delivery of Health Care Services: Methods and Applications, edited by Denise M. Oleske. Plenum Press, New York, 1995.

and threats posed by transmissible diseases. Also suggested are avenues for action in the prevention and control of these diseases in health care organizations.

Infectious Disease Concepts

In order to understand the manager's role in the control of transmissible diseases in health care organizations, a basic knowledge of terms and concepts is essential. To control transmissible disease, a health care manager must first understand how infectious diseases arise and are transmitted.

There are five elements involved in the emergence of an infectious disease. It is essential for managers to know these as they guide the decision-making process. The elements are: characteristics of the infectious agent, reservoir of the agent, mode of transmission, portal of entry/exit, and a susceptible host.

An infectious agent is characterized in terms of its biological classification, manifestation, and incubation period. The major categories of microbiological agents relevant to human diseases are **bacteria**, **fungi**, **parasites**, and **viruses**. Most human diseases caused by microbial factors are due to bacteria or viruses. Biological agents are classified according to the presence or absence of specific traits. For example, bacteria are classified based upon the mechanism of movement and character of the cell wall. Viruses are classified based upon the type of nucleic acid and the size, shape, substructure, and mode of replication of the viral particle. Tables 6.1 and 6.2 illustrate the classes of bacteria and viruses and their commonly associated diseases. In order to determine if a biological factor is causative in a disease, it must be isolated and identified in the host. Determination of the presence of microbial agents includes the following:

1. Morphological identification of the agent in sections of tissues or stains of specimens.
2. Culture isolation.
3. Detection of antigen from the agent by fluorescein-labeled antibody stains or by immunologic assay.
4. DNA–DNA or DNA–RNA hybridization to detect pathogen-specific genes in specimens.
5. Antibody- or cell-mediated immune responses.

Table 6.1. Classes of Bacteria and Commonly Associated Human Diseases[a]

Class	Disease
Staphylococci	Toxic shock syndrome
Streptococci	Streptococcal sore throat
Neisseriae	Gonorrhea
Legionellae	Pneumonia
Mycobacteria	Tuberculosis
Spirochetes	Syphilis
Rickettsia	Typhus
Chlamydiae	Urethritis

[a]Source: Jawetz et al. (1991).

Table 6.2. Classes of Human Viruses and Common Associated Diseases[a]

Nucleic acid core[b]	Viral type	Common pathology
DNA	Papovavirus	Chronic infections, tumors
	Adenovirus	Respiratory diseases, conjunctivitis
	Herpesvirus	Herpes simplex types 1 and 2 (oral and genital lesions); mononucleosis; chicken pox; shingles
	Poxvirus	Smallpox
	Hepadnavirus	Acute and chronic hepatitis
RNA	Picornavirus	Common cold
	Reovirus	Colorado tick fever
	Arbovirus	Yellow fever, encephalitis
	Togavirus	Rubella
	Arenaviruses	Lassa fever
	Coronaviruses	Acute upper respiratory infection
	Retrovirus	Acquired immunodeficiency syndrome
	Bunyavirus	Hemorrhagic fevers and nephropathy
	Orthomyxovirus	Influenza
	Paramyxovirus	Mumps, measles
	Rhabdovirus	Rabies

[a]Source: Jawetz *et al.* (1991).
[b]DNA, deoxyribonucleic acid; RNA, ribonucleic acid.

The most important components of accurately identifying an infectious agent are the specimen, the adequacy of material tested, the selection of the appropriate body area for testing, the method of collection, and the timeliness of the transport of the specimen to the laboratory. These steps are within the purview of the health manager and are essential processes to monitor in providing quality care to patients. In addition, the health care manager should have a knowledge of which diseases need to be reported to local health departments. A list of these is displayed in Table 6.3.

An agent can also be described in terms of **pathogenicity** and **virulence**. Pathogenicity is the ability of an organism to alter normal cellular and physiological processes. **Virulence** is the ability of an organism to produce overt infection. The **incubation period** is the time from the introduction of the agent into the host to the onset of the signs and symptoms of disease. Each infectious agent has its own unique incubation period that may be hours, days, weeks, months, or even years. For example, microbial agents that cause food poisoning typically have an incubation period of 24 to 72 hours; microbial agents that cause respiratory infections typically have an incubation period of 7 to 10 days; whereas hepatitis B and human immunodeficiency virus infections have incubation periods that may be several months long (American Public Health Association, 1990).

A **reservoir** is where the agent lives, grows, and multiplies. Reservoirs can be living (human, animal, plant) or inanimate (soil, water). Human reservoirs can be clinical cases or carriers. **Clinical cases** are those persons who manifest signs and symptoms of the disease (**acute cases**) or who are infected but who do not manifest signs and symptoms of the disease (**subclinical** or **inapparent cases**). **Carriers** are those persons who serve as a potential source of infections and harbor a specific infectious agent, but they themselves are not manifesting any signs or symptoms of the disease.

Table 6.3. Notifiable Diseases, United States

AIDS	Plague
Anthrax	Poliomyelitis (paralytic)
Botulism	Psittacosis
Brucellosis	Rabies
Cholera	Syphilis
Congenital rubella syndrome	Tetanus
Diphtheria	Toxic shock syndrome
Encephalitis, postinfectious	Trichinosis
Gonorrhea	Tuberculosis
Haemophilus influenzae (invasive disease)	Tularemia
Hansen's disease	Typhoid fever
Leptospirosis	Typhus fever, tick-borne (Rocky Mountain
Lyme disease	spotted fever)
Measles	

The process of producing disease from biological agents begins with the introduction and multiplication of the biological agent in the host. The **mode of transmission** is the mechanism by which an infectious agent is spread to a host or through the environment. There are three modes of transmission: (1) direct transmission is actual contact with an infected host such as through sexual intercourse; (2) indirect transmission occurs through contact with contaminated objects such as needles, and (3) droplet spread is the transmission of infected nuclei through sneezing or coughing. Some common infectious diseases, the reservoir, and route of transmission are displayed in Table 6.4.

The **portal of exit** is where the organism leaves the host. The **portal of entry** is where the organism invades the host. The portals of entry may be the respiratory (mouth and nose), gastrointestinal, or genitourinary tracts, or through the mucous membranes or skin. Usually, the portal of entry and the portal of exit are the same. For example, salmonella-contaminated feces could produce an infection via ingestion of food contaminated with the feces.

Host susceptibility is the level of resistance present to protect against a pathogenic agent once exposed to it. Susceptibility depends upon genetic factors, general health, and immunity. General health is influenced by nutrition and the presence of comorbidities. Disease caused by biological agents occurs when the normal immune response of the host is overcome and destruction of cells and tissues occurs producing physiological alterations in the host. **Immunity** is a resistance provided by the production of antibodies from lymphocytes or from monocytes having a specific action upon the microorganism or on its toxin. Immunity can be characterized as passive (natural or artificial) or active (natural or artificial). **Passive natural immunity** is the transplacental transfer of antibodies from mother to fetus. **Passive artificial immunity** is the inoculation of specific protective antibodies. Passive immunity has a short-term duration of efficacy (less than 2 months). **Active immunity** can be natural, as in the case of acquiring an infection (with or without clinical manifestation of disease), or artificial in which the agent itself in a killed or modified form is injected to stimulate protective antibodies. In fact, a relatively small subset of organisms causes disease.

Thus, to develop an infectious disease, an individual must be both susceptible and exposed. An exposure is a factor that, in the case of infectious disease transmission, is harmful, and allows for entry or interaction with the organism to produce harmful effects or clinical disease. However, just because an individual is both susceptible and exposed, does not mean

Table 6.4. Common Infectious Disease, Reservoirs, and Routes of Transmission

Infection	Reservoir	Route of transmission
Measles	Man	Respiratory
Hepatitis A	Man	Fecal–oral
Chlamydia	Man	Sexual intercourse
Hepatitis B	Man	Percutaneous and permucosal
Lyme disease	Wild rodents, deer	Vector, ticks
Encephalitis	Wild birds, rodents, bats, reptiles, amphibians	Vector, mosquitos
AIDS	Man	Sexual contact, percutaneous, permucosal, perinatal

that clinical (or overt) disease will develop. Circumstances and attributes of the exposure (frequency, dose, intimacy) and the degree of susceptibility of the host determine whether or not an infectious disease will emerge.

Managing Disease Outbreaks

In the health care setting, these elements guide practices to prevent the emergence of infection in patients and health care workers. However, circumstances may arise in which an epidemic may occur. An **epidemic** is the occurrence of cases of a condition in excess of what would be expected. An epidemic may occur for several reasons, including: an increase in the number of susceptible persons, the emergence of a new organism, changes in the environment, changes in behavior, new media for the growth of organisms, the migration of infected persons, animals, birds, or insects into an area, change in the virulence of an organism, and inadequate immunization levels. Some epidemics develop slowly in nature, such as the current epidemics of syphilis and tuberculosis. The increased incidence of these diseases has underlying causes in societal changes such as the increased use of illicit intravenous drugs and noncompliance with treatment plans. Noncompliance with treatment plans has led to new multidrug-resistant strains of TB. Other epidemics occur more suddenly and unexpectedly, such as an outbreak of *Salmonella*, whose root cause may be the improper handling of food.

Health care organizations that treat patients are susceptible to epidemics and must take precautions not only to prevent their occurrence, but also to respond to an epidemic in a quick fashion to decrease added risk to patients. As in the general population, both the patient population and health care providers are at risk in all hospital epidemics. An example of a slowly evolving hospital epidemic would be an increase in the incidence of needle-stick injuries among health care workers (HCW). Although each incident is documented, trends in incidence are typically noted over a longer period of time. An example of an epidemic with a faster incidence rate would be an outbreak of nosocomial infection among patients in an intensive care unit.

The health care organization's approach to epidemics must be both proactive and reactive. It is important to have the resources available to identify an epidemic and to respond accordingly. This requires specialized personnel such as an epidemiologist and safety experts. Additionally, the health care manager needs to understand how a hospital epidemic impacts other departments within the organization. It is important to remember that employees who do not have direct patient contact such as housekeeping, laundry, and laboratory staff are also at risk for infection. Aside from the infection control section, the outbreak of an epidemic in a health care setting also has the opportunity to affect:

1. Medical legal staff (possible lawsuits and litigation).
2. Health care costs (increased total treatment costs for a patient because of additional medical resources required to treat the patient, and increased length of stay).
3. New construction or renovation projects (identification of necessary air exchange systems, proper design of traffic flow patterns between isolation and nonisolation areas with transition areas between them, and Occupational Safety and Health Administration [OSHA] requirements).
4. Program development; has the organization adequately addressed these issues when considering expanding a service or offering a new treatment program?
5. Waste management; proper waste management assists in keeping the HCW safe from the spread of pathogens through penetrating injuries from contaminated needles or other sharp instruments.

Because of the broad impact that an epidemic can have, the fundamental role of the health care manager is to ensure that an organized strategy for the prevention of and response to an epidemic is in place. Elements of that strategy would include: define the case, screen with laboratory studies all exposed, quarantine the source, disinfect portals of exit, break the chain of transmission, defend portals of entry, immunize the host, investigate risk factors for developing the infection using an observational study design, and establish and maintain surveillance systems.

In addition to the prevention and control of epidemics, the health care manager also has general responsibilities in the control of transmissible diseases in health care service delivery settings. The tasks associated with this role are found in Table 6.5. Managers also have responsibilities for initiating appropriate policies and procedures regarding the specific aspects of infection control. Two areas of particular concern are blood-borne transmission and airborne transmission.

Blood-Borne Disease Transmission

An increased incidence of a number of blood-borne diseases has been observed, most notably hepatitis B (HBV) and acquired immunodeficiency syndrome (AIDS). With respect to

Table 6.5. Responsibilities of a Health Care Manager in the Control of Transmissible Diseases in Health Care Service Delivery Settings

1. Identify infectious disease risks associated with all job categories.
2. Offer training and education on work practices, protective clothing, and equipment related to job tasks to prevent exposure to transmissible diseases and on corrective action in the event of exposure.
3. Provide protective equipment and apparel and evaluate the efficacy of these periodically.
4. Monitor work practices with respect to compliance with hospital policies and procedures.
5. Provide care for work-related injuries and illnesses.
6. Support the investigation of epidemics within the health care organization and the introduction of control measures identified.
7. Monitor infection control indicators specified by accrediting bodies.
8. Establish and maintain surveillance system for transmissible diseases.
9. Support programs that provide immunization to health care workers.

HBV infections, the Centers for Disease Control and Prevention (CDC) estimated the total number of HBV infections in the United States to be 300,000 per year (1990), with approximately 25% of infected individuals developing acute hepatitis, and 6% to 10% becoming HBV carriers. This presents a risk of developing chronic liver disease and the potential of infecting others.

In addition to hepatitis B virus, HIV represents another virulent agent of concern to health care providers and managers. Human immunodeficiency virus is a retrovirus that, in the late stages of infection, gives rise to a condition known as AIDS; AIDS clinically manifests as a progressive destruction of the immune system and other organ systems, particularly the central nervous system. A number of opportunistic infections such as *Pneumocystis carinii* and several cancers, such as Kaposi's sarcoma are indicators of underlying AIDS (American Public Health Association, 1990). Since reporting began in June 1981, the number of AIDS cases has continued to increase dramatically (Fig. 6.1). Of the total number of documented cases, 220,871 individuals have died, and the U.S. Public Health Service has estimated that more than 1.0 million individuals in the United States are currently HIV-seropositive, or approximately one in every 250 individuals (CDC, 1993). The mode of transmission for HIV is through the exchange of body fluids such as blood, semen, feces, vaginal fluids, and urine. These fluids can be exchanged via sexual contact, the sharing of intravenous drug equipment, or other means where the integrity of the portals of entry, the mucous membrane and circulatory system are violated. Once infected, the host enters into a period of several months before having an immune conversion to test positive as a carrier of the virus. At this point, the carrier may or may not exhibit signs and symptoms of AIDS because of its long incubation time.

Because of the increased incidence of blood-borne diseases and the serious consequences of these diseases, CDC recommended **universal precautions** in 1987. **Universal precautions** outline steps that should be taken when handling blood and body fluids. These procedures are aimed at reducing the exposure of HCWs to HIV, HBV, and other blood-borne pathogens by minimizing their exposure to blood and body fluids that may be potentially infectious. Universal precautions stress two points. First, all patients are assumed to be potentially

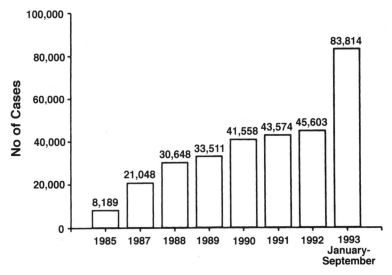

Figure 6.1. Acquired immunodeficiency syndrome (AIDS) cases, 1985–1993, United States. Source: U.S. Department of Health and Human Services Centers for Disease Control and Prevention (1994).

infectious for HIV and other blood-borne pathogens. Secondly, when body fluids are encountered under emergent, uncontrolled situations when the differentiation of body fluid types is not possible, all fluids should be treated as potentially hazardous. The responsibilities of health care managers regarding universal precautions are outlined in Table 6.6.

Health care workers are primarily protected through the use of barriers that reduce the risk of exposure of a HCW's skin or mucous membrane (ports of entry) to potentially infective materials. Barriers such as gloves, gowns, masks, and goggles should be easily accessible for any HCW who may come in contact with body fluids. Although the CDC has outlined which body fluids require mandatory universal precautions, current health care providers typically use barriers when handling any body fluids. Although these barriers provide front-line protection, the health care provider and manager must realize that they do not protect against penetrating injuries from needles, sharp instruments, or broken glass. Protective barriers should never be used more than once and should always be changed between patients.

Although the modes of transmission for both HBV and HIV are similar, the potential for HBV transmission in the workplace is greater than that of HIV because of the greater incidence of HBV in the population. However, protection from acute symptoms following exposure to HBV is greater than for HIV, since a hepatitis B vaccine is available. Health care managers should offer this vaccination to all HCWs at the beginning of their employment and draw immune titer levels periodically to verify immune response status.

Health care organizations must ensure that the management staff has designed a comprehensive exposure control plan for blood-borne pathogens (Table 6.7). All policies should comply with the U.S. Department of Labor, Occupational Safety and Health Administration Title 29, Code of Federal Regulations, Part 1910, *Occupational Exposure to Bloodborne*

Table 6.6. Management Responsibilities Regarding Universal Precautions

Prevention
    1. Classification of work activity
    2. Development of standard operating procedures
    3. Provision of training and education
    4. Development of procedures to ensure and monitor compliance
Management of workplace environment
    1. Needle and sharps disposal
    2. Handwashing facilities
    3. Cleaning, disinfecting, and sterilizing (equipment, room, laundry, body fluids)
    4. Provision of protective equipment
    5. Disposal of infective waste
Response to individual exposure
  Medical
    1. Blood sample at time of exposure
    2. Document in medical record circumstances of exposure (activities, work practices, protective equipment, source of exposure)
    3. Retest at 6 weeks, 12 weeks, and 6 months
    4. Provide treatment for febrile illness within 12 weeks after exposure
  Administration
    1. Report to OSHA and state health department
    2. Decision to have patient care duties depends on worker's personal physician and employer's medical advisors (Note: persons with impaired immune system are highly susceptible to contagious disease to which they may be exposed in patient care contact.)

Table 6.7. Elements of an Exposure-Control Plan for Blood-Borne Pathogens

List types of employees exposed to blood-borne pathogens by job classification.
Describe engineering controls implemented to handle sharp infected objects.
Provide directions outlining safe work practices.
Offer in-service programs on an annual basis to educate and train employees on following the safe work practices.
Describe types of risk exposure (sharp objects, splash or spray of infectious agents, etc.).
Describe and demonstrate the use of personal protective equipment.
Illustrate proper labeling and signage of high-risk areas and objects.
Assign responsibility for ensuring compliance with the safety plan and monitoring this compliance.

Pathogens: Final Rule, adopted in December 1991. In the event of exposure to potentially infectious materials, the health care organization should have in place policies that describe in detail the response to be taken. These steps should follow local laws regarding consent for testing individuals and should include legally valid steps for testing individuals when consent cannot be obtained (e.g., an unconscious patient). Because of the nature of a possible immune conversion following exposure, policies should be extremely sensitive to issues of confidentiality, and counseling should be available to the exposed individual both before and after testing. This counseling should actively be offered at any point during the incident. Policies should also ensure that the safety office, or appropriate recording department, should not only be notified of the incident, but the circumstances leading to the incident should also be reported. A review of this information can be helpful in changing practice, policies, and approaches to education in an attempt to decrease health care workers' exposure to blood-borne pathogens.

Airborne Disease

Since 1985, the reported cases of tuberculosis (TB; *Mycobacterium tuberculosis*) have exceeded the number of expected cases, thus, there is currently an epidemic of TB in the United States. In 1992, 26,673 cases of new TB, or 10.5 cases per 100,000 population were reported to the CDC (1993). The highest rate was observed in New York (Fig. 6.2). Between 1985 and 1992, an increased incidence of TB was seen in all racial and ethnic groups below age 50 years (Fig. 6.3). Increases among Hispanics, non-Hispanic blacks, and Asians/Pacific Islanders primarily reflect the greater prevalence of TB among persons infected with HIV (Barnes *et al.*, 1991; Theuer *et al.*, 1990), persons immigrating from countries with a high incidence of TB (CDC, 1986), and primary transmission between these groups. Other factors contributing to the spread of TB include substance abuse, limited access to health care, poverty, substandard housing, and homelessness (CDC, 1992).

As a result of immunosuppression, individuals coinfected with TB and HIV are at increased risk of developing active TB. In response to this, the Advisory Committee for the Elimination of Tuberculosis has recommended that individuals infected with HIV be screened for active and inactive TB. If the individual is infected, curative or preventive therapy should be offered. In addition to increased morbidity because of coinfection, strains of bacteria are able to mutate and become resistant to drug therapy. Over time, TB has become resistant to many of the antibiotics that had previously been used mainly as a result of noncompliance with treatment programs. New strains of multi-drug-resistant TB (MDR-TB) are spreading and creating a new challenge for the medical community.

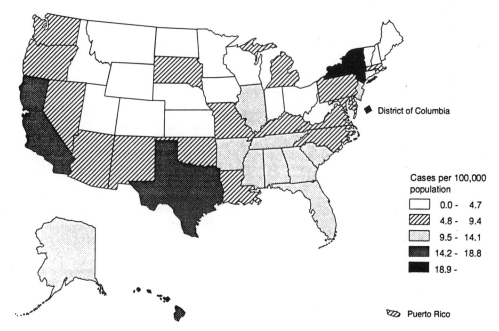

Figure 6.2. Rates of new tuberculosis cases in the United States, by state, 1991. Source: Office of Technology Assessment (1993).

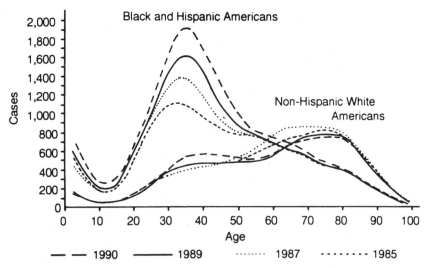

Figure 6.3. U.S. tuberculosis cases among black and Hispanic Americans compared with non-Hispanic white Americans, 1985, 1987, 1989, and 1990. Source: Office of Technology Assessment (1993).

As health care managers, we should be concerned about the transmission of TB within the environment. The most common method of TB transmission is exposure to bacilli in airborne droplet nuclei produced by infected persons who cough, sing, or sneeze. Infection occurs when an individual inhales droplet nuclei contaminated with *M. tuberculosis*. The bacteria then traverse the portal of entry (mouth or nasal passages) and deposit within the lungs. Usually the human immune system limits the multiplication and spread of the bacteria within 2 to 10 weeks. However, some of these bacteria remain dormant for many years, and this is known as latent TB infection. Individuals with latent TB usually have a positive response to the protein purified derivative (PPD) skin test, but are not symptomatic or infectious.

Factors affecting infection with TB are highly variable and depend on the virulence of the strain of TB, environmental conditions, and the health of the exposed individual. Outside the patients' rooms, infectious droplets may remain airborne and move within a building's air currents until inhaled by an another worker or patient, settled out of the air, or exhausted from the building. As a control measure, managers should ensure that the ventilation system is in compliance with the American Society of Heating, Refrigeration, and Air Conditioning Engineers Standard 62-1989. The use of ultraviolet radiation, disinfection, high-efficiency air filtration, and electrostatic precipitation are other control measures that can be used to control the level of droplet nuclei in the environment.

Recently, TB epidemics have been reported in health care facilities (Edlin *et al.*, 1992; Beck-Sague *et al.*, 1992). Some of these outbreaks have involved MDR-TB in both patients and HCWs. In these cases, a number of those persons were already HIV seropositive, and because of a suppressed immune system, the new infection progressed rapidly. The mortality associated with these outbreaks was extremely high with a range from 43% to 93%, and the time from diagnosis to death was very short, with a median interval of 4 to 16 weeks. Factors contributing to these outbreaks included:

1. Delayed diagnosis of patients with TB.
2. Delayed recognition of drug resistance.
3. Delayed initiation of effective therapy resulting in a prolonged contagious period.
4. Delayed initiation and inadequate duration of TB isolation.
5. Inadequate ventilation of TB isolation rooms.
6. Lapses in TB isolation practices.
7. Inadequate precautions for cough-inducing procedures.

These contributing factors indicate lapses in administrative (items 5 and 6), clinical care (items 1, 2, 3, and 4), and training (items 6 and 7) practice. The *Federal Register*, Volume 58, Number 195 (Tuesday, October 12, 1993) has updated the guidelines for preventing the transmission of TB in health care facilities. In attempting to reduce the incidence of TB transmission among individuals in health care settings, current guidelines emphasize the importance of *control measures* (administrative and engineering controls and personal respiratory protection), health care facility *risk assessment and development of a written TB control plan, early detection and management of persons with TB, skin-testing programs, and HCW education*. Health care managers should be intimately involved in each of the steps above.

Hierarchy of Control Measures

As an administrative control measure, managers should develop and implement written policies and procedures to ensure the early detection, isolation and treatment of patients with infectious TB, as well as implement effective work practices by HCWs in the facility.

A second level of control involves the use of engineering measures to prevent the spread of disease and reduce the concentration of infected droplet nuclei. The design and installation of all ventilation systems in the hospital should be supervised by a professional with expertise in ventilation who has also had hospital experience and knowledge of the setting. For instance, the design and installation of ventilation systems for general use areas of the hospital, such as nonisolation areas, waiting rooms, emergency rooms, etc., are different from systems necessary for TB isolation rooms or areas where cough-inducing procedures such as bronchoscopy or suctioning are performed. Areas such as these, which may have a higher concentration of airborne infected nuclei, need more air exchanges on an hourly basis to decrease the concentration of airborne nuclei. Additionally, health-care facilities that serve populations with a higher prevalence of TB may need to also supplement air-handling systems in general use areas.

Although the first two control levels attempt to minimize the number of areas in the health care facility where TB exposure may occur, they do not address those areas where exposure is at the highest, that is, TB isolation rooms and treatment rooms where cough-producing procedures are performed. In addition to the supplemental equipment described above, employees in this area need to be supplied with personal respiratory protective equipment.

Risk Assessment and Development of a Written TB Control Plan

Prior to developing any risk-assessment plan, an understanding of what the current risk of TB exposure is in the organization is necessary. Therefore, the very first step towards implementing a TB exposure control plan is an initial risk assessment of each hospital area and employee type. The risk assessment should receive input from qualified personnel such as an epidemiologist, infectious disease and pulmonary medicine specialists, engineers, and management. The assessment should include a review of the number of TB patients seen in the organization as a whole and for specialized areas such as TB, pulmonary, and HIV units. A review of the drug-susceptibility pattern of TB patients should be conducted along with an analysis of PPD skin-test results of HCWs across the organization.

After an initial risk assessment, a TB exposure-control plan should be implemented. Table 6.8 outlines an optimum TB control program for all health-care organizations, as recommended by the *Federal Register*, Volume 59, No. 195, Tuesday, October 12, 1993.

Early Detection and Management

Early detection and management is probably the most important step in the control of TB within a health care organization, and this measure relies heavily on the clinical expertise of HCWs assigned the responsibility for screening patients. Policies should be implemented that outline steps to be taken once an individual is suspected of having active TB, is in a high-risk group, or is symptomatic for active TB. The clinical skill of the HCW is critical since he or she has the first contact with patients.

Once a patient is positively identified as having active TB, proper patient management should quickly follow. This includes initiation of treatment and placement into isolation. Because of the restrictive nature of isolation, incentives should be provided for the patient to encourage compliance. These could include the provision of telephones, television, and other comforts to assist the patient in remaining in the room during the course of treatment. Additionally, it is important to educate the patient about the important role he or she plays in minimizing exposure to other individuals. These steps include instructing the patient about

**Table 6.8. Optimum Tuberculosis (TB) Control Program
for All Health Care Facilities**[a]

   I. Initial and periodic risk assessment
      A. Evaluate HCW PPD[b] skin test conversion data
      B. Determine TB prevalence among patients
      C. Reassess risk in each PPD testing period
  II. Written TB infection control program
      A. Document all aspects of TB control
      B. Identify individual(s) responsible for TB control program
      C. Explain and emphasize hierarchy of control
 III. Implementation
      A. Assignment of responsibility
      B. Risk assessment and periodic assessment of the program
      C. Early detection of patients with TB
      D. Management of outpatients with possible infectious TB
      E. Isolation for infectious TB patients
      F. Implement effective engineering controls
      G. Provide respiratory protection
      H. Contain/limit cough-inducing procedures
      I. HCW TB education
      J. HCW counseling and screening
      K. Evaluate HCW PPD test conversions and possible nosocomial TB transmission
      L. Coordinate efforts with public health department

---

[a]Source: *Federal Register* Volume 58, No. 195, Tuesday, October 12, 1993.
[b]HCW, health care worker; PPD, protein purified derivative.

covering the mouth and nose with a tissue while coughing or sneezing. A mask should be provided to patients when they are being transported within the health care facility for tests that cannot be performed inside the TB isolation unit.

Skin-Testing Programs and Health Care Worker Education

Skin testing (using protein purified derivative) should be required of all employees in a medical setting regardless of their role in the organization. The test should be part of a preemployment screening and be performed on a regular basis thereafter. The frequency of testing employees should be dependent on their level of risk to exposure to airborne nuclei contaminated with TB. Special circumstances, such as an increased incidence of TB in the population or a patient population in higher-risk categories for active TB infection, may necessitate modifying these policies. Policies should also be in place outlining steps to follow should a PPD convert (initial negative PPD reaction, followed by a positive reaction on follow-up testing) or active TB case in a HCW be identified.

As with testing, education should also be on a continuous schedule. At a minimum, all employees should be required to attend an annual in-service program that describes the risk of exposure to TB and the individual's responsibility to reduce his or her own probability of exposure. Educational programs may be required sooner than planned if an increase in active TB cases is noticed or if a lapse in clinical practice has caused the spread of disease. At all times, educational materials such as brochures, pamphlets, and federal, state, and local guidelines should be available to all employees upon request.

Special Considerations in Infectious Disease Control by Specific Health Care Service Setting

It is the responsibility and a special challenge to the health care manager to provide a safe work area for the organizations' employees as well as a treatment environment that reduces the additional burden on patients. Each health care arena presents circumstances specific to its setting. These are different between inpatient care facilities, ambulatory care centers, skilled-care facilities, home-care facilities, and hospice. Although concerns regarding communicable diseases exist in every health care setting, the types of disease that are of priority concern vary somewhat according to the setting. The specific settings addressed in this chapter are: inpatient, ambulatory care, long-term care, home-care, and hospice facilities.

Inpatient Acute-Care Facility

In the hospital, nosocomial infections are of special concern. A **nosocomial infection** is an infection that is acquired while one is in an inpatient setting and that is not part of the original disease process. The incidence of nosocomial infection varies according to organization characteristics, service area within a hospital, and anatomic site (Horan *et al.*, 1986). The highest nosocomial infection rate is attributable to urinary tract infection (12.9 cases per 1000 discharges). The consequences of nosocomial infection vary by type of infection, but overall they are responsible for 4.5 extra hospital days for a patient who develops nosocomial infection and as much as 4% of hospital deaths (Haley *et al.*, 1981).

Essential components of a hospital infection-control program include: an organized hospital-wide program of surveillance and control, a system of reporting wound infection rates to surgeons, a trained hospital epidemiologist, and one infection-control nurse per 250 beds (Haley *et al.*, 1985). The hospital control and surveillance program should collect and monitor data to evaluate conformance with the guidelines of accrediting bodies such as those of the local and state health departments, Health Care Financing Administration (if the hospital receives payment for Medicare patients), the Joint Commission for the Accreditation of Health Care Organizations (JCAHO), and others. Indicators that entered the β-testing phase by JCAHO to assist the general acute-care hospital assess its surveillance, prevention, and infection control activities are displayed in Table 6.9.

Ambulatory Care

Ambulatory care clinics should follow infection-control measures for the disposal of infectious waste that are the same as those for an inpatient treatment setting. For airborne pathogen transmission, HCWs should be aware of the risk of TB among their patient population and especially aware of coinfection of patients with HIV and TB. Patients who are infected with HIV should receive a PPD skin test during the first visit to an outpatient clinic. If the signs and symptoms of active TB occur, steps to diagnose infection should be undertaken. At the onset of symptoms, reverse isolation measures should be implemented to ensure that the patient's mouth and nose are covered while ambulating through the clinic.

All ambulatory care clinics should be equipped with either an isolation area or an area ventilated with the appropriate amount of air exchange to reduce the concentration of infected airborne nuclei for the examination and treatment of patients. Individuals who are known to have active TB infection should be provided, if possible, with a separate waiting and examination area or should be kept a maximum distance from other patients who may be immuno-compromised.

Table 6.9. Joint Commission on Accreditation of Health Care Organizations Infection Control (IC) Indicators[a]

IC-1
Indicator focus: Surgical wound infection
Numerator: Selected inpatient and outpatient surgical procedures complicated by a wound infection during hospitalization or after discharge
Denominator: Number of selected inpatient and outpatient surgical procedures
IC-2
Indicator focus: Postoperative pneumonia
Numerator: Selected inpatient surgical procedures complicated by onset of pneumonia during hospitalization but not beyond 10 postoperative days
Denominator: Number of selected inpatient surgical procedures
IC-3
Indicator focus: Urinary catheter usage
Numerator: Selected surgical procedures in inpatients who have catheters in place during perioperative period
Denominator: Number of selected inpatient surgical procedures in which patient had had a catheter in place during hospitalization
IC-4
Indicator focus: Ventilator pneumonia
Numerator: Inpatients receiving mechanical ventilation in whom pneumonia develops
Denominator: 1,000 (intensive care unit or ventilation therapy unit) patient ventilator days
IC-5
Indicator focus: Postpartum endometritis
Numerator: Inpatients in whom endometritis develops after cesarean section, observed until discharge
Denominator: Postpartum women who had cesarean section
IC-6
Indicator focus: Concurrent surveillance of primary bloodstream infection
Numerator: Inpatients with a central or umbilical line in whom primary bloodstream infection develops
Denominator: 1,000 (intensive care unit or nonintensive care unit) central or umbilical line days
IC-7
Indicator focus: Medical record abstraction of primary bloodstream infection
Numerator: Inpatients with a central or umbilical line and primary bloodstream infection, analyzed by method of identification
Denominator: Inpatients with a central or umbilical line and primary bloodstream infection, identified through either concurrent surveillance or medical record abstraction
IC-8
Indicator focus: Employee health program
Numerator: Hospital staff who have been immunized for measles (rubeola) or are known to be immune
Denominator: All hospital staff

[a]Reprinted from Nadzam (1992), with permission of the author and Mosby-Year Book, Inc., copyright 1992.

Home-Care Setting

There are two special concerns in preventing the spread of both blood-borne and airborne pathogens in the home-care setting. The first is to provide both the visiting health care provider and the patient adequately with the supplies necessary to handle infectious waste. Containers for contaminated sharps should be inside the home, and the home-care provider should educate the patient on what constitutes contaminated waste and how adequately to dispose of it.

In the event of the possible spread of pathogens via airborne transmission, the home-care provider should provide education to the patient. Methods to prevent the spread of disease to other individuals with whom the patient comes in contact should be described. This should include instructing the patient to cover the mouth and nose with tissue while coughing.

Long-Term Care/Skilled Nursing Facility

Infection control in a long-term care setting centers around admission of patients with infections, tuberculin testing of residents, employee health, use of immunizations, HIV-infected patients, and infection-control measures (Crossley et al., 1992). In nursing homes, the common sites of infection in patients are the respiratory tract, urinary tract, skin, and soft tissue. The major goals of surveillance in long-term care facilities should be to assist in early detection of outbreaks and to identify preventable endemic infections (Darnowski et al., 1991). The size of the institution also has an effect on the organization's ability to respond to an epidemic. In a recent survey of long-term care facilities, 79% of respondents had a limited infection control program in place defined as a part-time infection-control practitioner who spent less than 10 hours a week on infection-control activities. The survey also found that larger long-term care facilities spent more time on infection-control activities (Mylotte et al., 1992). Influenza, TB, and pneumonia are special concerns for managers of nursing homes given a patient population that is less resistant to other comorbidities.

In nursing homes, influenza, is a major source of morbidity and mortality and often occurs perennially. Because of crowded living conditions coupled with residents who are often in a compromised health status, influenza can rapidly affect as many as 60% of residents. The primary control measure is to provide vaccination against influenza for at least 70% of residents and to include staff, as well. This rate of vaccination can provide herd immunity. **Herd immunity** is the protection of entire populations from infection brought about by the presence of a critical number of immune individuals (Fine, 1993). To supplement control efforts, amantadine hydrochloride, a drug with antiviral activity, may be given to residents as well as staff prior to exposure to influenza or within 24 to 48 hours after the onset of symptoms. Other control measures include restricting visitors, delaying new admissions, quartering residents with signs, and symptoms of influenza, and implementing respiratory isolation measures for acutely ill patients. The health care manager must keep in mind that these efforts still may not prevent cases of influenza from occurring because of poor antibody response in the elderly, improper handling of vaccines during administration, and incompatibility between virus strain and vaccine.

Since the number of TB cases in the United States has ceased to decline and is rising in some populations, the likelihood of having long-term care patients become infected with TB is greater now, and it will only increase in the future given the demographics of the population now infected with TB. Additionally, there are many persons who are over the age of 65 who carry tubercle bacilli in dormant lesions acquired earlier. These individuals are still capable of spreading TB, and the possibility of latent infection becoming active increases as life forces wane. It is important for managers and providers in long-term care facilities to be aware of this possibility, since active TB is often incorrectly diagnosed as being either bronchitis or bronchopneumonia and could expose a number of health workers to TB (Stead and Dutt, 1991).

Infection control in long-term care facilities is becoming increasingly complex as the population ages, and the trend away from inpatient hospital care increases the number of persons treated in this type of facility. Reportedly, higher rates of nosocomial infection in these facilities, approximately 15% (Bentley and Cheney, 1990), and an environment of special risks, such as increased group activities and crowding, suggest that both health care providers and managers should outline procedures for: (1) the recognition of infection, (2) a knowledge of infection-control principles, (3) a review of immunization history of patients as they are admitted to the facility, and (4) an increase in communication among office, hospital, and long-term care facility. Once implemented, these policies should be reviewed on a scheduled basis. Efforts such as these, which aim at reducing the number of infections spread in the health care setting, should assist in reducing the additional risk placed on patients in long-term care.

Hospice

The emergence of AIDS presents health care providers with complex medical management issues. Hospice programs provide specialized care to persons who are in the final stages of the disease. As the epidemic grows, they increasingly also must respond to HIV-infected staff. A comprehensive workplace program prepares the hospice provider for these challenges and ensures an appropriate response. The four essential elements of such a program are policy development, staff education, supervisory training, and compliance monitoring. Policies to consider include the following: infection control, occupational exposure, confidentiality, and the response to HIV-infected patients and employees. Comprehensive education ensures quality care for AIDS patients. The education of managers and supervisors is crucial. After policy implementation and training, procedures must be instituted to monitor compliance and develop corrective action (Moga *et al.*, 1991).

Because of a compromised immune system, patients who are HIV positive or who have AIDS are more susceptible to coinfection with TB. Given that some hospices have inpatient services, precautions for the detection and prevention of the spread of TB should follow the same steps as those in place at an inpatient hospital setting. If the hospice is not associated with a larger hospital or does not have direct access to the infection-control staff of a larger organization, steps should be taken to ensure well-defined policies that detail steps to be taken for infection control. Additionally, if infection-control efforts are conducted on a part-time basis, there may be a need to contract supplemental help when necessary. Financial considerations such as this need to be addressed during the budget process to ensure that contracted services do not negatively affect the fiscal standing of the organization.

Conclusion

In addition to the administrative structure necessary to support infection control in a health care organization, the implementation of a comprehensive infection-control plan requires input from clinical specialists, engineering and physical-plant advisors. Also required is a work force that prioritizes the safety of both themselves and their patients.

One of the primary means to prevent the spread of disease is an educated work force. Instruction about universal precautions and isolation measures should be a dynamic experience. Records documenting proper training should be maintained for reporting to accrediting agencies, and a system for monitoring compliance with infection control protocols should be in place as a proactive aid in reducing the probability of unexpected disease exposure in the health care setting.

With health care shifting away from the inpatient setting and now being delivered in a variety of arenas such as hospice, home-care and increasingly in outpatient settings, infection-control practices need to be adapted to the unique characteristics of each of these settings. Since these settings often rely on the compliance of patients for successful treatment, education of the patient is also a factor. Specially, patients with TB need to be properly instructed about their role in preventing the spread of disease—namely, shielding others from exposure through the use of barriers when coughing or sneezing and a firm understanding of compliance with drug treatment. Long-term care and skilled nursing facilities face obstacles when working with the sick and elderly who already may have a compromised system. Hospice patients are at risk of comorbidities, especially those patients affected with HIV.

All of these issues must be addressed by the health care manager when determining how to meet regulatory agency requirement and how to keep their work force and patient population safe. Additionally, these issues must be addressed during stages of program development, renovation, and reconstruction. The financial and legal impact of an unsafe workforce and patient population cannot be underestimated. Given the rapidly changing environment of not only health care but of the financial, political, and legal framework in which it must function, the health care manager needs to be acutely aware of the importance of a properly designed infection-control program to prevent the spread of transmissible diseases in a health care organization.

Case Studies

Case Study No. 1
An Epidemic in a Neonatal Unit

On March 16, clinicians at Freeway Medical Center identified an outbreak of methicillin-resistant *Staphylococcus aureus* (MRSA) in the neonatal intensive care unit. Cultures were ordered on all 45 babies in the nursery. The cultures were taken from three body areas in the infants, rectum, oral cavity, and axillary area, as these were the likely portals of exit of the organism. Cultures were also taken from the clinical staff working in and servicing the unit as well as from the respiratory equipment used on the unit.

The results of the cultures confirmed the existence of the epidemic. There were 16 infants either actively ill or harboring the infection. One nurse tested positive for harboring the infection. The nurse who tested positive had apparently developed a *Staphyloccus* infection from a dermatitis on her hands. It was believed that the dermatitis was secondary to frequent handwashing and latex glove use.

Q.1. What should be the first action the manager takes?

Q.2. Upon confirmation of the epidemic, what should the manager do regarding operations of the unit?

Q.3. What should be done regarding staffing on the unit?

On April 10, the epidemic continued despite the measures introduced over the course of the last month since the identification of the epidemic, with one to two new cases developing each day. In addition, three more nurses had been found to be infected, and agency nurses had to be called in to replace the regular staff. The unit administration and the infectious-disease physicians reevaluated the problem, the previous responses, and the outcomes. This resulted in instituting the following measures: (1) all newborns had the drug Triple Dye® applied to the umbilical cord site (the most likely portal of exit for the organism) immediately after delivery; and Bactroban (mupirocin) was applied to the infant's nasal passages (the next most likely portal of exit of the organism) if any of the infant's cultures for MRSA were positive.

Q.4. Why did the epidemic continue?

Q.5. To prevent further cases of MRSA in the neonatal intensive care unit, what additional steps should be taken by the manager of this area?

Case Study No. 2
Evaluating Efficacy of Handwashing Systems

A major source of morbidity and mortality in the intensive care unit (ICU) is nosocomial infections. Nosocomial infections are a particular problem because patients in an ICU (1) are immunocompromised from the disease process, (2) have altered flora from treatment with high-dose and multidrug antibiotics, and (3) may have disrupted skin and mucosal membranes because of invasive procedures and devices. Among the organisms that these patients are susceptible to are those that may be transmitted by the hands. Thus, because many nosocomial infections can be prevented by interrupting their transmission by the hands, handwashing is an important intervention in health care settings. Doebbeling *et al.* (1992) describe a study to test the efficacy of hand-cleansing agents in preventing the transmission of pathogens from health care workers to patients. The two handwashing systems used in the study were (1) a 4% solution of chlorhexidine gluconate and (2) a 60% solution of isopropyl alcohol hand-rinsing agent with the optional use of a nonmedicated soap with a neutral pH. The setting for the study is a 902-bed teaching hospital. Patients for study were selected from the critical care unit (CCU), the surgical ICU, the medical ICU, and the cardiovascular ICU.

Q.1. Describe a study design to determine which of the two handwashing systems would be better to use in the hospital ICU.

Q.2. Propose a strategy to monitor the compliance with the handwashing protocols by hospital staff.

Q.3. List epidemiologic measures by which the efficacy of the handwashing system can be evaluated.

Case Study No. 3
Prevention of Needlestick Injuries in Hospital Employees

A major concern in the hospital setting is the transmission of blood-borne disease through the accidental puncture from needles. Direct handling of needles primarily involves nursing and laboratory personnel. Housekeeping personnel may also be involved because of needles inadvertently left in linens and trash. To determine if needlestick injuries were a problem at Freeway Medical Center (FMC), the hospital epidemiologist obtained all information on needlestick injuries in employees reported to the Employee Health Service during the last year. The human resource director of FMC provided information on the number of employees in each category of employee involved in nursing, laboratories, and housekeeping. The following data were obtained:

Job category	No. of needlestick injures	No. Full Time Equivalents (FTE)
RNs, full-time	26	262
RNs, part-time	15	69
LPNs, part-time	8	75
LPNs, full-time	24	125
Housekeeping, day shift	26	137
Housekeeping, night shift	9	50
Laboratory technicians	25	250

Q.1. What occupational groups of FMC are at highest risk of needlestick injuries?

Q.2. What interventions could be suggested to prevent needlestick injuries at FMC?

Case Study No. 4
An Outbreak of TB Infection in an HIV Unit

During January, a patient was admitted to a 25-bed HIV unit for long-term inpatient care. The patient was admitted for the treatment of multidrug-resistant *Mycobacterium bovis* (MDR-MB) TB and remained an inpatient for 6 months. During that time, eight additional patients and one healthy HCW exhibited signs and symptoms of active TB.

Diagnostic testing indicated that of the nine individuals who displayed symptoms of TB, five tested positive for MDR-MB TB, whereas the other four tested positive for another strain of TB.

Q.1. What factors make this patient population at increased risk for (MDR-MB) TB?

Q.2. Describe possible differences in the incubation period between the patients and the HCW.

Q.3. What measures should be initiated with the admission of patients with active TB?

Q.4. What measures should be initiated once other patients are found to have active TB?

Q.5. What measures should be initiated once the HCW displays signs of active TB infection?

Q.6. What should the health care manager do to prevent further outbreaks?

Case Study No. 5
An Outbreak of Hepatitis A among Health Care Workers

On December 9, a 32-year-old man and his 8-month-old son were admitted to a 16-bed burn treatment center. One month later he became jaundiced, and both were found to have hepatitis A. Although appropriate isolation precautions were initiated, 11 health care workers and one other burn patient became clinically ill with hepatitis A. According to Doebbeling *et al.* (1993), who investigated the epidemic, the typical nursing staff ratio is 1 : 3. A lounge and charting room located nearby is available to health care workers regularly assigned to the center. Snack food may be brought in by outpatients with burns to share with burn treatment personnel. At the entrance to the center, two sinks are located for handwashing.

Q.1. How would it be determined that an epidemic existed?

Q.2. What type of study design may be initiated to investigate behavioral risk factors for the development of hepatitis A?

References

American Public Health Association, 1990, *The Control of Communicable Diseases in Man*, APHA, New York.

Barnes, P. F., Bloch, A. B., Davidson, P. T., and Snider, D. E., 1991, Tuberculosis in patients with human immunodeficiency virus infection, *N. Engl. J. Med.* **234:**1644–1650.

Beck-Sague, C., Dooley, S. W., and Hutton, M. D., 1992, Outbreak of multidrug-resistant *Mycobacterium tuberculosis* infections in a hospital: Transmission to patients with HIV infection and staff, *JAMA* **268:**1280–1286.

Bentley, D. W., and Cheney, L., 1990, Infection control in the nursing home: The physician's role, *Geriatrics* **45:** 59–66.

Centers for Disease Control, 1986, Tuberculosis and acquired immunodeficiency syndrome—Florida, *Morbid. Mortal. Weekly Rep.* **35:**587–590.

Centers for Disease Control, 1990, Protection against viral hepatitis: Recommendations of the Immunization Practices Advisory Committee (ACIP), *Morbid. Mortal. Weekly Rep.* **39:**5–22.

Centers for Disease Control, 1992, Prevention and control of tuberculosis in U.S. communities with at-risk minority populations: Recommendations of the Advisory Council for the Elimination of Tuberculosis, *Morbid. Mortal. Weekly Rep.* **41**(no. RR-5):1–11.

Centers for Disease Control, 1993, Tuberculosis morbidity—United States, 1992, *Morbid. Mortal. Weekly Rep.* **42:**696–704.

Crossley, K., Nelson, L., and Irvine, P., 1992, State regulations governing infection control issues in long-term care, *J. Am. Geriatr. Soc.* **40:**251–254.

Darnowski, S. B., Gordon, M., Simor, A. E., 1991, Two year study of infection surveillance in a geriatric long-term care facility, *Am. J. Infect. Control* **19:**185–190.

Edlin, B. R., Tokars, J. I., and Grieco, M. H., 1992, An outbreak of multidrug-resistant tuberculosis among hospitalized patients with the acquired immunodeficiency syndrome, *N. Engl. J. Med.* **326:**1514–1521.

Fine, P. E. M., 1993, Herd immunity: History, theory, practice, *Epidemiol. Rev.* **15:**265–302.

Haley, R. W., Schaberg, D. R., Crossley, K. B., von Allmen, S. D., and McGowan, J. E., 1981, Extra charges and prolongation of stay attributable to nosocomial infections: A prospective interhospital comparison, *Am. J. Med.* **70:**51–58.

Haley, R., Culver, D. H., White, J. W., Morgan, W. M., Emori, T. G., Munn, V. P., and Hooton, T. M., 1985, The efficacy of infection surveillance and control programs in preventing nosocomial infections in US hospitals, *Am. J. Epidemiol.* **121:**182–205.

Horan, T. C., White, J. W., Jarvix, W. R., Emori, T. G., Culver, D. H., Munn, V. P., Thornsberry, C., Olson, D. R., and Hughes, J. M., 1986, Nosocomial infection surveillance, *Morbid. Mortal. Weekly Rep.* **35:**17SS–29SS.

Jawetz, E., Melnick, J. L., and Adelberg, E. A., 1991, *Jawetz, Melnick and Adelberg's Medical Microbiology*, 19th ed., Appleton & Lange, East Norwalk, CT.

Moga, D. N., Brodeur, S. E., and Beckman, P., 1991, AIDS in the workplace: Implications for hospice programs, *Hospice J.* **7:**151–169.

Mylotte, J. M., Karuza, J., and Bentley, D. W., 1992, Methicillin-resistant *Staphylococcus aureus*: A questionnaire survey of 75 long-term care facilities in western New York, *Infect. Control Hosp. Epidemiol.* **13:**711–718.

Office of Technology Assessment, U.S. Congress, 1993, *The continuing challenge of tuberculosis. OTA-H-574*, U.S. Government Printing Office, Washington, DC.

Shears, P., Rhodes, L. E., Syed, Q., and Watson, J., 1994, A pseudo outbreak of tuberculosis, *Commun. Dis. Rep. CDR Rev.* **4:**R9–10.

Smillie, W., 1952, The period of great epidemics in the United States (1800–1875), in *The History of American Epidemiology* (C. E. A. Winslow, eds.), C. V. Mosby, St. Louis.

Stead, W. W., and Dutt, A. K., 1991, Tuberculosis in elderly persons, *Annu. Rev. Med.* **42:**267–276.

Theuer, C. P., Hopewell, P. C., and Elias, D., 1990, Human immunodeficiency virus infection in tuberculosis patients, *J. Infect. Dis.* **162:**8–12.

U.S. Department of Health and Human Services Centers for Disease Control and Prevention, 1994, DHHS Pub. No. (PHS94-1232), National Center for Health Statistics, Hyattsville, MD.

7

Technology Assessment

Karl A. Matuszewski

With the continuous emergence of complex and expensive technologies for use in health care, how do health care managers decide which to support and which to reject. Technology assessment aids in that decision making. The assessment process considers technical characteristics of a new technology, as well as the clinical, economic, and social endpoints (Fuchs and Garber, 1990). Epidemiologic concepts and methods are utilized in technology assessment in determining the safety, clinical efficacy, and cost-effectiveness. Technology assessment can only be adequately performed with a thorough understanding of epidemiologic concepts. Specifically familiarity with study design, measures of effect, and statistical analyses for determining the significance of effect are required to assess a technology. This chapter describes the major components of technology assessment and the use of epidemiologic tools in that process. Case studies at the end of the chapter allow practice in the application of epidemiologic concepts and methods used in performing technology assessment.

Defining Technology Assessment and Its Function

Technology assessment is the process that examines the available evidence to form a conclusion as to the merits or role of a particular technology in relation to its possible use, purchase, or reimbursement in current medical practice. Results of clinical studies, expert opinion, theoretical performance, economic analyses, ethical considerations, and personal value judgments all enter into the final decision regarding whether or not the technology should be viewed as investigational or an accepted standard (or state-of-the-art) of practice. This decision will have a major impact on any institution involved in or planning to acquire the evaluated technology.

Technology assessment is often undertaken to maximize the quality of patient care and to control health care costs. To maximize quality is to ensure that the patient receives the most

Karl A. Matuszewski   Technology Assessment Program, University Hospital Consortium, Clinical Practice Advancement Center, Oak Brook, Illinois 60521, and Department of Health Systems Management, Rush University, Chicago, Illinois 60612.

Epidemiology and the Delivery of Health Care Services: Methods and Applications, edited by Denise M. Oleske. Plenum Press, New York, 1995.

effective health care services that medical science can provide at a given point in time. Technology assessment may also control costs by assisting in the identification of those medical technologies that do not provide any benefit to the patient and by promoting technologies that can increase the efficiency of patient diagnosis or treatment. For instance, the introduction of a new diagnostic test with a high sensitivity and a high specificity may obviate the need for other tests that yield the same results only if performed in parallel. As an example, positron emission tomography (PET) is useful in determining the extent of myocardial infarction damage. This technology has the ability to qualitatively and quantitatively characterize myocardial ischemic tissue damage, as compared to other diagnostic technologies such as magnetic resonance spectroscopy, thallium/technetium scanning, electrocardiography, echocardiography, and blood enzyme analyses, which allow only for either qualitative or quantitative analysis (AMA, 1988).

Reduced expenditures may be achieved, in some cases, if a technology replaces an older, more expensive one, or if significant decreases in the morbidity and/or mortality of the general population are achieved. Examples include the recent development of a new class of antibiotics called fluoroquinolones, that may be dosed less frequently, but often with greater therapeutic effectiveness compared to other classes of antibiotics (Hooper and Wolfson, 1991) and renal extracorporeal shock-wave lithotripsy, which, compared to percutaneous ultrasonic lithotripsy and conventional surgery for the removal of kidney stones, is more cost-effective on selected patients because of a reduction in morbidity (Hatziandreu *et al.*, 1990).

Caution, however, should be used when claims of superiority are made for a new technology. The clinical effects found to be statistically significant should be considered with the confidence intervals for those effects (Braitman, 1991). In addition, the measurement of immediate outcomes in some studies may not always be the best indicator of ultimate clinical superiority. Likewise, statements of efficacy in the controlled study environment do not always translate into proven effectiveness in the "real world" (Diamond and Denton, 1993). Naylor *et al.* (1992) in a survey study found that readers of clinical studies are often influenced in judging the therapeutic effectiveness of an intervention, based on the summary results presentation method. A relative risk reduction (RRR) $\{RRR = [(I_O - I_I)/I_O] \times 100\%\}$ of 33% for instance, might also be reported as an absolute risk (AR) reduction $(AR = I_O - I_I)$ of 5% when the event rates (I) in two groups compared are actually 15% and 10%.

Together, these two factors of maximal quality and reasonable cost promote the appropriate and efficient use of health care resources. Payers of medical costs, either the federal government (i.e., Medicare and Medicaid) and numerous private insurers have a strong incentive to pay only for the use of cost-efficient medical services and to limit increases in taxes or higher employer/subscriber insurance premiums, respectively. At an organizational level (e.g., hospital or third-party payer), dedicated and thorough technology assessment can offer an advantage in extremely competitive markets. It enables the provider or payer to limit the selection of available technologies to those that are the most effective options and further assists in controlling the costs of providing health care (Veluchamy and Saver, 1990).

Categories of Technology

The United States Department of Health and Human Services' Office of Technology Assessment (OTA) defines medical technology as "the set of techniques, drugs, equipment and procedures used by health care professionals in delivering medical care to individuals, and the systems within which such care is delivered" (OTA, 1976). Systems are often not addressed by the majority of assessors of technology because of the complexity of such projects. Examples of medical technology systems include methods of healthcare delivery (e.g., health maintenance organizations [HMOs] and preferred provider organizations [PPOs]), clinical information networks, and ambulatory care. Therefore, in most cases, **technology assessment includes the evaluation of the safety, effectiveness, efficiency, and appropriateness of devices, medical and surgical procedures, and pharmaceuticals promoted as improving a patient's condition or quality of life**. The technologies considered for assessment include: **devices, procedures, pharmaceuticals, and combinations thereof**. These are defined as follows.

Devices

Medical devices remain the major focus of technology assessment efforts (Radensky, 1991). Recent explosive developments in the diagnostic imaging field have brought forth a multitude of machines so complicated that they are almost instantaneously given acronyms for use as descriptors in general conversation. CAT (computed axial tomography), MRI (magnetic resonance imaging) and SPECT (single photon emission computed tomography) are examples of widely accepted diagnostic modalities. PET (positron emission tomography) and MRA (magnetic resonance angiography) are two examples of emerging diagnostic technologies.

Advances in therapeutic devices also are occurring at a rapid pace. For example, lasers are being used to reopen clogged coronary arteries and offer an alternative to the traditional options of open-heart surgery and coronary bypass or balloon angioplasty. Lasers, in conjunction with improving laparoscopic techniques, promise new ways of doing common standard surgical procedures (e.g., laparoscopic laser cholecystectomy for gallbladder disease or intra-uterine laser ablation of endometrial tissue), with an expected reduction in the morbidity associated with the standard surgery. Device miniaturization has also made it possible to perform many complex medical interventions outside of the hospital setting. Examples of this trend include the increasing use of portable cardiac-monitoring devices and implantable drug infusion units.

Procedures

Medical and surgical procedures may be the subject of technology assessment. Examples of these include: radial keratotomy, an operation that alters the shape of the cornea to improve vision; chorionic villus sampling, a first trimester prenatal genetic testing technique; and autologous or allogeneic bone marrow transplantation for the treatment of various cancers. Many other therapeutic diagnostic procedures would benefit from early critical evaluation before becoming widely accepted as standards of medical practice.

Pharmaceuticals

An important emerging role of technology assessment is to determine the efficient and appropriate clinical uses for drugs that are approved (labeled) by the United States Food and Drug Administration (FDA) and non-FDA-approved (off-label) indications, as well as those of promising new investigational agents not yet approved for marketing. The term **labeling** refers to the exact language used to delineate the clinical use of a drug (indications, dosage, adverse effects, etc.) as determined by the FDA on all promotional materials related to a drug once it has received final market approval. The need for technology assessment in the pharmaceutical area is being spurred by manufacturers who are producing increasingly sophisticated and expensive pharmaceuticals, by such means as recombinant DNA techniques, for ever broader clinical applications.

The future clinical uses of these drugs, however, will not be completely controlled by the FDA, which has stated that it is only responsible for, and interested in, initial drug marketing and not in the control of the practice of medicine (Young, 1988). The use of expensive approved drugs for unsubstantiated and unapproved indications, and pressure by various groups to allow more widespread use of drugs still undergoing clinical trials, are two reasons why the proactive assessment of drug efficacy and cost-effectiveness offer potentially great benefits to managed care systems (Detsky, 1989). Existing authoritative sources of evaluative drug information include the three major U.S. drug compendia:

1. United States Pharmacopeia—Drug Information (USP-DI) for the Health Care Professional
2. American Hospital Formulary Service—Drug Information
3. American Medical Association—Drug Evaluations (to be merged with USP-DI in 1995)

Technology Life Cycle

Regardless of the technology category, all medical technologies are subject to a predictable life cycle characterized by five distinct phases (Fig. 7.1). In the first phase of **investigation**, laboratory and clinical studies attempt to discover or create, refine, and package a new diagnostic or therapeutic modality. In the second phase of **promotion**, the technology is introduced to the buying community (i.e., patients, physicians, hospitals, and third-party payers) and is promoted by the sponsoring company's marketing efforts to achieve a profitable return on the investment of the first phase. A third phase, **acceptance and utilization**, is entered if the technology becomes incorporated into general medical practice. The fourth phase, **decline**, is achieved as a technology is supplanted by a superior new technology and falls out of general use or becomes a second- or third-line treatment choice. Finally, in the fifth

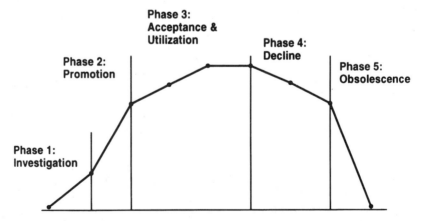

Figure 7.1. Technology life cycle. Reprinted from Matuszewski and Vermeulen (1994), with permission of the University Hospital Consortium, Oak Brook, IL, copyright 1994.

phase of **obsolescence**, the technology is considered obsolete and is no longer appropriate, because newer technologies offer greater benefits and/or less harm. Banta *et al.* (1990) have remarked that the "diffusion of technology over time generally has been found to follow a sigmoid, or "S"-shaped, curve, in which initial diffusion is slow, followed by a rapid phase, and finally ended by a flattening as saturation occurs." This corresponds to phases one through three. Murphy (1991) describes the evolution of medical technology in nine stages: invention, evaluation of safety and efficacy, implementation, marketing, general evaluation, comparison to existing alternatives, evaluation of long-term effects, modification, and replacement.

The timing and length of the phases vary for each type of technology. Some technologies never develop sufficient inertia to leave the investigational phase (e.g., orthomolecular therapy, which advocates high doses of vitamins), whereas other technologies may enjoy a perpetual position in the acceptance and utilization phase (e.g., X-rays). Rarely, some technologies are considered obsolete and are no longer considered to be an acceptable standard of care (e.g., Garren Gastric Bubble for the treatment of severe obesity). Blue Cross and Blue Shield Association's Medical Necessity Program, started in 1976, was one of the earliest formal efforts to identify obsolete practices with the intent to eliminate reimbursement and change practice patterns (Banta and Thacker, 1990). Often new technologies are found to be additive, and they cannot eliminate the need to perform the previous standard (Schwartz, 1987). For example, when magnetic resonance imaging (MRI) was developed, it was promoted as the ultimate imaging technology that would replace computed tomography (CT) scans (Larson and Kent, 1989). Yet, in actual clinical practice, multiple imaging technologies (e.g., MRI, CT, X-ray, ultrasound) are often performed to take advantage of incremental improvements in the available diagnostic information.

Technology assessment probably is most effective when applied in the late first phase (investigation), early second phase (promotion) or the fourth phase (decline). It is at these critical points that practices can be evaluated for possible changes to existing clinical practices and reimbursement policies (i.e., full, partial, or no payment) to achieve the greatest positive impact on patient care.

Targeting Technologies for Assessment

One difficulty in performing technology assessment lies in selecting technologies that merit an in-depth, resource-consuming evaluation. Criteria have been developed by the Council on Health Care Technology of the Institute of Medicine (IOM) for the priorization of technology assessment topics. Primary IOM selection criteria include those technologies that have the potential to: (1) improve individual patient outcome, (2) positively affect a large population, (3) reduce treatment costs, and (4) reduce unexplained treatment variation. Secondary IOM criteria are that the assessments should address ethical/social issues, advance medical knowledge, affect policy decision making, enhance the national assessment capacity, and be easily conducted (IOM, 1990). Additionally, organizational criteria for selecting technologies for assessment by the Health Care Financing Administration, Georgetown's Institute for Health Policy Analysis, the National Institutes of Health Office of Medical Applications of Research, the American College of Physicians, and the American Medical Association have been published (Eddy, 1989b).

Based on the review of selection criteria used by many of the major technology assessment organizations, three core criteria are proposed for targeting new medical technologies for evaluation:

1. High utilization
2. High potential for harm
3. High cost

High Utilization

Rapidly increasing or highly variable rates of utilization of a technology across geographic areas may signal inappropriate or excessive utilization (Leape, 1989). For example, the sharp rise in the rate of birth by the cesarean procedure without major changes in the characteristics of the women delivering, and the wide variation in the cesarean birth rates according to geographic region, payer, and hospital characteristics raised questions regarding the appropriateness of some of the procedures that were performed (National Center for Health Statistics, 1993). High utilization of a technology for common conditions may also be inappropriate when the cost benefit or cost-effectiveness of the technology cannot be justified. The use of mammography in screening young women at low risk of developing breast cancer is an example. For women less than 50 years of age, the incidence of breast cancer among white females is 33 per 100,000 population, whereas among those age 50 years and over, the incidence rate is 359.3 per 100,000 population, a greater than tenfold difference (USDHHS, 1991a). Eddy (1989a) calculated the cost per health life-year provided by annual mammography at $30,000 for women over 40 years of age, $20,000 for women over 50, and $15,000 for women over 65. This compares to a $1000 cost per healthy life-year for annual Pap smears and fecal occult blood tests. A "dollars-per-extra-years-of-life" analysis would provide medical policy formulators the opportunity to fairly judge the merits of such expenditures against other competing resource requirements that might have greater positive health impacts (e.g., prenatal nutrition counseling).

Data from the National Hospital Discharge Survey may assist in identifying the procedures that are frequently utilized (National Center for Health Statistics, 1990). Provider purchasing data and third-party payer claims data are also useful for this purpose.

High Potential for Harm

Common sense dictates that different standards and assessment priorities should exist for the evaluation of technologies that have widely differing rates of risk and harm (e.g., tongue depressors versus implantable heart valves). Similarly, the proposed use of aspirin for myocardial infarction prophylaxis may be viewed differently from the investigational use of interleukin-2 for the treatment of a cancer that has not yet been fully evaluated by rigorous clinical drug efficacy trials. Although some advocate the necessity of assuming unknown or greater risks for severe, life-threatening conditions (e.g., AIDS), the existence of effective treatment alternatives may not justify the use of unproven or equivocal technologies.

High Cost

The time of unlimited health care spending is over. The amount of money society is willing to spend on health care services, as measured by the increasing percentage of GNP spent for health care, is now the subject of much debate. Payers of health care services are demanding accountability and value for their expenditures on behalf of consumers and subscribers (Maloney, 1988). Although no specific price has yet been proposed by any group as being too much to pay, every new technological innovation that increases overall health care spending has a direct effect on future taxes and insurance premiums. For assessment purposes, technology costs may be examined at either the unit-of-service level or as an aggregate expense for treating an entire patient population. The results of special surveys, such as those conducted by state agencies that collect and disseminate information from the hospital discharge abstract form (UB-82 or UB-92 form), are useful in determining high-cost procedures such as can be available from the Illinois Health Care Cost-Containment Council, the Massachusetts Rate-Setting Commission, the Florida Agency for Health Care Administration, and the Washington State Department of Health, to name a few.

Numerous technologies enter the marketplace each year, and health care managers are confronted with difficult decisions regarding which to adopt for their organization. The process of technology assessment is dynamic. Technologies that were previously assessed may be considered for possible reevaluation because the role of a technology may change over time. Displayed in Fig. 7.2 is a method for how health care systems could prioritize technologies to assess.

How Is Technology Assessment Performed?

There is a wide range and complexity of methods for technology assessment (Fig. 7.3). The most common approaches include literature review and synthesis, consensus panels, decision criteria, meta-analyses, outcomes assessment, and clinical trials. Although these methods are described below as individual processes, in actual practice, combinations may be used.

Literature Review and Synthesis

A thorough review of the pertinent primary medical literature is a requirement for almost every evaluation effort. Although secondary sources (review articles and textbooks) may

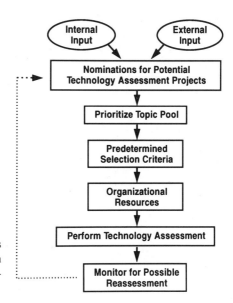

Figure 7.2. Framework for prioritizing technologies to assess. Reprinted from Matuszewski and Vermeulen (1994), with permission of the University Hospital Consortium, Oak Brook, IL, copyright 1994.

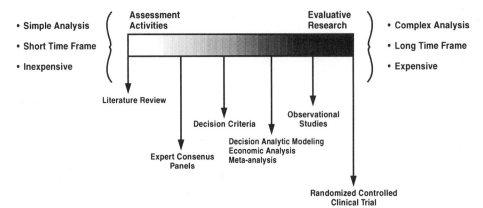

Figure 7.3. Range and relative complexity of methods for technology assessment. Modified from Matuszewski and Vermeulen (1994).

provide some useful interpretations of existing knowledge, articles presenting original research are the most important sources of information. Quantitative measures, particularly the results of statistical analyses, are among the most important in evaluating the effectiveness of a technology. Traditionally, a statistically significant finding is declared if the p value is less than 0.05. In accepting this value in technology assessment, this would mean that the chances are 5 out of 100 that the technology would be declared efficacious when in fact it is not. In evaluating research reports, p values as well as confidence intervals should be considered. The confidence interval conveys the range of the magnitude of the effect that can be expected if the chance occurrence of the effect has been statistically excluded. Neither the p value nor the confidence interval should be considered the sole indicators of clinical importance (Brown and Newman, 1987). Additional detail on the use of statistical criteria in evaluating data can be found in Thompson (1987) and Bailar and Mosteller (1988).

In reviewing the literature, one must be aware of the type of study from which the information was derived. Table 7.1 summarizes the level of evidence provided by common epidemiologic study designs. The optimal design for evaluating a health event is a randomized clinical trial. Yet, even this design can be flawed if the study is not performed in a double-blind manner, the sample is too small, or the drop-out rate or follow-up rate among the study groups is different. Guidelines for evaluating scientific studies are proposed by Schecter and Birnbaum (1989) and include the following questions:

Table 7.1. Level of Evidence about the Efficacy of a Technology Provided by Various Study Types

Strength of evidence	Level	Study type
Strong	1	Randomized clinical trial
	2	Quasiexperimental study
	3	Longitudinal (or cohort study)
	4	Case-control study
	5	Cross-sectional study
Weak	6	Case series

- How and why was the study performed?
- What interventions were made during the study?
- Who were the study subjects?
- How was the study analyzed?
- Were the results of the study meaningful?

Consensus Panels

In the **consensus approach**, experts review information from the scientific literature and seek input from consumers and medical professionals. These experts then convene to reach an agreement on responses to key questions posed in advance of the consensus conference. The expert panel may comprise members of subspecialty groups or may be multidisciplinary. Ultimately, the panel issues a consensus statement that contains recommendations for a particular health care practice. Consensus conferences have made recommendations concerning coronary artery bypass surgery (Stocking and Jennett, 1984), intravenous immunoglobulins (NIH Consensus Conference, May 1990), and have recommended that vaginal delivery after a previous cesarean, with a few clinical exceptions, is safe (USDHHS, 1981).

Decision Criteria

Decision criteria may be either quantitative or qualitative. Qualitative criteria may be standards or guidelines, either published or unpublished, against which a technology is tested (e.g., BCBSA TEC Criteria). This method relies heavily on the examination of the peer-reviewed literature, with the final recommendation of a technology evaluation directly related to the fulfillment of the criteria.

Quantitative criteria, such as measures of specificity, sensitivity, and positive predictive value are important in assessing the value of a new diagnostic technology. Although sensitivity (true positive) and specificity (true negative) of the test are independent of the characteristics of the population examined, the prevalence rate of the disease affects the positive predictive value of the test. The lower the disease rate, the lower the positive predictive value, and the lower the yield in finding cases with the condition. Thus, if a population has a low disease rate, the diagnostic technology may not be suitable for it despite the fact that the technology used to assess the disease has a high sensitivity and specificity. The use of decision criteria in technology assessment is illustrated by the work by Turner *et al.* (1988) in which magnetic resonance imaging is compared to xeromammography for detecting breast cancer. The assessment utilizes receiver operating characteristic (ROC) curves that are constructed from plots of $1-$specificity (on the x axis) versus sensitivity (on the y axis) to assess diagnostic accuracy (Fig. 7.4). The values for the curve associated with the technology that yields the highest peak in the upper-left-hand corner of the graph (the highest ratio of true positives to false negatives) has the greatest diagnostic accuracy, in this case, xeromammography.

Quantitative and qualitative criteria can be combined to facilitate achieving consensus about a technology. LeGales and Moatt (1990) describe a multicriteria decision-analysis model to assess the value of screening for hemoglobinopathies. Quantitative criteria included measures of effectiveness (specificity and sensitivity of various screening measures) and cost. Qualitative measures included the rating of technical and practical feasibilities, ethical acceptability, information about follow-up time, and impact on the provision of health education.

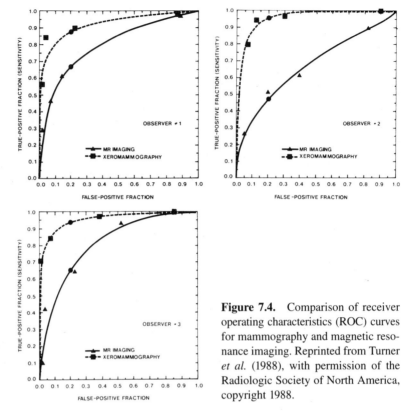

Figure 7.4. Comparison of receiver operating characteristics (ROC) curves for mammography and magnetic resonance imaging. Reprinted from Turner *et al.* (1988), with permission of the Radiologic Society of North America, copyright 1988.

Meta-Analyses

Increasingly, a quantitative approach is being used to evaluate the body of literature on a new technology to overcome the limitations of small sample sizes often associated with randomized clinical trials (RCTs) (Type II error and the inability to detect subgroup responses). A **meta-analysis** summarizes the treatment effect obtained from a comprehensive determination of the pool of available published studies that meet predetermined criteria for inclusion in the analysis (Dickerson and Berlin, 1992). The measures of treatment effect that are summarized vary according to the nature of the problem being assessed and the availability of published data. The most common measure is the odds ratio. Table 7.2 illustrates the statistics for meta-analysis of data in which the odds ratio is the measure of effect. Data for studies of antithrombolytic agents in Table 7.3 are used in the example. The statistical components of the meta-analysis determine if the effect is consistent across all trials or studies (test of heterogeneity) and also whether or not there is a treatment effect. The test statistic for heterogeneity is that described in Yusef *et al.* (1985). The significance of the treatment effect can be determined from the Mantel-Haenszel-Peto test or from evaluation of the confidence intervals if the odds ratios can be expected to be similar across studies evaluated. The methods for computing the treatment effect are detailed in Yusef *et al.* (1985). The results of the meta-analysis reveal that the treatment effect is significant, with antithrombolytic therapy resulting in a significant reduction of the odds of myocardial infarction (OR = 0.75, 95% CI, 0.69, 0.81), and that the treatment results are consistent across all studies (i.e., χ^2 heterogeneity is not significant).

Table 7.2. Statistics Used in Meta-Analysis

For a single study (for PARIS II in Table 7.3):

	Intervention	Control	Total
MI	189 (*a*)	249 (*b*)	438 (*D*)
No MI	1374 (*c*)	1316 (*d*)	2690
Total	1563 (*n*)	1565	3128 (*N*)

Observed $(O) = 189$

Expected $(E) = (1563 \times 438)/3128 = 218.86$

Total number of events $(D) = 438$

Number treated $(n) = 1563$

$\mathrm{Var}\,(O - E) = E(1 - n/N)(N - D)/(N - 1)$
$= 218.86(1 - 1563/3128)(3128 - 438)/(3128 - 1) = 94.2$

Over all studies (in Table 7.3):

$\chi^2_{\mathrm{heterogeneity}} = \mathrm{Sum}\,[(O_i - E_i)^2/\mathrm{Var}_i] - GT^2/SIV$, with df of $n_{\mathrm{trials}} - 1$
$= 64.14 - 50.00 = 14.2$, df $= 9$, NS

Odds ratio (OR) $= \exp(GT/SIV) = \exp(-171.1/585.5) = 0.75$

95% CI of OR $= \exp(GT/SIV) \pm 1.96/(SIV)^{1/2} = \exp\,[(-171.1/585.5) \pm 1.96/(585.5)^{1/2}]$
$= 0.69, 0.81$

Problems in drawing conclusions from a meta-analysis include variation in treatment protocols, different patient populations treated, and insufficient detail to identify treatment response in subgroups. Additional background on the performance of meta-analyses can be found in Dickerson and Berlin (1992).

Because meta-analysis is a retrospective look at data, its results should be carefully reviewed before accepted as fact. Table 7.4 lists several questions that should be considered in critiquing the results of a meta-analysis. Meta-analyses have been utilized to evaluate a variety

Table 7.3. Studies of Randomized Clinical Trials of Antiplatelet Treatment[a]

Trial name	Myocardial infarction		$O - E$	$\mathrm{Var}\,(O - E)$	Crude OR[b]
	Antiplatelet group	Control group			
AMIS	416/2267	458/2257	−22.0	176.3	0.88
PARIS-II	189/1563	249/1565	−29.9	94.2	0.73
PARIS-I	287/1620	93/406	−16.9	49.5	0.72
Cardiff-II	128/832	186/850	−27.3	63.9	0.65
ART	117/806	153/814	−17.3	56.3	0.73
CDP-A	79/758	100/771	−9.7	39.5	0.72
GDR	50/672	100/668	−25.2	33.3	0.46
Cardiff-I	60/615	76/624	−7.5	30.3	0.78
ARIS	41/365	60/362	−9.7	21.8	0.64
GAMIS	43/317	53/309	−5.6	20.4	0.76
TOTAL	1410/9815	1528/8626	−171.1 (GT)	585.5 (SIV)	

[a]Data from Antiplatelet Trialists' Collaboration (1988).
[b]Odds ratio.

**Table 7.4. Questions in
Critiquing a Meta-Analysis**

Are sample sizes similar for all studies evaluated?
Are treatment protocols comparable?
What are the patient selection criteria for each study?
What are the outcomes measured in each study?
Are any studies excluded from the analysis? If yes, why?

of technologies, including coronary artery bypass surgery (Wortman and Yeaton, 1985) and neonatal intensive care units (Ozminkowski *et al.*, 1987).

Outcomes Assessment

Outcomes assessment compares the performance of a technology against standards established or recommended by expert bodies. Many organizations are developing various guidelines or practice parameters in an attempt to promote the use of outcomes assessment in evaluating new clinical technologies. Cost and intensity of care are related to real-world results using such measures as recovery speed, quality of life, ability to work, and patient preferences. Stated another way, outcomes assessment attempts to answer such practical questions as . . . "When a physician has a few spare minutes to spend with a patient, should that time be devoted to a blood pressure check, a counseling session about dietary fat, an inquiry about possible symptoms of transient cerebral ischemia, or a demonstration of how to use nicotine chewing gum" (Laupacis *et al.*, 1988). This method seeks to maximize outputs related to limited inputs, as measured and valued by the patient or health care payer. The essential elements of performing outcomes assessment as described by Laupacis *et al.* are:

1. Comparing the consequences of doing nothing against the potential benefits of doing something.
2. Summarizing the harmful effects of the technology (e.g., side effects and toxicity).
3. Identifying patients who are at high risk and those most likely to respond to therapy.
4. Incorporating measures that allow clinicians and their patients to evaluate directly the benefits and risks of alternative therapies.

Specific outcomes of a technology can be assessed through an evaluation of changes in the relative risk, odds ratio, absolute risk, excess risk and time to event (relapse, cure, death, etc.). Health-status assessment instruments, such as the *Short-Form Health Survey* (Ware and Sherbourne, 1992), the Sickness Impact Profile, the General Well-Being Index, and the Nottingham Health Profile, may also be used (Schwartz and Lurie, 1990).

The Agency for Health Care Policy Research is at the forefront of promoting outcomes analysis as the preferred method for technology assessment (Radensky, 1991). Health care cost savings and the reduction of variations in treatment are the ultimate goals of outcomes assessment, when new technologies are directly compared to existing alternatives. One such example is the notion that laparoscopic cholecystectomy is superior to conventional gall bladder surgery and saves money by reducing the length of hospitalization. Currently available evidence to support such a contention, however, is limited (Wagner, 1991) or disputed by preliminary cost analyses (Jordan, 1991).

Randomized Clinical Trials

Focused, randomized, controlled clinical trials are the "gold standard" of any assessment undertaking if certain criteria are met. A high-quality RCT should include blinding of physicians and patients regarding treatment assignment (double-blind), hard end points not susceptible to other therapy, prior analysis of how many participants are required for study, and appropriate statistical analysis. Chalmers *et al.* (1981) describe other factors that add to the quality of a RCT. The resources required to conduct such studies may be considerable and make them impractical for all cases where additional information is required. However, the ability to prospectively structure a trial to address specific issues essential to the assessment of the role of a technology in clinical practice may make this the most efficient method for conducting future assessments on controversial technology questions. An example of this is demonstrated in the finding that optic nerve decompression surgery is not effective, but potentially harmful (The Ischemic Optic Neuropathy Decompression Trial Research Group, 1995).

Other Methods

Other types of analytic socioeconomic approaches have been proposed to support technology assessment efforts. These methods are explained in Bootman *et al.* (1991), Luce (1990), and Detsky and Naglie (1990) and include the analysis of cost benefit, cost-effectiveness, cost utility, cost minimization, quality of life, and cost of illness. As these methods increasingly gain acceptance, attention must be focused on their proper use. Udvarhelyi *et al.* (1992) cited the general lack of adherence to fundamental economic analytic principles in a retrospective review of 77 published journal articles.

Who Does Technology Assessment?

Technology assessment, either through formal programs or as an informal medical policy function, is performed by many groups. The perspective of the evaluating organization should be important to the reader and can be categorized in one of the following groups (the five "Ps"): payer, provider, patient, producer, or public (i.e., society). A distinction must be made, however, in that most nonprofit technology assessment programs generally publish their evaluations and often provide a forum for public comments. Private programs, such as those created by insurance companies, generally consider their evaluations proprietary information and do not publish or broadly circulate their technology assessment conclusions. A directory of organizations involved in medical technology assessment in the United States has been published (Goodman, 1988). Several of the major technology assessment organizations and programs are discussed below.

U.S. Food and Drug Administration

The U.S. Food and Drug Administration (FDA) assesses through the drug review and approval process and device regulation system. New pharmaceutical products require an "investigational drug exemption" (IDE) by the FDA before a sponsor may proceed with human clinical trials. Drugs are then scrutinized in three phases of clinical trials. Based on the strength of the data from these trials, a sponsor submits a "new drug approval" (NDA) application to the FDA, who either approve or reject that drug for general marketing. Devices are reviewed through the 510(k) approval process for substantial equivalence or by "pre-market approval" (PMA) applications for unique, complex devices that require clinical studies to show positive effects. Device manufacturers are required to meet specified performance standards.

The new drug approval process is extremely rigorous and has, for the most part, been accepted as the authoritative final word on the marketing and distribution of new drugs. This role is now changing as the result of tremendous societal pressures for new cures at any cost or at any risk to certain patient groups. New strategies developed by the FDA to deal with these external pressures are "treatment investigational new drug (treatment IND) status" and expedited drug review. Additionally, parallel track development for AIDS drugs allows patients easier access to investigational agents outside of the restrictions imposed by conventional clinical trials (*Federal Register*, 1992).

On the other hand, the FDA process for *device* approvals is considered by many to be inadequate. It has been in reality, a rubber stamp for marketing approval when a device is not expected to cause grievous harm or injury to an individual. Studies of safety and effectiveness are usually not required for the majority of devices before they can be sold, except for devices needing a PMA application (McGivney and Hendee, 1990). Of approximately 3000 devices introduced into the market place every year, 99% of devices go through a 510(k) approval process that essentially approves a device on the basis of its similarity to previously marketed devices, and only 1% require proof of safety and effectiveness (personal communication with the FDA, January 1991). This system is slowly changing—in part because of recent problems associated with FDA-approved heart valves and breast implants. The FDA's Center for Devices and Radiological Health is now focusing its resources on fast track evaluation of life-saving devices, while delaying (and more carefully analyzing) noncritical products (Anonymous, 1993).

Agency for Health Care Policy and Research

Formerly the National Center for Health Services Research (NCHSR), the Agency for Health Care Policy and Research (AHCPR) was established in 1989 through Public Law 101-239 to facilitate "the development, review, and updating of clinically relevant guidelines to assist health care practitioners in the prevention, diagnosis, treatment, and management of clinical conditions" (USDHHS, 1990a). The Medical Treatment Effectiveness Program (MEDTEP) is the multiagency program with AHCPR responsible for examining the relationships between health care and clinical patient outcomes. An example of MEDTEP initiatives include 11 large-scale patient outcomes research teams (PORTs) whose charge is to combine an analysis of the literature and Medicare data to issue recommendations on selected clinical practices (Raskin and Maklan, 1991). Examples of reports by AHCPR include an assessment of thermography for indications other than breast cancer, criteria for heart–lung transplantation and cardiac catheterization in a freestanding setting (USDHHS, 1990b, 1994).

American College of Physicians

The American College of Physicians (ACP), through a program called the Clinical Efficacy Assessment Project (CEAP), performs comprehensive consensus-driven assessments of various technologies. Comments are solicited from all specialty groups having an interest in the technology under review. Most CEAP reports eventually lead to position papers published in the *Annals of Internal Medicine*.

American Medical Association

The American Medical Association (AMA) performs technology assessment through the Diagnostic and Therapeutic Technology Assessment (DATTA) Program. This program uses a selected group of medical consultants from a large pool of AMA physicians, who are polled on their opinions as to the safety and effectiveness of a particular technology for the specific clinical indication. The technology is also assessed to determine if it is established, promising, investigational, doubtful, or unacceptable. The results are published in *The Journal of the American Medical Association*, along with a brief summary of the selected technology reviewed (McGivney and Hendee, 1988).

Blue Cross and Blue Shield Association

The Blue Cross and Blue Shield Association (BCBSA) evaluates new technologies through the Technology Evaluation Center (TEC), using defined criteria (Table 7.5) as a framework for the consistent evaluation of many types of technologies (Schaffarzick, 1987). In 1994, BCBSA collaborated with Kaiser Foundation Health Plan and Southern California

Table 7.5. Blue Cross and Blue Shield Association Technology Evaluation Center Criteria[a]

1. The technology must have final approval from the appropriate government regulatory bodies.
   - This criterion applies to drugs, biological products, devices, and diagnostics.
   - A drug or biological product must have final approval from the Food and Drug Administration.
   - A device must have final approval from the Food and Drug Administration for those specific indications and methods of use that Blue Cross and Blue Shield Association is evaluating.
   - Any approval that is granted as an interim step in the FDA regulatory process is not sufficient.
2. The scientific evidence must permit conclusions concerning the effect of the technology on health outcomes.
   - The evidence should consist of well-designed and well-conducted investigations published in peer-reviewed journals. The quality of the body of studies and the consistency of the results are considered in evaluating the evidence.
   - The evidence should demonstrate that the technology can measure or alter the physiological changes related to a disease, injury, illness, or condition. In addition, there should be evidence or a convincing argument based on established medical facts that such measurement or alteration affects the health outcomes.
   - Opinions and assessments by national medical associations, consensus panels, or other technology assessment bodies are evaluated according to the scientific quality of the supporting evidence and rationale.
3. The technology must improve the net health outcome.
   - The technology's beneficial effects on health outcomes should outweigh any harmful effects on health outcomes.
4. The technology must be as beneficial as any established alternatives.
   - The technology should improve the net health outcome as much as or more than established alternatives.
5. The improvement must be attainable outside the investigational settings.
   - When used under the usual conditions of medical practice, the technology should be reasonably expected to satisfy criteria 3 and 4.

[a]Source: BCBSA (1994).

Permante Medical Group to expand the resources devoted to technology assessment for these groups. This joint venture allows for the purchase of TEC assessment documents by external organizations for the first time (Blue Cross and Blue Shield Association, 1994).

ECRI (Formerly the Emergency Care Research Institute)

ECRI is a nonprofit organization, established in 1955 and chartered by the Commonwealth of Pennsylvania. ECRI's Health Technology Assessment Information Service provides summary reports on selected technologies published in *Executive Briefings*, a subscription service. Complete comprehensive reports are also available for a fee. Technology overviews are provided in the monthly newsletter *Health Technology Trends*. ECRI's assessments reflect the opinions and interpretations of ECRI staff and are targeted primarily at the hospital industry to facilitate device technology planning and acquisition needs. In 1993, ECRI was contracted by the United States National Library of Medicine (NLM) to develop and maintain a comprehensive international data base on health care technology assessment. This data base is available online through the NLM's Medical Literature Analysis and Retrieval System (MEDLARS).

Office of Health Technology Assessment (OHTA)

As a component of AHCPR, the Office of Health Technology Assessment (OHTA) evaluates the risks, benefits, and clinical effectiveness of new or unestablished medical technologies being considered for Medicare coverage at the request of the Health Care Financing Administration (HCFA). Evaluations include a review of the medical literature, and participation in the assessment process is open to all interested parties. Input is sought through announcements for comments in the *Federal Register*. Final publication leads to "Health Technology Assessment Reports," with an example being a report on carotid endarterectomy (USDHHS, 1991b).

Office of Technology Assessment

The Office of Technology Assessment (OTA) was established by Congress to provide congressional committees with analyses of emerging, complex, and often highly technical issues. Although a multidisciplinary staff prepares the assessments, it draws from the expertise of academia, state and local governments, public interest groups, and the citizenry at large. The OTA reports often address major public policy issues that may involve multiple technologies, as well as political, societal, and ethical concerns. Among the issues that OTA has addressed in the past are the costs and effectiveness of screening for cholesterol in the elderly and the costs and effectiveness of cervical cancer screening in the elderly (Congress of the U.S., OTA, 1989, 1990).

University Hospital Consortium

An alliance of over 65 academic medical centers, the University Hospital Consortium has a program within the Clinical Practice Advancement Center called the Technology Assessment Program. Started in 1989, the program produces guidelines, monographs, assessments, and reports on new or existing medical technologies using an extensive network of medical and administrative experts and/or consultants from UHC member institutions. The assessment information is used by UHC institutions to assist in the adoption, acquisition, and utilization of new and expensive technologies. Because of its organizational structure, UHC has also been able to pursue multicenter technology surveillance projects that provide a "snapshot" view. Two completed projects include ondansetron (Vermeulen *et al.*, 1994) and colony-stimulating factors (Yim *et al.*, 1995), which compared actual drug use against "model" UHC guidelines developed by national expert panel consensus. NHC "model" guidelines are often submitted for peer-review publication, with an example being consensus guidelines on albumin, nonprotein colloid, and crystalloid solutions (Vermeulen *et al.*, 1995). Assessment documents have been available to non-UHC members for a modest fee since April 1994.

Others

The Rand Corporation, a private company, is noted for its extensive experience in evaluating the appropriateness of medical procedures (Park *et al.*, 1986). Examples of private, not-for-profit academic health centers that have medical assessment programs include Duke University Center for Health Policy Research and Education and Johns Hopkins Program for Medical Technology and Practice Assessment. For-profit consulting groups, such as Health Technology Associates, Inc. and Technology Diffusion Associates, often specialize in new product reimbursement and marketing assessments. Finally, most health insurance companies and health plans, to some degree, conduct technology assessment to control the premium expenditures and benefits design for health care services.

International Efforts

Technology assessment is not unique to the United States. Numerous technology assessment projects are under way in many foreign countries. The Netherlands has created an advisory body known as the Health Council to begin a systematic approach toward technology assessment (Gelijns and Rigter, 1990). In Australia, the National Health Technology Advisory Panel was created in 1982 to examine technology issues (Gross, 1989). French efforts, to date, at assessing medical technology are evolving. Responsibilities for technology decision-making are shared by the Ministry of Health and the National Health Insurance Fund (Weill *et al.*, 1989). The Swedish Council on Technology Assessment in Health Care was established in 1987, and nine areas of interest were identified. Assessment is carried out by the consensus conference approach (Calltorp and Smedby, 1989). The Swiss health care system has a Medical Advisory Service to consider the safety, efficacy, advantages, costs, and other aspects of medical technology (Koch, 1987). Norway and Australia have also convened expert panels to develop consensus statements on mammography and extracorporeal membrane oxygenation, respectively (Perry *et al.*, 1991). Canada, in mid-1989, created the Canadian Coordinating Office for Health Technology Assessment (CCOHTA) to "encourage the appropriate use of health technology by influencing decision makers through the collection, analysis, creation and dissemination of information concerning the effectiveness and cost of technology and its impact on health" (background information received from CCOHTA, July 1991). The International Society for Technology Assessment in Health Care describes ongoing developments in its quarterly journal.

In addition to those described above, various technology assessment initiatives are found in the United Kingdom, Italy, Japan, Israel, South Korea, China, Finland, and Germany (Koch, 1987; Stocking, 1988). As compared to the United States, efforts in technology assessment in other nations are in their infancy, often underfunded, and are more likely to be initiated in response to budgetary concerns.

Technology assessment projects in foreign countries are conducted by governmental, academic, as well as private organizations. International differences in the focus and application of the results of new technology evaluations can be related to the differences in the mechanism by which health care services are paid. Long-range planning and fixed budgeting in countries with national health programs set well-defined limits to the acquisition of any new technologies. Since one central source often holds most of the policy making and reimbursement authority, tight utilization standards can be imposed on health care providers. The United States' pluralistic health care system, from the standpoint of payers and providers, is less focused. No central policy making authority exists to set payment and utilization limits. The assessment of new technologies, therefore, tends to be duplicative, since many organizations perform their own evaluations with little or no coordination or input from other assessment entities.

Problems in Performing Technology Assessment

Several factors affect the conclusions that may be drawn when performing technology assessment. They include the following:

Lack of Evidence

Evidence on efficacy and cost-effectiveness for some new technologies is slow in accumulating for a variety of reasons, such as difficulty in performing randomized controlled trials, rarity of certain conditions to be treated, or lack of economic incentive. Even when published studies are available, problems can occur with the quality of these studies. The major study limitations most often encountered are: (1) small number of published clinical trials (excluding review articles, company promotional materials, and animal or cadaver studies); (2) small sample sizes (excluding case reports, where $n = 1$); (3) lack of quantitative detail in the results section of published studies; (4) no control or randomization included in the study design; (5) emphasis on intermediate outcome results (e.g., tumor shrinkage) instead of the ultimate desired clinical outcome (e.g., survival, cure, measurable functional improvement); and (6) no comparisons to alternative therapies.

Lack of Agreement on How to Perform the Assessment

As described earlier, there are a variety of methods of performing technology assessment (i.e., consensus panels, decision criteria, meta-analysis, or outcomes assessment). Each method has strengths and weaknesses for which its proponents will stress the positive features. No single method of performing technology assessment is universally accepted for all potential topics. There is also no guarantee that two organizations using the same method would arrive at similar conclusions.

Inconsistent Evidence

Differences in sample sizes, study populations, and treatment protocols are among the factors that contribute to inconsistent or inconclusive evidence. The inconsistent evidence on the effectiveness of electronic fetal monitoring (EFM) is an example of this problem. Although EFM may be useful in identifying infants at risk of neonatal seizures (MacDonald *et al.*, 1985), EFM has also been identified as being associated with an increased risk of cerebral palsy (Shy *et al.*, 1990).

Legal Interference

Increasingly, individuals with little or no medical or scientific background are making decisions on incredibly complex technology issues. In numerous cases (primarily in the area of bone marrow transplantation for various cancers), a judge or jury, after hearing extensive conflicting testimony from medical experts, have decided on the appropriateness of its use (Anderson *et al.*, 1993; Ferguson *et al.*, 1993).

Several states currently have regulations that mandate third-party payer coverage of cancer drug therapies cited in the major drug compendia (cited earlier) or even mentioned in the literature as possibly effective. Medicare has a similar policy for unlabeled cancer chemotherapies. Anecdotal evidence, emotion, and contract language often supersede hard scientific evidence in these cases.

Breadth of Topics

It seems that there always will be more topics in need of assessment than resources available to evaluate them. The introduction of new technologies to the health care marketplace shows no signs of slowing in the near future (Lumsdon, 1991). If anything, the pace has accelerated. There is, unfortunately, tremendous duplication in the resources expended to evaluate a handful of controversial technologies by multiple organizations. No central coordinating body exists to maximize the information pool on all the possible technologies in need of assessment. Lacking such coordination, many marginal technologies are never evaluated.

New Information

New knowledge is constantly being presented and published. Since a technology assessment document is really a review of what is known about a technology up to its publication date, the assessment process must be ongoing to capture changes in evidence, either positive or negative (Banta and Thacker, 1990). Approval by the FDA alone for a technology is not the ultimate eternal level of proof of appropriateness, particularly for many devices, and additional evaluation through independent studies is often necessary to form a rational, informed conclusion.

Future of Technology Assessment

There is every indication that technology assessment will become a common part of management practice as a core service of a health care delivery institution in the same manner as strategic planning and marketing (Veluchamy and Saver, 1990). Changes in clinical services and reimbursement practices will increase the need for timely technology assessment information (Sussman, 1991). Future clinical services will include biotechnology products, advances in imaging, and the use of genetics to identify, monitor, and alter disease processes. Changes in the methods of reimbursement, such as capitation, outpatient DRGs, and structured physician payment (e.g., Medicare's RBRVS) are designed to limit unnecessary use of advanced technology. Cost-effectiveness evaluations and "restricted use criteria" for specific patient populations will become more common in medical practice as technology assessment matures as a discipline. Automated decision making will support this trend.

Monetary support for technology assessment efforts will most likely come from government, private foundations, and third-party payers. Funding sources might include a percentage of future premiums paid by individuals covered by health insurance (Fuchs and Garber, 1990) or special revenue taxes and fees to manufacturers and employers. Providers, both hospitals and physicians, through alliances (e.g., University Hospital Consortium's Clinical Practice Advancement Center) and professional organizations (e.g., American Medical Association's DATTA Program) are themselves undertaking the assessment of medical technologies to protect their interests and to advance medical practice. Collaborative (e.g., BCBSA and Kaiser) efforts and broader distribution of assessment documents will strengthen technology decision implementation.

There will be an increasing use of unpublished studies and/or a greater reliance on organized treatment registry data in the evaluation of future technologies (Steinbrook and Lo, 1990; Rimm *et al.*, (1991). Because analysis will often be undertaken in the early developmental stages of a technology, this information should be used cautiously, since it will not have the benefit of extensive peer review (Davis, 1990). Postmarketing trials and third-party payer claims data bases will also be used to assess patient outcomes and to determine the cost-effectiveness of alternative medical technology interventions (Schwartz and Lurie, 1990). Multicenter technology surveillance using practice guidelines may become a critical method for monitoring a technology to evaluate actual practice against predefined standards.

Despite numerous established organizational processes for performing technology assessment (Goodman, 1988), individuals with no clinical or scientific background are increasingly making decisions on incredibly complex medical technology issues (Sugarman, 1990). An example to illustrate this point is a case from Washington, D.C., where a U.S. District judge ruled that HCFA could not implement a policy to deny coverage of non-FDA-approved artificial lenses to Medicare cataract patients. The judicial override of FDA approval as a minimal coverage standard suggests a lack of understanding by the courts of the ultimate purpose of drug and device regulation, which exists solely to protect the public from technologies that are not yet conclusively proven to be safe and effective (Appleby, 1991). Other technologies for which court-ordered reimbursement has been granted despite the lack of evidence for effectiveness include amygdalin (i.e., laetrile), immunoaugmentative therapy, and thermography (Ferguson *et al.*, 1993). This trend is disturbing.

What must be avoided in the future is an antagonistic attitude among the patient, provider, producer (i.e., the manufacturer), and third-party payer. Technology assessment offers a rational and conservative approach to the use of new medical services. However, if patients feel that they are being denied the "best" possible care, if physicians feel that their clinical actions are being unnecessarily limited, or if third-party payers use technology assessment as a shield to deny the coverage of promising medical advances, then the recommendations of technology assessment reports will be worthless, and the health care system will operate at a less than optimal level.

Technology Assessment and Health Care Reform

The realization of the eventual (inevitable) arrival of health care reform has created a debate about the value and role of technology assessment activities in the new health care system. Unfortunately, no consensus has emerged, partly because no one is certain of the final form of the system. Important issues to be addressed regarding future technology assessment include:

- How will it be performed? Which method?
- Who will perform it? A single centralized national body or many local alliances?

- What will be the effects on medical innovation and future research?
- When and how often will new information be incorporated in technology evaluations?
- How will rare conditions be treated by the system? (Effectiveness evidence accumulates slowly.)

The current direction of the debate seems to bode well for formal technology assessment in the future U.S. health care system. Managed care, spending caps, global budgeting, practice guidelines, and the lack of opportunities to shift costs to other payers all enhance the need to know the most appropriate and efficient forms of care to minimize resource consumption. Patient satisfaction may also be improved by providing the level of care necessary or desired, thus preventing iatrogenic complications from current system incentives to try to do anything and everything.

State-of-the-art technology will most likely be limited to a smaller number of medical centers in the future. Networking, alliances, and joint ventures will result in a decline in full-service providers and an increase in specialty hospitals (Ronning, 1994). Projected improvements in health care information systems will make every case part a larger ongoing clinical trial of outcome effectiveness and efficiency. The dissemination of this technology information will be rapid and complete. Manufacturing principles of maximizing output will need to coexist with concerns of the U.S. population for access to timely and comprehensive medical services. The fields of pharmacoeconomics and health system economics will spur health care providers, producers, and payers to act in concert to achieve input-to-output patient care results that use resources in a "prudent buyer" fashion.

Summary

Who should ultimately decide what is standard therapy, state-of-the-art, or investigational: juries, judges, politicians, scientists, providers, or payers? This question has no clear answer. This chapter strongly recommends that health care administrators, providers, and payers should all be familiar with the elements of technology assessment as a means of monitoring the quality and cost-effectiveness of health care delivery. Future health care administrators, as important decision-makers in new technology acquisition, must possess a comprehensive understanding of the issues involved in the process of technology assessment as well as the ability to interpret the primary medical literature knowledgeably, using epidemiologic methods to assess the relative merits and limitations of new technologies. In this way, proactive technology decisions will be made, not reactive decisions based on external pressures.

Case Studies

Case Study No. 1
Extracorporeal Shock-Wave Lithotripsy for Kidney Stones

Extracorporeal shock-wave lithotripsy (ESWL) is a noninvasive procedure for breaking up kidney stones. High-intensity shock waves are produced electrically and focused radiographically or ultrasonically on the treatment area. The ESWL treatment consists of approximately 500–1500 shocks delivered over 30–60 min. The size and number of stones to be treated usually determine the extent of therapy. The patient may be either submerged in a water bath (wet-method device) or have water-filled compressible pads positioned in the appropriate area (dry-method device). General, spinal, or epidural anesthesia is usually administered with this procedure. Several machines under investigation require only local anesthetics. The ESWL treatments can be performed on an inpatient or outpatient basis. Following ESWL, most kidney-stone fragments are eventually eliminated in the urine. Adjunctive procedures (e.g., pre-ESWL stent placement or stone manipulation and post-ESWL endoscopy or surgery) are estimated to be required in 7–15% of patients to ensure the complete removal of the stone fragments.

Q.1. Is ESWL more effective than surgical intervention? Propose a study design to answer this question.

Q.2. What criteria could be used to determine which treatment is more effective?

Q.3. What factors could reduce the quality of the study?

Case Study No. 2
Chorionic Villus Sampling

Chorionic villus sampling (CVS) is a prenatal genetic testing procedure that may be performed in the first trimester of pregnancy. CVS is performed by obtaining a sample of villus tissue, the thread-like projections growing in tufts on the external surface of the chorion. Methods of sampling include the transcervical (TC) route or the transabdominal (TA) route, with both methods requiring ultrasonic guidance to ascertain proper positioning within the chorion frondosum. Samples are drawn by aspiration of villus tissue through a catheter (TC method) or a needle (TA method). CVS permits the diagnosis of genetic disease in the fetus as early as the eighth week of gestation, as compared to amniocentesis, which is performed following the 16th week.

Q.1. How can the diagnostic accuracy of CVS be determined?

Q.2. What factors influence the accuracy of this diagnostic test?

Q.3. Under what circumstances would you make CVS routinely available for the persons covered by a Health Maintenance Organization (HMO)?

Q.4. What are the ethical implications of performing CVS?

Case Study No. 3
Ambulatory Uterine Monitoring

Ambulatory home uterine monitoring is a diagnostic procedure performed in the patient's home to detect changes in uterine activity with the goal of initiating early tocolytic therapy, if necessary, to arrest preterm labor and prevent premature delivery. A sensor is attached to the pregnant woman's abdomen at prescribed time intervals, and uterine activity data are recorded for subsequent daily telephone transmission to a monitoring center. At the monitoring center, the data are analyzed and assessed as to the need for medical intervention based on the ambulatory home uterine monitoring results (e.g., tocolysis or conservative management, such as bed rest or hydration).

Q.1. Propose a study design to determine if home monitoring can reduce the incidence of adverse pregnancy outcomes within a health plan.

Q.2. What epidemiologic measures would be important in assessing this technology?

Case Study No. 4
Positron Emission Tomography

Positron emission tomography (PET) is a diagnostic imaging modality that uses radiopharmaceuticals generated by a cyclotron or nuclear generator, which are introduced into the body by intravenous infusion and finally recorded by a scanner to produce images of biochemical reactions and physiological functions. This is accomplished by measuring the concentrations of radioactive isotopes that are partially metabolized in the body region of interest. Primary areas of clinical imaging include the brain and heart. The acquisition of this device is extremely expensive, with estimates ranging from $2 to $5 million per installation.

Q.1. What are some of the alternative diagnostic imaging technologies to PET, and what factors should managers consider when comparing technologies?

Q.2. Describe a study design to determine the effectiveness of PET.

Case Study No. 5
Thrombolytic Therapy

Thrombolytic therapy is the therapeutic delivery of one of three pharmaceuticals, alteplase (t-PA), anistreplase or streptokinase (SK), to dissolve blood clots in the coronary vasculature following an acute myocardial infarction (AMI). These agents are administered intravenously and achieve the most favorable outcomes if administered immediately after the AMI. The difference in cost between the most expensive thrombolytic and the least expensive is approximately a factor of ten. Several large-scale multinational clinical trials have not shown any major differences among the three agents (GISSI, 1990; ISIS, 1992). The most recent study, GUSTO (1993), however, demonstrated a 1% 30-day survival advantage with the most expensive agent.

Q.1. In analyzing the available studies, what features would you identify as being important in comparing the studies' results?

Q.2. If the t-PA group's mortality was 6.3% at 30 days, and the SK group's was 7.4%, what are the absolute risk and relative risk reduction for using t-PA?

Case Study No. 6
Treatment of Benign Prostatic Hyperplasia

Benign prostatic hyperplasia (BPH) is a nonmalignant disease primarily affecting elderly males. The gradual overgrowth of the prostate gland, blocking the urethra, leads to increasingly painful and difficult voiding. The "gold standard" of treatment for this condition has been transurethral resection of the prostate (TURP), a surgical procedure that has a fairly high rate of complications. New approaches to treating BPH include surgical procedure modifications, stents, drug therapies, ultrasonic aspiration, and thermotherapy.

Q.1. Describe a study design to determine which treatment strategy should be adopted in a managed care environment?

Q.2. What would be the "ideal" characteristics for a BPH treatment technology to possess in order to be performed safely on an ambulatory basis?

References

American Medical Association, Council on Scientific Affairs, 1988, Application of positron emission tomography in the heart, *JAMA* **16:**2438–2445.

American Medical Association, 1993, *Drug Evaluations*, AMA, Chicago.

American Society of Hospital Pharmacists, Inc., 1993, *American Hospital Formulary Service Drug Information*, ASHP, Bethesda, MD.

Anderson, G. F., Hall, M. A., and Steinberg, E. P., 1993, Medical technology assessment and practice guidelines: Their day in court, *Am. J. Public Health* **83:**1635–1639.

Anonymous, 1993, The new queue at the CDRH, *In Vivo* **November:**5–9.

Antiplatelet Trialists' Collaboration, 1988, Secondary prevention of vascular disease by prolonged antiplatelet treatment, *Br. Med. J.* **296:**320–331.

Appleby, C. R., 1991, HCFA told to cover lenses still in clinical trials, *HealthWeek* **5:**4.

Bailar, J. C., and Mosteller, F., 1988, Guidelines for statistical reporting in articles for medical journals, *Ann. Intern. Med.* **108:**266–273.

Banta, H. D., and Thacker, S. B., 1990, The case for reassessment of health care technology: Once is not enough, *JAMA* **264:**235–240.

Blue Cross and Blue Shield Association, Technology Evaluation Center, 1994, *TEC Criteria*, The Association, Chicago.

Bootman, J. L., Townsend, R. J., and McGhan, W. F., 1991, *Principles of Pharmacoeconomics*, Harvey Whitney Books, Cincinnati.

Braitman, L. E., 1991, Confidence intervals assess both clinical significance and statistical significance, *Ann. Intern. Med.* **114:**515–517.

Brown, W. S., and Newman, T. B., 1987, Are all significant *p* values created equal? The analogy between diagnostic tests and clinical research, *JAMA* **257:**2459–2463.

Calltorp, J., and Smedby, B., 1989, Technology assessment activities in Sweden, *Int. J. Technol. Assess. Health Care* **5:**263–297.

Chalmers, T. C., Smith, H., Jr., Blackburn, B., Silverman, B., Schroeder, B., Reitman, D., and Ambroz, A., 1981, A method for assessing the quality of a randomized control trial, *Control. Clin. Trials* **2:**31–49.

Congress of the United States, Office of Technology Assessment, 1989, *Costs and Effectiveness of Screening for Cholesterol in the Elderly*, GPO No. 052-003-01151-4, Government Printing Office, Washington, DC.

Congress of the United States, Office of Technology Assessment, 1990, *Costs and Effectiveness of Screening for Cervical Cancer in the Elderly*, GPO No. 052-003-01176-0, Government Printing Office, Washington, DC.

Davis, K., 1990, Use of data registries to evaluate medical procedures, *Int. J. Technol. Assess. Health Care* **6:**203–210.

Detsky, A. S., 1989, Are clinical trials a cost-effective investment? *JAMA* **262:**1795–1800.

Detsky, A. S., and Naglie, I. G., 1990, A clinician's guide to cost-effectiveness analysis, *Ann. Intern. Med.* **113:** 147–154.

Diamond, G.A., and Denton, T. A., 1993, Alternative perspectives on the biased foundations of medical technology assessment, *Ann. Intern. Med.* **118:**455–464.

Dickerson, K., and Berlin, J. A., 1992, Meta-analysis: State-of-the-science, *Epidemiol. Rev.* **14:**154–176.

Eddy, D. M., 1989a, Screening for breast cancer, *Ann. Intern. Med.* **111:**389–399.

Eddy, D. M., 1989b, Selecting technologies for assessment, *Int. J. Technol. Assess. Health Care* **5:**485–501.

Ferguson, J. H., Dubinsky, M., and Kirsch, P. J., 1993, Court-ordered reimbursement for unproven medical technology: Circumventing technology assessment, *JAMA* **269:**2116–2121.

Food and Drug Administration, New drug, antibiotic, and biological drug product regulations: Accelerated approval, *Federal Register*, April 15, 1992, Vol. 57, no. 73, p. 13234.

Fuchs, V. R., and Garber, A. M., 1990, The new technology assessment, *N. Engl. J. Med.* **323:**673–677.

Gelijns, A. C., and Rigter, H., 1990, Health care technology assessment in the Netherlands, *Int. J. Technol. Assess. Health Care* **6:**157–174.

Goodman, C., ed., 1988, *Medical Technology Assessment Directory: A Pilot Reference to Organizations, Assessment, and Information Resources*, National Academy Press, Washington, DC.

Gross, P. F., 1989, Technology assessment in health care in Australia, *Int. J. Technol. Assess. Health Care* **5:**137–153.

Gruppo Italiano per lo Studio della Sopravivenza nell'Infarto Miocardico, 1990, GISSI-2: A factorial randomized trial of alteplase versus streptokinase and heparin versus no heparin among 12,490 patients with acute myocardial infarction, *Lancet* **336:**65–71.

[The] GUSTO Investigators, 1993, An international randomized trial comparing four thrombolytic strategies for acute myocardial infarction, *N. Engl. J. Med.* **329:**673–682.

Hatziandreau, E. E., Carlson, K., Mulley, A. G., and Weinstein, M. C., 1990, Cost-effectiveness study of the extracorporeal shock-wave lithotripter, *Int. J. Technol. Assess. Health Care* **6:**623–632.

Hooper, D. C., and Wolfson, J. S., 1991, Fluoroquinolone antimicrobial agents, *N. Engl. J. Med.* **324:**384–394.

Institute of Medicine, Council on Health Care Technology, 1990, *National Priorities for the Clinical Conditions and Medical Technologies, Report of a Pilot Study*, National Academy Press, Washington, DC.

[The] Ischemic Optic Neuropathy Decompression Trial Research Group, 1995, Optic nerve decompression surgery for nonarteritic anterior ischemic optic neuropathy (NAION) is not effective and may be harmful, *JAMA* **273:** 625–632.

ISIS-3 Collaborative Group, 1992, ISIS-3: A randomized comparison of streptokinase vs. tissue plasminogen activator vs. anistreplase and of aspirin plus heparin vs. aspirin alone among 41,299 cases of suspected acute myocardial infarction, *Lancet* **339:**753–770.

Jordan, A. M., 1991, Hospital charges for laparoscopic and open cholecystectomy, *JAMA* **266:**3425–3426.

Koch, P. W., 1987, Government reimbursement policy and medical technology assessment: The case of Switzerland, *Int. J. Technol. Assess. Health Care* **3:**607–612.

Larson, E. B., and Kent, D. L., 1989, The relevance of socioeconomic and health policy issues to clinical research, *Int. J. Technol. Assess. Health Care* **5:**195–206.

Laupacis, A. L., Sackett, D. L., and Roberts, R. S., 1988, An assessment of clinically useful measures of the consequence of treatment, *N. Engl. J. Med.* **318:**1728–1733.

Leape, L., 1989, Unnecessary surgery, *Health Serv. Res.* **23:**351–407.

LeGales, C., and Moatt, J. P., 1990, Searching for consensus through multicriteria decision analysis: Assessment of screening strategies for hemoglobinopathies in southeastern France, *Int. J. Technol. Assess. Health Care* **6:** 430–449.

Luce, B. R., 1990, The risk manager's role in cost-effectiveness studies of new technology, *Perspect. Healthcare Risk Manage.* **Spring:**13–16.

Lumsdon, K., 1991, Biotechnology drugs create new maze of concerns for hospitals, *Hospitals* **December:**32–35.

MacDonald, D., Grant, A., Sheridan-Pereira, M., Boylan, P., and Chalmers, I., 1985, The Dublin randomized controlled trial of intrapartum fetal heart rate monitoring, *Am. J. Obstet. Gynecol.* **152:**524–539.

Maloney, J. V., 1988, Technology in health care: The social impact and economic cost, *Med. Prog. Technol.* **14:**109–114.

Matuszewski, K., and Vermeulen, L., 1994, Medical technology assessment, *Critical Issues Shaping Medical Practice*, University Hospital Consortium, Oakbrook, IL.

McGivney, W. T., and Hendee, W. R., 1988, Technology assessment in medicine: The role of the American Medical Association, *Arch. Pathol. Lab. Med.* **112:**1181–1185.

McGivney, W. T., and Hendee, W. R., 1990, Regulation, coverage, and reimbursement of medical technologies, *Int. J. Radiat. Oncol. Biol. Phys.* **18:**697–700, 1990.

Murphy, J. R., 1991, The assessment process: A microscopic view, *Med. Prog. Technol.* **17**(2):77–83.

National Center for Health Statistics, 1990, *1989 Hospital Discharge Survey*, NCHS, Hyattsville, MD.

National Center for Health Statistics, 1993, Rates of cesarean delivery—United States, 1991, *Morbid. Mortal. Weekly Rep.* **42:**285–289.

National Institutes of Health, 1990, *Intravenous Immunoglobulin: Consensus Statement 8, no 5*, NIH, Bethesda, MD.

Naylor, C. D., Chen, E., and Strauss, B., 1992, Measured enthusiasm: Does the method of reporting trial results alter perception of therapeutic effectiveness? *Ann. Intern. Med.* **117:**916–921.

Office of Technology Assessment, 1976, *Development of Medical Technology: Opportunities for Assessment*, U.S. Government Printing Office, Washington, DC.

Ozminkowski, R. J., Wortman, P., and Roloff, D., 1987, Evaluating the effectiveness of neonatal intensive care: What can the literature tell us? *Am. J. Perinatol.* **4:**339–347.

Park, R. E., Fink, A., Brook, R. H., Chassin, M. R., Kahn, K. L., Merrick, N. J., Kosecoff, J., and Solomon, D. H., 1986, Physician ratings of appropriate indications for six medical and surgical procedures, *Am. J. Public Health* **76:**766–772.

Perry, S., Hanft, R., and Chrzanowski, R., 1991, Technology assessment reports, *Int. J. Technol. Assess. Health Care* **7:**68–105.

Radensky, P., 1991, Federal activities related to health and economic outcomes, *Administrative Radiology* **54:**53–55.

Raskin, I. E., and Maklan, C. W., 1991, Medical treatment effectiveness research: A view from the inside the agency for health care policy and research, *Eval. Health Prof.* **14**(2):161–186.

Rimm, A. A., Barr, J. T., Horowitz, M. M., and Bortin, M. M., 1991, Use of a clinical data registry to evaluate medical technologies, *Int. J. Technol. Assess. Health Care* **7:**182–193.

Ronning, P. L., 1994, The impact of health care reform on technology, *ECRI's Hosp. Technol. Scanner* **January:**5–8.

Schaffarzick, R. W., 1987, Health care technology and quality of care, *Am. Coll. Util. Rev. Physicians* **2:**84–89.

Schecter, M. T., and Birnbaum, D., 1989, Technology assessment, *J. Healthcare Mater. Manage.* **Nov/Dec:**66–72.

Schwartz, J. S., and Lurie, N., 1990, Assessment of medical outcomes: New opportunities for achieving a long sought-after objective, *Int. J. Technol. Assess. Health Care* **6:**333–339.

Schwartz, W. B., 1987, The inevitable failure of current cost-containment strategies, *JAMA* **257:**220–224.

Shy, K. K., Luthy, D. A., Bennett, F. C., Whitfield, M., Larson, E. B., van Belle, G., Hughes, J. P., Wilson, J. A., and Stenchever, M. A., 1990, Effects of electronic fetal heart rate monitoring, as compared with periodic auscultation, on the neurologic development of premature infants, *N. Engl. J. Med.* **322:**588–593.

Steinbrook, R., and Lo, B., 1990, Informing physicians about promising new treatments for severe illness, *JAMA* **263:**2078–2082, 1990.

Stocking, B., and Jennett, B., 1984, Consensus development conference—coronary artery bypass surgery in Britain, *British Medical Journal of Clinical Research* **288:**1712.

Stocking, B., 1988, Medical technology in the United Kingdom, *Int. J. Technol. Assess. Health Care* **4:**171–183.

Sugarman, S. D., 1990, The need to reform personal injury law leaving scientific disputes to scientists, *Science* **248:**823–827.

Sussman, J. H., 1991, Financial considerations in technology assessment, *Top. Health Care Financ.* **17:**30–41.

Thompson, W. D., 1987, Statistical criteria in the interpretation of epidemiologic data, *Am. J. Public Health* **77:** 191–194.

Turner, D. A., Alcorn, F., Shorey, W. D., Stelling, C. B., Mategrano, V., Merten, C. W., Silver, B., Economou, S. G., Straus, A. K., Witt, T. R., and Norusis, M., 1988, Carcinoma of the breast: Detection with MR imaging versus xeromammography, *Radiology* **168:**49–59.

Udvarhelyi, I. S., Colditz, G. A., Rai, A., and Epstein, A. M., 1992, Cost-effectiveness and cost–benefit analyses in the medical literature: Are the methods being used correctly? *Ann. Intern. Med.* **116:**238–244.

United States Pharmacopoeial Convention, Inc., 1993, *Drug Information for the Health Care Professional*, Rockville, MD, 1993.

USDHHS, NIH, 1981, *Cesarean Childbirth: Report of the NICHD Task Force on Cesarean Childbirth*, NIH Pub. No. 82-2067, DHHS, Bethesda, MD.

USDHHS, PHS, Agency for Health Care Policy Research, 1990a, *AHCPR Program Note*, DHHS, Rockville, MD.

USDHHS, PHS, Agency for Health Care Policy Research, 1990b, *Health Technology Assessment Reports: Abstract of Office of Health Technology Reports, 1988–1989*, DHHS Pub. No (PHS)90-3459, Rockville, MD.

USDHHS, PHS, National Cancer Institute, 1991a, *Cancer Statistics Review 1973–1988*, NIH Pub. No. 91-2789, Bethesda, MA.

USDHHS, PHS, Agency for Health Care Policy Research, 1991b, *Health Technology Assessment Report: Carotid Endarterectomy*, DHHS Pub. no. (PHS)91-0029, Rockville, MD.

USDHHS, PHS, Agency for Health Care Policy Research, 1994, *Health Technology Assessment. Institutional and Patient Criteria for Heart–Lung Transplantation*, AHCPR Pub. No. 94-0042, Rockville, MD.

Veluchamy, S., and Saver, C. L., 1990, Clinical technology assessment, cost-effectiveness adoption, and quality management by hospitals in the 1990s, *Quality Rev. Bull.* **16:**223–228.

Vermeulen, L. C., Matuszewski, K. A., Ratko, T. A., Burnett, D. A., and Vlasses, P. H., 1994, Evaluation of ondansetron prescribing in U.S. academic medical centers, *Arch. Intern. Med.* **154:**1733–1740.

Vermeulen, L. C., Ratko, T. A., Erstad, B. L., Brecher, M. E., and Matuszewski, K. A., 1995, A paradigm for consensus: The University Hospital Consortium guidelines for the use of albumin, nonprotein colloid, and crystalloid solutions, *Arch. Int. Med.* **155:**373–379.

Wagner, M., 1991, Outcome research affecting devices, *Mod. Healthcare* **February:**54.

Ware, J. E., and Sherbourne, C. D., 1992, The MOS 36-item short-form health survey (SF-36), *Med. Care* **30:** 473–483.

Weill, C., Fagnani, F., and LeFaure, C., 1989, The assessment of medical technology: The case of France, *Int. J. Technol. Assess. Health Care* **5:**144–150.

Wortman, P., and Yeaton, W. H., 1985, Cumulating quality of life results in controlled trials of coronary artery bypass graft surgery, *Controlled Clinical Trials* **6:**289–305.

Yim, J. M., Matuszewski, K. A., Vermeulen, L. C., Ratko, T. A., Burnett, D. A., and Vlasses, P. H., 1995, Surveillance of colony-stimulating factor use in U.S. academic health centers, *Ann. Pharmacotherapy* (in press).

Young, F. E., 1988, *Paying for Progress: Reimbursement and Regulated Medical Products*, Presented to the Blue Cross and Blue Shield Technology Management Conference, Chicago, November.

Yusuf, S., Peto, R., Lewis, J., Collins, R., and Sleight, P., 1985, Beta blockade during and after myocardial infarction: An overview of the randomized trials, *Prog. Cardiovasc. Dis.* **27:**335–371.

8

Epidemiology and Health Care Quality Management

Marie E. Sinioris and Kevin L. Najafi

Epidemiology has a critical role to play in health care quality management, since health care quality management involves analyzing variation and determining the structural and process features of health care organizations that affect health outcomes in populations. Epidemiology provides a conceptual orientation and methods to assist in performing these activities. In this chapter, we describe quality management and how to assess and improve quality in the health care setting. We also consider the impact of quality management on the overall performance of health care systems. Case studies at the end of the chapter further illustrate the relationship between epidemiology and health care quality management.

Theory of Quality Management

The ultimate aim of health care is to produce beneficial **outcomes** for patients, providers, and society. There are several types of outcomes to consider, including morbidity, mortality, functional status, and quality of life. Economic outcomes refer to such elements as cost of care, resource utilization, and lost earnings to patients and employers. Satisfaction with health care is another type of outcome. These outcomes occur at the levels of individuals, families, communities, and broader populations.

The achievement of desired outcomes depends on the **processes of care** that are employed because process and outcome are intertwined. The way care is delivered influences the results that are obtained. Both are important dimensions of the definition of quality in health care developed by the Institute of Medicine:

> Quality of care is the degree to which health services for individuals and populations increase the likelihood of desired health outcomes and are consistent with current profes-

Marie E. Sinioris   Department of Health Systems Management, Rush University, and Rush-Presbyterian-St. Luke's Medical Center, and ArcVentures, Inc., Chicago, Illinois 60612.   **Kevin L. Najafi**   Department of Health Systems Management, Rush University, and ArcVentures, Inc., Chicago, Illinois 60612.

Epidemiology and the Delivery of Health Care Services: Methods and Applications, edited by Denise M. Oleske. Plenum Press, New York, 1995.

sional knowledge . . . How care is provided should reflect appropriate use of the most
current knowledge about scientific, clinical, technical, interpersonal, manual, cognitive, and
organizational and management elements of health care. (Lohr, 1990)

An important part of this definition is the focus on **appropriateness** as a critical factor in
determining the quality of care. Appropriateness is defined as an intervention's expected
level of benefit for a patient given current knowledge (Berwick, 1994). In other words, based
on the available evidence, to what degree can a preventive measure, diagnostic test, or surgical
treatment be expected to lead to a desirable outcome for the patient? Depending on the health
characteristics of the patient and available scientific knowledge, there may be a great deal of
uncertainty about what constitutes appropriate care or there may be little or no uncertainty.
Moreover, there may be multiple modalities of care that are considered appropriate, without
definitive evidence on which is most appropriate for a given patient. For example, there
may be insufficient evidence to know whether medication or surgery will be more effective in
improving the patient's health. **Effectiveness** is the extent to which care in the real world of
everyday practice achieves theoretically attainable outcomes as determined by experimentation.

In essence, inappropriate care includes the misuse, overuse, or underuse of health care
resources (Brook *et al.*, 1991). An example of misuse is to perform surgery when medication is
known to be a more effective way to help the patient. Performing a diagnostic test that is not
indicated in a given situation is an example of overuse. An example of underuse is the lack of
vaccination in instances where it is known to be beneficial. In all of these cases, the process of
care is ineffective, leading to suboptimal outcomes.

If two types of care are equally effective, the less costly one is the more efficient means of
achieving health improvement (Donabedian, 1990). **Efficiency** is a dimension of quality that is
of growing concern to all stakeholders in the health care system. Individual patients and their
families perceive inefficiency when the cost of the same level of health care coverage increases
over time. Managed care organizations are often at financial risk for the health of defined
populations of covered lives. Health care providers are under intensifying pressure to keep
costs down while improving the value of the services they provide. And society as a whole
sees health expenditures consuming an ever increasing fraction of the gross national product,
despite the fact that the uninsured population is growing.

Interrelationship between Health Care Quality Management and Epidemiology

Donabedian has defined the **epidemiology of health care quality** as the "study of the
distribution of quality at any given time and of changes in its distribution through time. Time,
place, and person, the traditional triad of descriptive epidemiology, apply to the study of the
quality of medical care as well" (Donabedian, 1985). From this perspective, health care quality
management is a process to do one or both of the following:

1. Assess and improve the *average* level of quality. For example, a health maintenance
   organization (HMO) reduces the average number of nonacute inpatient days for a
   certain diagnosis-related group (DRG). Nonacute inpatient days are a wasteful and
   inappropriate use of resources and, therefore, are a sign of suboptimal quality.
2. Assess *variability* and improve quality through the reduction of unwanted variation.
   Continuing the example, the HMO also reduces unwanted variation in nonacute days
   per patient episode. If most cases grouped into this DRG have similar severity of

illness and risk of poor outcomes such as complications or mortality, then a large standard deviation of nonacute days may indicate that the process of care is uncontrolled. Perhaps the sequence and timing of interventions by clinicians and other staff is poorly coordinated. This is a sign of inefficiency and, therefore, suboptimal quality. The unwanted variation is over and above inherent variation in nonacute days due to real differences in patient acuity and risk.

By reducing unwanted variation and the average number of nonacute days, the HMO improves the efficiency of managing patients in this DRG. Even if experimentation is not feasible or possible, efficiency should be inferred by comparing a given level of performance against the best that has been achieved elsewhere. In the case of the HMO, efficiency in minimizing nonacute days may be assessed through comparisons to the results achieved by other institutions.

The essence of quality management is the assessment of variation in processes and outcomes, the elimination of unwanted variation, and the improvement of average levels of performance. The application of epidemiologic techniques is integral to answering the following questions in quality management: How do we describe variation in quality? What causes variation in quality of care? What methods do we use to reduce unwanted variation and improve the average level of quality? How can health care organizations and systems apply these methods to improve performance? By designing, refining, and redesigning structures and processes, organizations may improve outcomes.

Epidemiologic tools are useful in both quality assessment and improvement. They now include a variety of powerful techniques that originated in industrial settings and have been adapted to the health care setting during the past decade (Batalden and Nelson, 1989; Laffel and Blumenthal, 1989; Berwick *et al.*, 1990; James, 1990; Melum and Sinioris, 1992; Gaucher and Coffey, 1993). These methods fall collectively under the name Total Quality Management or Continuous Quality Improvement (TQM/CQI): TQM is a strategic, systematic, and customer-centered approach to health care management with the aim of never-ending improvement in quality of care; CQI is often used as a synonym, but may also refer to specific techniques of process improvement that fall within the broader framework of TQM. Like traditional epidemiologic methods, TQM/CQI is concerned with reducing unwanted variation in processes and outcomes. However, TQM/CQI extends beyond the bounds of epidemiology to encompass the whole array of activities, both clinical and support, that interact to determine the level of quality delivered to customers by an organization or system. This spirit of a never-ending drive for innovation and improvement in everything that impacts the customer is the basis for assigning strategic importance to the quality management function.

Quality Assessment

Assessing quality is a prerequisite to improvement. Both quantitative and qualitative information are pertinent to the overall evaluation of quality. Techniques that are useful in this endeavor range from basic to sophisticated. Most assessment activities employ a variety of techniques either in series or in parallel. Techniques useful in quality assessment include **rate measures, small area analysis**, and **quality control tools**.

The most common method for measuring quality in a population is determination of a **rate** (see Chapter 3 for a description of rate measures). Rate measures may be used to assess the quality of a health care system in terms of structure, process, and outcome. With respect to structure, an example is the prevalence of board-certified physicians in a multispecialty group. A higher prevalence of board-certified physicians is desirable because the credentialing is intended to reflect a higher level of competence that should, in turn, lead to better outcomes. The follow-up rate for a tumor registry is an example of a process indicator of quality. Follow-up will ensure that the patient returns to the system to prevent disease recurrence and complications. The postsurgical wound infection rate is an example of an outcome measure. A low or zero postsurgical wound infection rate indicates high quality. In addition to measuring rates that represent adverse outcomes, rates associated with indicators of population health status, such as immunization rates and cholesterol screening rates, and patient satisfaction should also be measured to assess the quality provided within health care systems. Rate measures are useful for **benchmarking**, which is the identification of "best-in-class" performance and analysis of the process by which that performance is achieved. Thus, HMOs with low immunization rates may use HMOs with high immunization rates for benchmarking purposes.

Small area analysis (SAA) is a method of comparing utilization rates in populations from small geographic areas. The highest rates of the small areas are compared to the lowest rates, the degree of difference is evaluated and an attempt is made to explain the variability in terms of service availability or the uncertainty regarding the optimal treatment approach. In the early 1980s, Wennberg and Gittelsohn (1982), McPherson et al. (1982), and Connell and others (1981) used rate measures to illustrate the highly variable nature of medical care delivery, in particular at the local level. Their approach to investigating this variability has been termed small area analysis: SAA has identified marked differences in the rates of hospitalization and the use of various procedures in populations despite age-adjustment. This variability has been attributed to differences in physician practice styles, differences in the adequacy of community, ambulatory, and preventive care, and lack of medical consensus about the optimal treatment strategy for conditions demonstrating wide variability in rates.

There are various approaches for conducting SAA (Connell et al., 1981; Wennberg and Gittelsohn, 1982; Spitzer and Caper, 1989; Tedeschi et al., 1990; Diehr et al., 1990; McPherson et al., 1982). The first step is to define the small area (SA). The SA may consist of a group of counties or smaller units such as zipcodes. The assignment of units to an SA can be based upon a determination of where the simple plurality of patients go. For example, if 51% of a hospital's discharged patients originate in a particular zipcode, that zipcode is assigned to an SA. The SA may also be comprised of geographic areas aggregated to achieve some minimum number of persons (McPherson et al., 1982). Typically, SAs are contiguous units. The third step is to determine the "event" and evaluate whether or not an individual can experience the event more than once. The last step is to select a descriptive measure of the degree of variability and to assess its statistical significance. One method for measuring the degree of variation in SAs is to compute the coefficient of variation (CV). The CV is the mean divided by the standard deviation. Smaller values of the CV indicate lesser variation. In evaluating the rates of three procedures in various geographic areas, Leape et al. (1990) computed the age-adjusted rate for each area using the indirect method. The mean and standard deviation of these rates were used to compute the CV. In their study, the highest procedure variability was found for coronary angiography in rural areas, with a CV = 0.49 (Table 8.1). To assess the variance of the rates among the SAs, an F-test was used. The F-test for rural areas was found to be statistically significant indicating that a larger variation in the utilization rates occurred than was expected by chance alone. Another means of comparing rates across small areas is to construct a $2 \times k$ contingency table (persons with the procedure, yes/no by k number of SAs) and to compute a $k - 1$ degree of freedom χ^2 test (Diehr et al., 1990). The χ^2 test is appropriate when the person is counted only once in the numerator and the

**Table 8.1. Comparison of Rates of Use of Three Study
Procedures in Large and Small Areas**[a]

	No. of procedures per 10,000 medicare enrollees		
Use rate	Coronary angiography	Carotid endarterectomy	Upper gastrointestinal tract endoscopy
Among 13 large areas			
High	50	23	149
Low	22	5	102
High–low ratio	2.3	4.6	1.5
Coefficient of variation	0.32	0.39	0.16
Among 23 small areas (counties)			
High	158	41	165
Low	13	5	42
High–low ratio	12.1	8.2	3.9
Coefficient of variation	0.49	0.41	0.21

[a]Reprinted from Leape *et al.* (1990), with permission from American Medical Association, copyright 1990.

In both large and small areas, for all three procedures, there is more variance in use rates than would be expected by chance alone ($p < 0.01$, χ^2). Standard deviations used in the calculation of coefficients of variation are weighted by the number of beneficiaries in each area. There is significantly more variance among small areas than there is among large areas for angiography ($p < 0.01$; F test with 21, 12 df) but not for endarterectomy ($p > 0.05$; F test with 20, 12 df) or endoscopy ($p > 0.10$; F test with 20, 12 df).

expected number of events per SA is at least five. Other methods for assessing small area variation are currently being evaluated, including various regression methods (Elston *et al.*, 1991; Diehr *et al.*, 1993).

   Quality control (QC) **tools** are a set of graphical methods specifically designed for analysis of the variation in processes to promote achievement of statistical process control (Fig. 8.1). **Flow charts** and **cause-and-effect diagrams** are examples of qualitative graphical methods. A flow chart is a visual depiction of every step in a process emphasizing steps where variation may occur, including the sequence in which the steps occur. A cause-and-effect diagram is a pictorial representation of the relationship between an effect and all of its potential causes. Quantitative graphical techniques include **checksheets, histograms, pareto charts, scatter diagrams, and run charts/control charts**. A checksheet is a simple form for making sample observations such as counting the occurrence of events. A histogram is a two-dimensional graph with vertical bars representing the frequency of values in a continuous distribution. A pareto chart represents a frequency distribution of discrete events in descending rank order. A scatter diagram is a two-dimensional plot of points representing observations of what happens to one variable when another variable changes. A run chart is a plot of sample data in the form of a line graph, with time indicated on the *x* axis and a measure of the outcome of the process on the *y* axis. A control chart is a run chart with three lines, two of which represent the upper and lower control limits, and a center line representing the mean of the sample means or proportions. The steps in preparing a control chart are as follows:

1. Operate the process under normal conditions without any adjustments.
2. Take samples of measurements at successive time intervals.

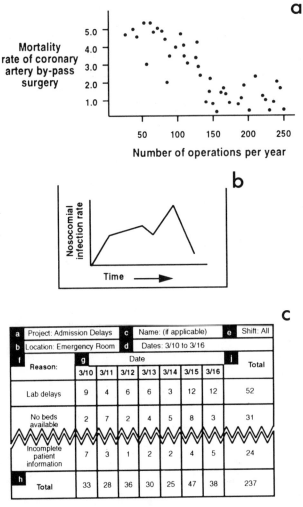

Figure 8.1. Quality control tools. (a) Scatter diagram. (b) Run (trend) chart. (c) Check sheet. (d) Histogram. (e) Cause-effect diagram. (f) Flow chart. (g) Pareto chart. (c) and (e) adapted with permission from GOAL/QPC, 13 Branch Street, Methuen, MA 01844-1953. Tel: 508-685-3900. Source: *The Memory Jogger II: A Pocket Guide of Tools for Continuous Improvement and Effective Planning* © GOAL/QPC 1994.

3. Calculate the control limits and the center line.
4. Plot the control chart.

There are a number of methods for constructing the lines of the control chart, depending on the form of the data (continuous or categorical), the variability of sample size per time period, and the existence of a standard for the process (which would *de facto* determine the center line) (Montgomery, 1985; Wadsworth *et al.*, 1986). In health care, the sample per month (i.e., number of patients) is highly variable, and the process is often monitored in terms of the rate of health events (r). The first step in the construction of this type of control chart is to obtain the average sample size. For the data in Table 8.2, the average sample size is:

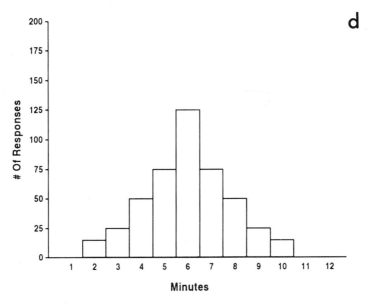

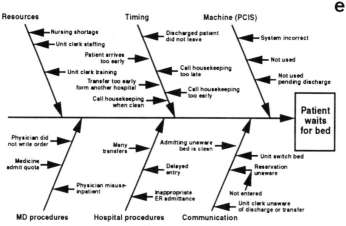

Figure 8.1.   (*Continued*)

$$\bar{n} = \Sigma \, n/12 = 2410/12 = 201$$

The equations for the control chart are as follows:

$$\text{Centerline} = \bar{r}$$
$$\text{UCL} = \bar{r} + 3 \sqrt{\bar{r}(100 - \bar{r})/\bar{n}}$$
$$\text{LCL} = \bar{r} - 3\sqrt{\bar{r}(100 - \bar{r})/\bar{n}}$$

Using the data in Table 8.2, the lines of the control chart graphed in Fig. 8.2 are obtained:

$$\text{Centerline } \bar{r} = 28.8 \text{ per } 100$$
$$\text{UCL} = 28.8 + 3\sqrt{(28.8)(71.2)/201} = 38.4 \text{ per } 100$$
$$\text{LCL} = 28.8 - 3\sqrt{(28.8)(71.2)/201} = 19.2 \text{ per } 100$$

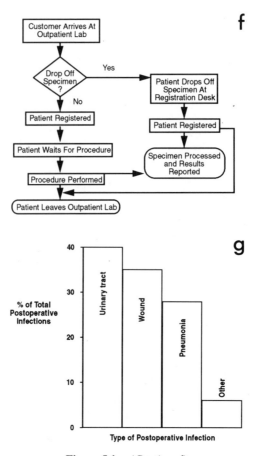

Figure 8.1. (*Continued*)

The centerline represents the average cesarean section rate at Freeway Medical Center. The control chart indicates that the process is in control. The members of the quality improvement team may now initiate steps to reduce the cesarean birth rate in order to achieve the level for the year 2000 recommended in the National Health Objectives (USDHHS, 1990).

In analyzing variation, QC tools help to identify the two sources of variation in health care delivery: **special causes** and **common causes**. The QC tools, in particular control charts, are useful in distinguishing between these two causes. Common causes are random sources of variation that are inherent to a process. In general, they are identified by random distributions of points occurring within the control limits of a control chart, as seen in Figure 8.2. Examples of common causes include the physical layout of facilities, organizational policies and procedures, and information systems. In order to reduce common causes of variation, changes in the design of the process must occur.

Special causes of variation are nonrandom events or circumstances that are not inherent to the process as designed (Deming, 1986). They produce deviations from expected values beyond variation from common causes. Special causes tend to occur according to person, place, and time. When they are identifiable and recurring, special causes may often be removed directly, without redesign of the process. Examples of special causes of variation include miscalibrated laboratory equipment, introduction of new staff, and electrical power

**Table 8.2. Data for a Control Chart of Cesarean Section
Rates with Variable Sample Size**

Month (i)	Number of births (n_i)	Number of cesarean sections (e_i)	Cesarean rate (r): $r_i = e_i/n_i \times 100$
January	190	56	29
February	180	52	29
March	210	63	31
April	188	44	23
May	213	60	28
June	216	52	24
July	224	66	29
August	202	51	25
September	205	63	31
October	195	59	30
November	216	63	29
December	180	53	29
Total	2410	682	28

failures. On a control chart, a special cause usually appears as a point outside of the control limits. However, a persistent upward or downward trend within the control limits may also be indicative of special cause variation. There are other rules for identifying special causes for points inside the control limits (Nelson, 1984).

Upon the identification of type of variation, quality improvement efforts may be undertaken. The first step in quality improvement is to achieve statistical process control (i.e., elimination of all special causes). Once achieved, the remaining variation is random, which

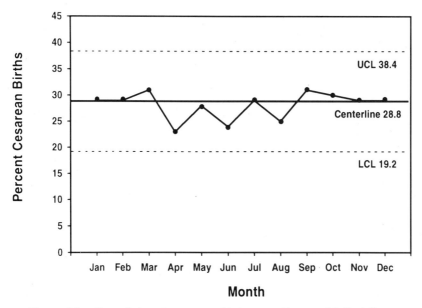

Figure 8.2. Control chart for cesarean birth rate at Freeway Medical Center.

means that the process has a defined capability as measured by the vertical distance between the upper and lower control limits on a control chart. If, after achieving statistical process control, it is determined that the capability or actual performance of the process is unacceptable, corrective action is necessary to eliminate common causes of variation. Thus, the second step in quality improvement is to improve process capability through changes in the design of the process in order to yield better outcomes.

Quality Improvement Techniques

Although rate measures and small area analysis aid in identifying problems and prioritizing them for intervention, they are not useful in identifying the cause of the variation nor do they indicate the type of corrective action needed. Newer health care quality-management techniques incorporate both assessment and improvement strategies into their methods. This shift has changed the emphasis in quality management from inspection techniques and identification of outliers (such was the traditional focus of quality assurance programs) to prevention of quality problems and a focus on reducing variation and improving average levels of performance. Just as there are a variety of quality assessment techniques, there are numerous quality improvement strategies. This chapter emphasizes those strategies that have applicability to improving the quality of health care for populations. Quality improvement techniques include: **pilot tests without control groups** (**PDSA cycle**), **analytic studies**, and **practice guidelines** and **critical paths** (or **clinical pathways**).

Before broad implementation of changes to improve a process, strategies should be pilot-tested systematically on a small scale using the **Plan, Do, Study, Act (PDSA)** cycle (Deming, 1993). The main purpose of the PDSA is to remove special causes efficiently. This assumes that a rigorous method has been used to identify which process from among many should be targeted for improvement (e.g., Delphi technique). The elements of the PDSA cycle are as follows:

- *Plan Phase.* A project team is appointed that makes a flow chart of the process as it currently operates. The team identifies and correlates customer requirements and expectations with process characteristics. Team members collect data to identify sources of process variation, distinguish special from common causes, and hypothesize potential changes to the process that could eliminate the special causes of variation. The team also defines measures by which the success of the improvement may be evaluated.
- *Do Phase.* The team implements the change to the process on a small scale in an effort to remove special cause variation.
- *Study Phase.* The team observes the effects of the pilot test through data and qualitative observations. They evaluate whether there was reduced process variation and utilize the performance measures specified in the plan phase to assess whether a better average level of performance was achieved. If performance improved, they evaluate whether the changed process led to improved and less variable outcomes.
- *Act Phase.* If appropriate, the change is instituted widely and the process is thereafter monitored in order to maintain the gains. If further improvement is needed, there should be a return to the plan phase, and the whole cycle should be repeated until suitable progress is achieved. Even after broad implementation of change, further PDSA cycles are undertaken to continuously improve the process.

The PDSA cycle is a simple yet powerful model for applying a systematic approach to quality improvement. Kantutis *et al.* (1992) used a PDSA cycle to implement activities designed to improve the quality of outpatient laboratory services after removing special cause variation identified through a control chart (Fig. 8.3). Too often, changes are hastily implemented, and processes are tampered with without sufficient understanding of the causes of variation. Any change to a process that is not in statistical control is just as likely to lead to poorer rather than better performance as a result of even greater variation.

In addition to the QC tools, there are **management and planning** (MP) tools that are useful in carrying out the PDSA cycle (Plsek, 1993). The MP tools add discipline to planning and promote teamwork in decision making throughout the quality-improvement process. In addition, these tools are a method of organizing and analyzing qualitative data. The most common MP tools used in health care are the **affinity diagram**, **tree diagram**, and **activity network diagram**. An affinity diagram is a technique for organizing a large volume of qualitative data derived through brainstorming. To produce an affinity diagram, the project team brainstorms, without debate or rebuttal, about possible causes of unwanted variation, writing each idea regarding a cause on a separate card. In silence and in turn, individuals place related ideas in "affinity" groups that are subsequently named aloud by the participants according to their theme. Figure 8.4 shows an affinity diagram of possible causes for variable waiting times in an outpatient laboratory. A tree diagram represents all of the processes, tasks, events, and decisions that lead to a single goal or outcome and every subgoal or intermediate outcome along the way. An activity network diagram (or arrow diagram) is a tool to sequence, time, and monitor a complex task and all related subtasks. This technique assists in scheduling and monitoring the implementation of a process and in determining the critical path (the

Figure 8.3.   Plan, do, study, act (PDSA) cycle for investigating possible causes of variable waiting time in an outpatient clinical laboratory. Modified from Kantutis *et al.* (1992).

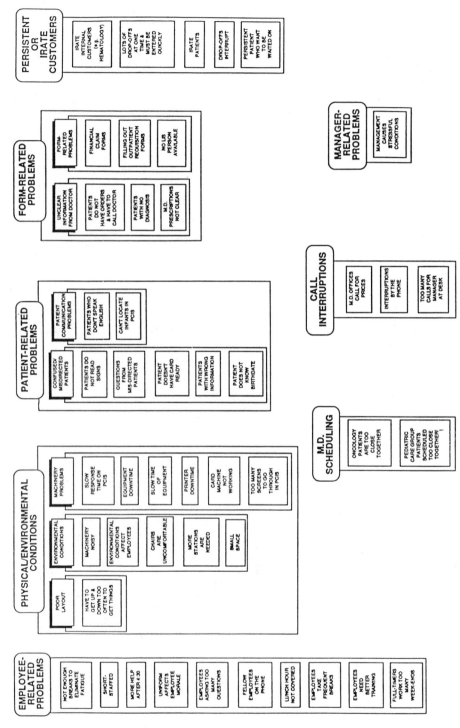

Figure 8.4. Affinity diagram of possible causes of variable waiting time in an outpatient clinical laboratory. Reprinted from Kantutis *et al.* (1992), with permission of the American Hospital Association, copyright 1992.

specific sequence of tasks within the overall process that determines the minimum time to complete the process).

In assessing variation, it is likely that data acquired in an investigation of the cause of process variation may be evaluated using more than one QC or MP tool in series or in parallel. For example, the output of information from the affinity diagram in Fig. 8.4 may be used to construct a cause and effect diagram of all of the possible reasons for variable waiting times in the outpatient laboratory. After data have been collected over time on the occurrence of specific causes, a pareto chart may be constructed to show which causes are most frequent.

The PDSA cycle focuses on the achievement of statistical process control as well as on the improvement of process capability. Once the process is stable, if the system is still performing at an unacceptable level, then one option is to repeat the PDSA cycle testing other improvements to address common causes. In addition, more powerful methods, such as the application of **analytic studies** (see Chapter 5), may be implemented as an efficient means of determining the effectiveness of various quality-improvement strategies. A variety of study designs may be used to assess the relationship between the structure and process of care to various health outcomes and, hence, to determine the factors to modify in order to improve health care. Hospital patient satisfaction surveys are examples of the use of cross-sectional study designs (Nelson and Niederberger, 1990). The Burlington Study is an example of the use of an experimental design to compare the quality of care provided by a nurse practitioner and an internist (Sackett *et al.*, 1974). In this study, eligible families were randomized to receive services from a nurse practitioner group or from a family physician. Outcomes measured were mortality rates, physical function, emotional function, and social function. Since no statistically significant differences between the group of patients managed by the nurse practitioner group and the physician were found, it was concluded that the process of care provided by a nurse practitioner was both safe and effective. Mohide *et al.* (1988) provide an example of an analytic study designed to assess quality of care. Nursing homes were randomly allocated to receive or not to receive a quality assurance intervention. Since the patient was the unit of measurement for the quality indicators studied, such as the prevalence of constipation and skin breakdown, the study was quasiexperimental. Analytic studies, however, typically focus on only one aspect of the care episode. Regardless of the particular type of analytic study design employed, the application of these methods is used to identify structural or process components of a health care system that could be modified to improve the average level of quality.

Pooling information from various analytic studies may provide the basis for formulating an overall approach to the management of care that is felt to be appropriate to the patient population. Two major categories of quality-improvement methods that may address the entire care episode are **practice guidelines** and **critical paths** (also called **clinical pathways**). These methods are tools for implementing effective practice patterns and discouraging variation from those patterns. In both methods, actions are based on research findings or consensus among experts about the relationship between process and outcomes. However, these methods are distinguished from each other with respect to the timing for initiating the course of action.

Practice guidelines are criteria or linkages of criteria in sequence to form algorithms. Practice guidelines are derived from consensus expert opinion supplemented with varying degrees of scientific evidence (Marder, 1990). Practice guidelines, which may be represented in narrative or graphical forms, do not specify the timing of implementation of actions. Illustrated in Fig. 8.5 is the Agency for Health Care Policy's flow chart of a pain-management practice guideline.

In health care, critical paths have been defined as the "optimal sequencing and timing of interventions by physicians, nurses, and other staff for a particular diagnosis or procedure,

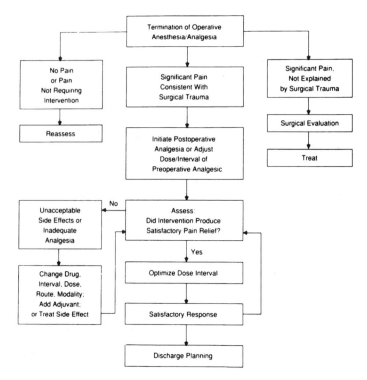

Figure 8.5. Practice guideline for postoperative pain management. Source: Acute Pain Management Guideline Panel (1992).

designed to minimize delays and resource utilization and to maximize the quality of care" (Coffey *et al.*, 1992) (see Fig. 8.6). A critical path is a special form of the activity network diagram. Ideally, a critical path should be developed using decision analysis (Eckman *et al.*, 1991), which uses a tree-diagram to depict in increasing detail the complete set of alternative outcomes that arise as a result of a primary event in a process and from every related subsequent event. Decision analysis determines appropriate segments of the critical path and provides a method for solving complex sequential problems. The components of decision analysis are decision alternatives, a probability representing each of the various outcomes, and the utility value associated with these outcomes (Fig. 8.7) (Carpenter, 1986). Decision analysis defines each branch of the tree in probabilistic terms based on empirical evidence such as the results of epidemiologic studies, randomized clinical trials, and meta-analyses. Probabilities from these studies are computed to characterize risks, complications, treatment effectiveness, and probable prognosis. The lack of data for both probabilities and utilities limits the widespread use of decision analysis in the provision of patient care. Moreover, even if data are available for characterizing short-term and long-term clinical outcomes, the patient's valuation of the health state (utility) may change over time. Lastly, decision analysis should also consider the characteristics of the patient population served, patient preferences and choices (utilities), and costs associated with each endpoint.

     Not only are critical paths useful for controlling the process of care and reducing variation, they are also valuable for framing hypotheses concerning the cause–effect relationship between processes of care and patient outcomes. These hypotheses can then be formally

Patient Name: _____ Age _____

Medical Record Number: _____

Admission Date: _____ Discharge Date: _____ Physician: _____ Procedure: _____

SIT Admit Date/Time: _____ 9K Admit Date/Time: _____ Date: _____

DAY/ LOCATION	OR Day	SIT Day #1	SIT Day #2	9 Kellogg Day #1	9 Kellogg Day #2	9 Kellogg Day #3	9 Kellogg Day #4
ACTIVITY	•Bedrest	•Passive/Active ROM •Dangle	•Up to chair •Walk 40 ft.	•Up to chair TID •Walk 40-80 ft:	•Walk 80-160 ft:	•May shower •Up ad lib •Walk > 160 ft •Stairs - 1 flight	•Home
TUBES/LINES	Pt has: •ET •Swan Ganz •2 peripheral IV's •Arterial Line •Chest tube •Foley catheter •NG •Pacer wires	•D/C Swan Ganz •Heplock peripheral IV x 2 •D/C A-line: •D/C NG:	•D/C Chest tubes: Date/time: •D/C foley: •D/C Cordis:			•D/C pacer wires: •D/C telemetry:	•D/C heplock prior to discharge •D/C pacer wires: •D/C telemetry:
RESPIRATORY	Ventilated	•Weaning protocol Y N •Extubated Date/time: •Reintubated Date/time: •Heated aerosol mask/ Nasal cannula •Incentive spirometer	•Nasal cannula •Incentive spirometer	•O2 Nasal Cannula •Incentive spirometer	•O2 Nasal Cannula •Incentive spirometer	•O2 Nasal Cannula •Incentive spirometer	•O2 Nasal Cannula PRN •Incentive spirometer
TESTS	STAT ON ARRIVAL TO SIT: •ABG, K+, Hct, Ca •Venous O2 for calibration •PT, PTT, SMA-6 •Cardiac Isoenzymes •EKG •CXR •ABG, K+ q 6 hrs •Glucosan q 6° (diabetics)	WEANING PROTOCOL •CBC, Plat CT, SMA-6 •Cardiac Isoenzymes •EKG •CXR	•CBC, Plat CT, SMA-6 •Cardiac Isoenzymes •CXR after CT removal	•CBC, SMA-6		•EKG •CXR- PA/Lat	•CBC, SMA-6
CLINICAL OUTCOMES	•None of the following: reintubation re-operation wound infection wound dehiscence post-op AMI cardiac arrest mortality	•None of the following: reintubation re-operation wound infection wound dehiscence post-op AMI cardiac arrest mortality	•None of the following: reintubation re-operation wound infection wound dehiscence post-op AMI cardiac arrest mortality return to SIT •Pt transferred to 9K	•None of the following: reintubation re-operation wound infection wound dehiscence post-op AMI cardiac arrest mortality return to SIT	•None of the following: reintubation re-operation wound infection wound dehiscence post-op AMI cardiac arrest mortality return to SIT	•None of the following: reintubation re-operation wound infection wound dehiscence post-op AMI cardiac arrest mortality return to SIT •Ambulate up to 160 ft	•None of the following: reintubation re-operation wound infection wound dehiscence post-op AMI cardiac arrest mortality return to SIT •Discharge
EDUCATION/ DISCHARGE PLANNING				•Nursing to contact Utilization Management •Nutrition consult		•Discharge Instructions	
ON/OFF Pathway							

Figure 8.6. Post-open-heart-surgery clinical pathway. M, met on schedule; N, not met on schedule. Courtesy of Rush-Presbyterian-St. Luke's Medical Center, Chicago.

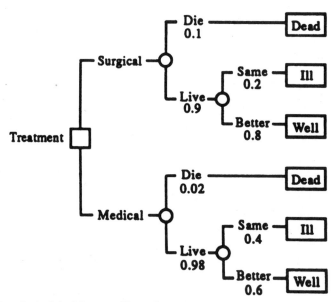

Figure 8.7. Hypothetical decision tree. Note: the square represents a decision or choice node, circles represent chance nodes, and rectangles represent terminal or outcome nodes. The numbers at each chance node are probabilities of each event occurring given that the decisions and events to the left of that chance node have occurred. Reprinted from Goel *et al.* (1992), by permission of the publisher.

evaluated through epidemiologic studies. By outlining the crucial steps in the delivery of care, guidelines may serve as devices for collection of data that can be used to assess the effectiveness and efficiency of specific courses of action. The visual nature of the critical path provides a map for determining where and when to collect data on risk factors, severity of illness, intermediate outcomes of care, cost, therapeutic alternatives, and so forth. Feedback of epidemiologic findings from the use of critical paths facilitates may also improve practice patterns through modifications to the guidelines (e.g., revised guidelines could reduce the incidence of pain or the incidence of postoperative complication).

Improving System Performance

In anticipation of health reform and widespread adoption of managed care, health care organizations are rapidly forming strategic alliances, partnerships, and networks that will be accountable for serving defined populations. This trend implies an evolving role for epidemiology and quality management. Although the role of quality management in the formation of a provider network is limited, quality management can play a major role in bringing the organizations together as a team once a network is formed. To function as an integrated health system, each component must overcome organizational barriers to teamwork that might inhibit meeting customer needs and achieving desired outcomes (G. Laffel, personal communication, 1994).

Quality management serves an integral function in integrated health systems. Two complementary approaches exist to assist health care systems in evaluating overall performance. One is the Malcolm Baldrige National Quality Award criteria (U.S. Department of Commerce, 1992). Often referred to as a *de facto* definition of TQM, the criteria and accompanying scoring guidelines are useful for self-assessment in health care delivery (Reimann, 1992). The Baldrige criteria encompass the related functions and processes that determine whether an organization or system is satisfying the needs and expectations of its customers in an efficient manner. The other is the National Committee for Quality Assurance's Health Plan Employer Data and Information Set (HEDIS 2.0). HEDIS is a performance assessment tool for health plans covering defined populations (National Committee for Quality Assurance, 1993). Quality measures that have an epidemiologic basis are a major subset of the assessment of the overall performance of health systems in optimizing the outcomes of health care. For example, high blood cholesterol is linked to the development of coronary artery disease, the leading cause of mortality in the United States. If the proportion of individuals with high cholesterol in a population is reduced, the incidence of cardiovascular events will also likely be reduced. It behooves a health plan to monitor not only the prevalence of high blood cholesterol and initiate programs to reduce it but also to develop a strategy for ensuring that all adults within a plan have had their cholesterol checked. Thus, a quality performance measure of a health plan would be the percentage of adults who were screened for high blood cholesterol within the preceding five years. Assessing system performance using these or similar approaches provides a mechanism for identifying strengths and weaknesses of a health care system, prioritizing areas for improvement, and monitoring the effectiveness of improvement efforts.

Summary

Descriptive epidemiologic methods in conjunction with tools from industrial quality control help assess and monitor the health status of populations served by health care systems. However, measurement in itself is insufficient; it must be part of a process to continuously improve the performance of a health care system. Analytic epidemiologic study designs and the results of these coupled with techniques such as the PDSA cycle, practice guidelines, critical paths, and total quality management should become part of a health system's total strategy to promote beneficial outcomes in the population served. In the forthcoming era of integrated health systems, epidemiology will enable the application of quality assessment and improvement approaches to the entire continuum of care, from the measurement of a community's health status to surveillance of the effects of a new technology.

Case Studies

Case Study No. 1
Reducing the Nonacute Inpatient Days at Random Medical Center for DRG 182 (Esophagitis, Gastroenteritis, and Miscellaneous Disorders; Age > 17 Years with Complications)

Random Medical Center is attempting to promote the effective, efficient, and appropriate use of the hospital's resources. A team of physicians, nurses, and ancillary personnel seeks to decrease the hospital's overall average length-of-stay (LOS), without compromising the quality of inpatient care. The routine monitoring of hospital length-of-stay information assists the team in achieving its goal.

Preliminary data from the previous five calendar years reveal that DRG 182 (esophagitis, gastroenteritis, and miscellaneous digestive disorders; age > 17 years, with complications) consistently had the highest rate of nonacute days among all DRG's. After reviewing this information, the team decided to investigate the reasons for the excess in nonacute days.

Q.1. The first step in the investigation was to characterize the variation in the length of stay for DRG 182. Propose methods to characterize the variation.

Q.2. How could an initial assessment be made to determine if attending physician characteristics affected variation in LOS?

Q.3. The investigation showed that the timing of diagnostic tests and digestive consults affected the variation in LOS for DRG 182. How might the team direct an effort to reduce the variation?

Q.4. How could the team determine if the implementation of a process guideline reduced the length of stay for DRG 182?

Q.5. What outcomes might the team consider to evaluate the critical path's effect on quality of care?

Q.6. How else might LOS be appropriately reduced for these patients?

Case Study No. 2
Lowering the Rate of Postsurgical Wound Infection

By reducing postoperative wound infections, a hospital not only improves the quality of patient care but also lowers costs. Antimicrobial prophylaxis accounts for as much as half of hospital antibiotic utilization. Classen *et al.* (1992) examined the relationship of practice patterns associated with antimicrobial prophylaxis on the subsequent occurrence of surgical-wound infection at a hospital. Utilizing a longitudinal observational study design, the investigators measured the time of antibiotic prophylaxis and the occurrence of surgical-wound infection in 2847 patients who underwent elective, clean or clean-contaminated procedures at a large community hospital. The patients who were administered antibiotics during the two hours prior to the incision served as the reference group, with 0.6% having surgical-wound infections postoperatively. Of the patients who began early prophylaxis (two to 24 hours before the surgical incision), 3.8% subsequently developed wound infection (relative risk = 6.7, 95% confidence interval: 2.9 to 14.7, $p < 0.001$). Prophylaxis starting zero to three hours after the incision yielded with a wound infection rate of 1.4% ($p = 0.12$; relative risk = 2.4, 95% confidence interval: 0.9–7.9). Of the patients who started prophylaxis postoperatively (more than three hours after the incision), 3.3% had wound infections (relative risk = 5.8, 95% confidence interval: 2.6 to 12.3, $p < 0.001$). Classen *et al.* concluded that there is considerable variation in the practice of prophylactic administration of antibiotics in surgical patients and that the administration in the two hours before surgery is statistically associated with a reduced risk of postoperative wound infection.

Q.1. Explain how the researchers examined the relationship between process and outcomes to assess quality.

Q.2. Compare and contrast the design used in this study to a randomized controlled design addressing the same problem. What are the advantages of this type of study over a randomized controlled trial on the efficacy of surgical antibiotic prophylaxis?

Q.3. How might the study findings be used to convince the hospital's surgeons to alter their practice patterns?

Case Study No. 3
Significant Differences in Individual Provider Outcomes

Health care regulators and purchasers are increasingly intrigued with the idea of statistically comparing outcomes among the populations served by individual physicians. The dilemma is that most outcomes of interest, such as mortality, are relatively rare in the experience of any particular physician, and the patient volume (the denominator in the rate calculation) is typically low. Luft and Hunt (1986) estimated that, if a given provider treats 200 patients having a condition with an expected death rate of 1%, it would take only five deaths to show a poor outcome that is statistically significant at the 0.05 level. On the other hand, if a provider treats only 200 patients, it would be impossible to show better than expected outcomes for this provider that are statistically significant. At most, a rate of one death in 500 patients would have to be achieved to demonstrate a statistically significant reduction in mortality among patients served by this provider.

Q.1. As the medical benefits manager for a Fortune 500 company, you are looking for ways to trim the company's escalating costs for coronary artery bypass, organ transplant, and other expensive procedures. What do you need to know to make intelligent judgments about data comparing the performance of individual physicians?

Q.2. Assume that, as medical benefits manager, you have identified several coronary-artery bypass providers that show poor mortality outcomes that are statistically significant at the 0.05 level. How will you respond to their possible objection that "my patients are sicker"?

Q.3. What is the potential role of the severity-of-illness adjustment in provider comparisons such as these? How might providers go about making valid arguments against severity-adjusted data?

Case Study No. 4
Reducing Infant Mortality

Throughout the world, infant mortality (death during the first year of life) is widely viewed as an indicator of a population's health status. Recent efforts to reduce the infant mortality rate have centered on infants born weighing less than 2500 g, since mortality risk increases with decreasing birthweight. Accounting for two-thirds of neonatal deaths, low birthweight (LBW) infants are known to be a primary determinant of neonatal mortality and morbidity and, by extension, infant mortality. Those LBW babies who live through the first year are at an increased risk of learning disorders, neurodevelopmental problems, respiratory infections, and other serious ailments.

Siu *et al.* (1992) report that the potential impact of primary prevention of LBW births on infant mortality is probably very large. Whereas some maternal risk actors for LBW such as race, socio-economic status, and age are outside the realm of medical intervention, others are modifiable to varying degrees. Modifiable risk factors include smoking, alcohol consumption, drug usage, and diet. The most cost-effective method of improving pregnancy outcomes is thought to be early initiation of prenatal care. In the future, primary prevention will have a much greater expected impact on infant mortality than secondary prevention, such as specialized treatment of LBW infants in neonatal intensive care units and specialized centers for delivery of high-risk infants. Most experts believe secondary prevention has already attained the majority of its potential impact.

Q.1. Given these facts, how should a corporate benefits manager go about choosing an HMO for its employee population, a large percentage of whom are females of child-bearing age, based upon quality indicators?

Q.2. Given the evidence in the case, what quality-of-care measures are most appropriate for an HMO concerned with preventing LBW infants?

Case Study No. 5
Assessing Quality of Care for Chronic Illness in a Health Maintenance Organization

The Vice President of Quality Management at Sunnyside HMO is producing a Health Plan Employer Data and Information Set (HEDIS) report to help employers assess the HMO's performance on a broad range of dimensions, including quality. One of the quality measures in HEDIS is the "Asthma Inpatient Admission Rate." This rate and another measure, "Diabetic Retinal Exam Rate," are intended to indicate a health plan's quality of care for chronic illness.

The Asthma Inpatient Admission Rate is the percentage of HMO members with inpatient admissions for the care of asthma during the calendar year. Separate rates are calculated for members aged 1–19 years and 20–39 years. The rationale for using this measure is that many, if not most, inpatient admissions for asthma care are preventable with optimal outpatient care, according to medical expert consensus and the scientific literature.

The denominator of the rate is the number of members in the appropriate age category who were enrolled continuously during the prior 12-month period as of December 31 of the most recent calendar year. The numerator is the number of members in the denominator with one or more inpatient admissions for asthma treatment during the calendar year. In addition, a readmission rate for each age category is calculated by using the same denominator, but replacing the numerator with the number of members in the denominator with *two* or more admissions for asthma treatment.

The Vice President collects the data from a data base containing the hospital/billing discharge summaries of all members. For both age categories and for admissions and readmissions, the results compare very favorably to standards set by the U.S. Department of Health and Human Services (1990).

Q.1. Should the Benefits Manager of an employer negotiating a contract with Sunnyside conclude from the data that Sunnyside HMO has a high quality of care for asthma patients?

Q.2. What are the limitations of the data as an indicator of quality of care for chronic illness in an HMO?

Q.3. Should the Benefits Manager compare Sunnyside's rates to those of other HMOs in assessing quality of asthma care?

Q.4. Is this rate appropriate for quality assessment in a hospital?

References

Acute Pain Management Guideline Panel, 1992, *Acute Pain Management: Operative or Medical Procedures and Trauma. Clinical Practice Guideline. AHCPR Pub. No. 92-0032.* AHCPR, Rockville, MD.

Batalden, P., and Nelson, E., 1989, Hospital quality: Patient, physician, and employee judgments, *Int. J. Healthcare Qual. Assur.* **3**:7–17.

Berwick, D. M., 1994, Improving the appropriateness of care, *Qual. Connect.* **3**:1–6.

Berwick, D., Godfrey, B., and Roessner, J., 1990, *Curing Healthcare*, Jossey-Bass, San Francisco.

Brassard, M., 1994, *The Memory Jogger* II, Goal/QPC, Methuen, MA.

Brook, R. H., Kamberg, C. J., Mayer-Oakes, A., *et al.*, 1991, Appropriateness of acute medical care for the elderly: An analysis of the literature, in *Health Care Quality Management for the 21st Century* (J. B. Couch, ed.), pp. 151–176, American College of Physician Executives, Tampa, FL.

Carpenter, T. E., 1986, Decision-tree analysis using a microcomputer, *Am. J. Epidemiol.* **124**:843–850.

Classen, D. C., Evans, R. S., Pestotnik, S. L., Horn, S. D., Menlove, R. L., and Burke, J. P., 1992, The timing of prophylactic administration of antibiotics and the risk of surgical-wound infection, *N. Engl. J. Med.* **326**:281–286.

Coffey, R. J., Richards, J. S., Remmert, C. S., LeRoy, S. S., Schoville, R. R., and Baldwin, P. J., 1992, An introduction to critical paths, *Qual. Manage. Health Care* **1**:45–54.

Connell, F. A., Day, R. W., and LoGerfo, J. P., 1981, Hospitalization of medicaid children: Analysis of small area variations in admission rates, *Am. J. Public Health* **71:**606–613.

Deming, W. E., 1986, *Out of the Crisis*, Massachusetts Institute of Technology Center for Advanced Engineering Study, Cambridge.

Deming, W. E., 1993, *The New Economics*, Massachusetts Institute of Technology Center for Advanced Engineering Study, Cambridge.

Diehr, P., Cain, K., Connell, F., and Volinn, E., 1990, What is too much variation? The null hypothesis in small-area analysis, *Health Serv. Res.* **24:**741–777.

Diehr, P., Cain, K., Zhan, Y., and Abdul-Salam, F., 1993, Small area variation analysis, *Med. Care* **31:**YS45–YS53.

Donabedian, A., 1990, The seven pillars of quality, *Arch. Pathol. Lab. Med.* **114:**1115–1118.

Eckman, H. E., Wong, J. B., and Pauker, S. G., 1991, The role of clinical decision analysis in medical quality management, in *Healthcare Quality Management for the 21st Century* (J. B. Couch, ed.), pp. 253–280, American College of Physician Executives, Tampa, FL.

Elston, J. M., Koch, G. G., and Weissert, W. G., 1991, Regression-adjusted small area estimates of functional dependency in the noninstitutionalized American population age 65 and over, *Am. J. Public Health* **81:**335–343.

Gaucher, E. J., and Coffey, R. J., 1993, *Total Quality in Health Care: From Theory to Practice*, Jossey-Bass, San Francisco.

Goel, V., and the Health Services Research Group, 1992, Decision analysis: Applications and limitations, *Can. Med. Assoc. J.* **147:**413–417.

James, B. C., 1990, TQM and clinical medicine, *Front. Health Serv. Manage.* **7:**42–46.

Kantutis, C. A., Chang-Vizon, M., and Strode, S. R., 1992, Fitting ME/IE tools into the total quality management puzzle: An outpatient laboratory case study, in *Proceedings of the 1992 Annual HIMSS Conference*, pp. 161–174, American Hospital Association, Chicago.

Laffel, G., and Blumenthal, D., 1989, The case for using industrial quality management science in healthcare organizations, *JAMA* **262:**2869–2873.

Leape, L. L., Park, R. E., Solomon, D. H., Chassin, M. R., Kosekoff, J., and Brook, R. H., 1990, Does inappropriate use explain small-area variations in the use of health care services? *JAMA* **263:**669–672.

Lohr, K. N., ed., 1990, *Medicare. A Strategy for Quality Assurance*, Vol. 1, Institute of Medicine, National Academy Press, Washington, DC.

Luft, H.D., and Hunt, S. S., 1986, Evaluating individual hospital quality through outcome statistics, *JAMA* **255:**2780–2784.

Marder, R. J., 1990, Relationship of clinical indicators and practice guidelines, *Quality Rev. Bull.* **16**(2):60.

McPherson, K., Wennberg, J. E., Hovind, O. B., and Clifford, P., 1982, Small-area variations in the use of common surgical procedures: An international comparison of New England, England, and Norway, *N. Engl. J. Med.* **307:**1310–1314.

Melum, M. M., and Sinioris, M. K., 1992, *Total Quality Management: The Healthcare Pioneers*, American Hospital Publishing, Chicago.

Mohide, E. A., Tugwell, P. X., Caulfield, P. A., Chambers, L. W., Dunnett, C. W., Baptiste, S., Bayne, J. R., Patterson, C., Rudnick, V., and Pill, M., 1988, A randomized trial of quality assurance in nursing homes, *Med. Care* **26:**554–565.

Montgomery, D. C., 1985, *Introduction to Statistical Quality Control*, Wiley, New York.

National Committee for Quality Assurance, 1993, *Health Plan Employer Data and Information Set and Users' Manual*: version 2.0, NCQA, Washington, DC.

Nelson, C. W., and Niederberger, J., 1990, Patient satisfaction surveys: An opportunity for total quality improvement, *Hospital and Health Services Administrator* **35:**409–427.

Nelson, L. S., 1984, The Shewhart control chart—tests for special causes, *J. Qual. Technol.* **16:**237–239.

Plsek, P. E., 1993, Tutorial: Management and planning tools of TQM, *Qual. Manage. Health Care* **1:**59–72.

Reimann, C. W., 1992, Malcolm Baldrige national quality award criteria, in *Total Quality Management: The Healthcare Pioneers* (M. Melum and M. Sinioris, eds.), American Hospital Publishing, Chicago.

Sackett, D. L., Spitzer, W. O., Gent, M., Roberts, R. S., 1974, The Burlington randomized trial of the nurse practitioner: Health outcomes of patients, *Ann. Intern. Med.* **80:**137–142.

Siu, A. L., McGlynn, E. A., Morgenstern, H., Beers, M. H., Carlisle, D. M., Keeler, E. B., Beloff, J., Curtin, K., Leaning, J., Perry, B. C., Selker, H. P., Weiswasser, W., Wiesenthal, A., and Brook, R. H., 1992, Choosing quality of care measures based on the expected impact of improved health, *Health Serv. Res.* **27:**619–650.

Spitzer, M., and Caper, P., 1989, *Quality Measurement through Small-Area Analysis Techniques*, American Hospital Publishing, Chicago.

Tedeschi, P., Wolfe, R. A., and Griffith, J. G., 1990, Micro-area variation in hospital use, *Health Serv. Res.* **24:**729–740.

U.S. Department of Commerce, 1992, *1992 Award Criteria, Malcolm Baldrige National Quality Award*, USDC, Gaithersberg, MD.

U.S. Department of Health and Human Services, 1990, *Healthy People 2000—Full Report with Commentary*, U.S. Government Printing Office, Washington, DC.

Wennberg, J.E., and Gittelsohn, A., 1982, Variations in medical care among small areas, *Sci. Am.* **246:**120–134.

Wadsworth, H. M., Stephens, K. S., and Godfrey, A. B., 1986, *Modern Methods for Quality Control and Improvement*, Wiley, New York.

9

Managing Health Care Systems from an Epidemiologic Perspective

Wayne M. Lerner

The recent submission of health care legislation by the President of the United States represents completion of a process begun in the early 1980s to solidify the purchasing power of both public and privately financed payers. The reform measures embodied in the legislation would force health care organizations to assume both fiscal and health status risk for their defined populations. Diagnosis-related group (DRG) systems would be phased out for all but Medicare beneficiaries as capitation payment is implemented for all health care product lines encompassing outpatient, psychiatric, long-term care, prevention, hospice, and rehabilitation services. Physicians would receive payment for inpatient and outpatient care based on conditions placing them at risk for both the price of the services delivered and the utilization experience of their patients. The legislation also includes provisions to encourage providers to participate in health services research designed to measure disease trends and the effects of various treatment patterns. In other words, clinical outcomes research would eventually provide payers a means of assessing if the services they purchase actually improve the health status and if they are being delivered in a cost-beneficial (value-added) manner.

Public and private payers expect reform legislation to promote cooperation between physicians and hospitals and among a community's health care organizations by aligning economic incentives and prohibiting service duplication except when a single provider cannot satisfy defined needs. Reform measures would force consolidation of institutions and services by encouraging the development of health care systems, increasing local market competition, and decreasing the rate of operational and capital spending. Implementation of proposed legislation has the potential to achieve economies of scale and improved access to health services—the central themes of the myriad of health care proposals offered for legislation over the past several decades.

Late in 1994, the support for federal health reform diminished in the face of competing bills and fears of increased administrative costs, and bureaucracy to oversee such a massive

Wayne M. Lerner　　The Jewish Hospital of St. Louis, BJC Health System, and Washington University School of Medicine, St. Louis, Missouri 63110.

Epidemiology and the Delivery of Health Care Services: Methods and Applications, edited by Denise M. Oleske. Plenum Press, New York, 1995.

change. In spite of this experience, reform plans, based in general on the principles espoused by President Clinton, have been enacted in some states (Hawaii, Tennessee, Minnesota) and are in the formulation stage in others (Missouri, Kansas). Each of these plans proposes important changes in pricing and insurance coverage. Typically, pricing for a defined set of benefits would be based on community, rather than experience, rating, and the "preexisting condition" clause would be eliminated. In addition to state-based efforts, local markets are enacting changes similar to the reform principles described above. Purchasing cooperatives of small and large businesses are buying employee health services from providers and insurers on the premise that, by linking health status with financial risk, not only will their losts be reduced, but also, in the end, they will employ a substantially healthier population.

With the anticipated loosening of the constraints affecting provider operations in such related areas as tort awards and antitrust regulations, the scene has been set for a massive overhaul of the health care delivery system. Although the results of reform may not be known for years to come, it is clear that price and quality indicators promulgated by local integrated systems (accountable health plans) will allow consumers to make a more informed choice than ever before about the plan they will join. Further, the roles of physicians (generalists and specialists), hospitals, medical schools, ambulatory and posthospitalization organizations, insurance companies, and regulators will change. Whether the integrated system is based in a PHO, an HMO or a hospital network, long-term survival will initially be directly related to price. Ultimately, however, the quality of the services as managed by the plan and perceived by the beneficiaries will be the final arbiter of success (The Governance Committee, 1993a, b). Thus, the linking of financial risk with responsibility for a population's health status will cause providers to focus on disease prevention and health promotion rather than traditional acute care services (Lewin, 1993; Kaufman and Waterman, 1993).

The above scenario poses the following challenge to the health care executive: How can he or she lead the organization to successfully respond to such massive changes in the health care system? The executive's leadership role requires the use of epidemiology to identify and address the complex issues related to the delivery of care to two distinct populations— one currently receiving services and one potentially receiving them. This chapter illustrates how the health care executive should view the application of epidemiology for managing a health care system. Case studies at the end of this chapter reflect the types of problems that a health care manager may seek to resolve through the use of epidemiologic approaches.

Application of Epidemiology in Managing the Delivery of Health Care

Epidemiology is the discipline that will enable health care executives to manage the complex processes associated with the delivery of services to larger populations. Essential to their leadership task are the ability to: (1) measure and act upon information pertaining to a system's performance; (2) organize intra- and interinstitutional systems with the patient as the unit of output; (3) provide opportunities for linkages between practitioners and institutions to effectively deliver services responsive to the needs of a defined population; and (4) develop a common language and perspective of the problems each of the providers face.

An epidemiologic framework can provide a paradigm for action and analysis that is predicated on knowledge of population characteristics, patterns of health problems, and risk factors. A health care executive utilizing such a framework is in a better position to ensure that an institution or system continues to provide quality patient care and community services regardless of the changes in the environment. To fulfill a leadership role effectively, the health care executive must draw on an integrated model for decision making. Epidemiology and other disciplines (such as economics, social anthropology, organizational behavior, and systems theory) provide the tools for problem analysis and evaluation of alternatives to resolve problems facing the organization and the community to be served. An epidemiologic framework relies on the interdependencies of these disciplines for promoting a joint recognition of the opportunities, objectives, and obstacles surrounding a health system's performance. Use of an epidemiologic approach enables the health care executive to increase the probability that the system and its professionals can positively influence the service population's health status.

Since the primary focus of both payer and system efforts should be to maximize a population's health, epidemiology, supplemented by consumer research information, can derive a baseline of the health needs and health status for the defined population. Measurable health status proxies can be identified (e.g., high heart disease rates, high rates of pregnancy complications), and the organization can focus intervention efforts on significant health problems that are optimally addressed through health care services. Problem analysis may suggest the need to modify resource availability and supply, system design or medical practices. The organization's goal should be to define a model of care that allows for the measurement and analysis of each aspect of the delivery process in terms of the desired outcomes. The key questions that a health care executive must address in managing the organization or a health care system from an epidemiologic perspective are displayed in Table 9.1.

A health care organization has responsibility for ensuring that the services delivered match the health care needs of the population served. An epidemiologic framework and the methods of epidemiology can be applied to the following organizational activities to ensure that a health care organization can achieve the goal of matching services and needs: (1) linking national or regional policy initiatives with institutional efforts; (2) strategically developing new services or planning changes in existing ones; (3) projecting the human resources necessary to provide care to a population; (4) monitoring system performance with respect to

Table 9.1. Questions for Health Care Executives when Managing Systems from an Epidemiologic Framework

1. Who is the population served?
   a. How should the service population be defined?
   b. From what distances do individuals travel to receive health care?
2. How can the population's health care needs be measured?
   a. What explicit or implicit factors can be reliably and validly measured to determine need?
   b. What confounders or modifiers in the health promotion–disease treatment continuum exist that affect the ease by which need is identified?
3. What are the health care needs?
   a. Are the population's needs latent or overt?
   b. Are the needs limited or assisted by other socioeconomic factors (such as availability of primary care physicians, public transportation, or employment levels)?
4. What interventions can the health care organization make available to address these needs?
5. Do the interventions improve the health status of the population served?
   a. Which risk factors exist within the various populations that are immutable to change?
   b. Which factors can be modified by the health care system, individual, governmental, or society-wide actions?
   c. Which study designs can be used to identify risk factors?
   d. How can a new program's effects on a population's health status be measured over time?

patient outcomes; and (5) measuring the success of institutional linkages and/or system configurations to effect changes in the health status of the population. How epidemiology is used in each activity is described below.

Linking National or Regional Policy Initiatives with Local Health Systems

Government initiatives have attempted to improve the delivery of health care through the promotion of planning and the initiation of various funding mechanisms. Institutions, on the other hand, have directed their efforts to the planning of services for a defined population having the need for the services offered or the population contained within the geographic area traditionally served by the institution.

The reimbursement provisions for a patient's stay have changed over recent years from an "*a la carte*" payment program to a fixed-price orientation, from an "all you can charge" payment plan to one that places financial risk for the costs incurred firmly on the institution. Recently, this "bundling" concept has been extended to physician services in selected areas. A multitude of new organizations has been evolving at the same time and perhaps as a response to the new payment system. These organizations are designed to deliver patient care more efficiently than in the past and to increase the orientation of service delivery to the patient as a consumer. These HMOs, PPOs, home health care agencies, durable medical equipment firms, and outpatient surgery centers have been established to maximize both efficiency and effectiveness. They can also be characterized as a logical economic response to the regulation of inpatient care.

In conjunction with the developments discussed above, management techniques have been initiated to control costs by controlling service utilization. Patients are being encouraged to assume greater responsibility for personal actions that could negatively affect their health status by benefit modification, adding incentives for positive health behaviors, and supplementing incentives with health education. As a organization experiences changes in reimbursement provisions, it is necessary for the organization to assess carefully the relationships among the level of services provided, the needs of the target population and the expected outcomes from both provider- and patient-initiated actions. In other words, in a fixed-price environment, the breadth and intensity of services should be consistent with the expected effects on the patient's health status, not just the presenting complaint.

A population's need, both latent and observed, for medical and health care services, and the demand for these services, expressed or implied, can be incorporated into an epidemiologic model that accounts for such variables as population characteristics, disease trends, or geographic location. Epidemiology can provide institutional executives and their community leaders with a method for evaluating the impact of new reimbursement systems that link health status and financial incentives. The latter is particularly important because, in addition to HMOs, other institutions are entering into an increasing number of point-of-service contracts with large companies proposing to measure the value of health care expenditures through changes in mortality, morbidity, and lost work days as well as the effects of new practices or technologies on health care utilization and cost. These assessments, which are designed to influence a company's selection of a provider or system, are beginning to impact the manner in which health care services are being provided.

A prime example of this changing orientation to health care delivery can be found in the Rochester region of New York. Through the direct involvement of business, community organizations, and the provider community, population-based planning was used to promote efficiency and effectiveness of the health care system. Through the collaborative efforts of com-

Table 9.2. Selected Characteristics of the Rochester, New York, Hospital System Compared with New York State and U.S. Averages, 1991[a]

Area	Beds per thousand	Occupancy (percent)	Hospital cost per capita (dollars)	Hospital admissions per thousand per year	Full-time-equivalent staff per occupied bed
Rochester	3.18	87.8%	$775	103.4	3.28
New York State	4.14	85.9	1,064	112.7	3.74
U.S. average	3.73	66.7	811	109.5	4.20

[a]Source: Hall and Griner (1992).

munity leaders, a single plan was established as the principal health insurance carrier for the entire community. The population-based planning and monitoring encompassed by these efforts (as described in Chapters 4 and 5) resulted in the number of hospital beds per population being minimized (to 3.2 per 1000 residents) with the result that hospital occupancy was maintained at an 87.8% level. One areawide risk pool was created (enabling community rating) so that all employers paid the same rates for the same benefits, rendering health insurance more affordable and allowing more people to be covered. Population-based monitoring sought information regarding the cost, quality, and access to care. The results of this on-going initiative indicate that consumer satisfaction with the health care system is high (with 73% of plan members being satisfied or very satisfied), access is markedly better, and premiums and hospital costs are less than elsewhere (Leitman et al., 1993; Hall and Griner, 1993).

Various health care policies and regulations (e.g., state certificate of need laws, PL 92-603, PL 93-641) enacted over the past three decades have attempted to link national planning with local planning and delivery efforts. At the national level, epidemiologic data were used in conjunction with the objectives outlined in "Healthy People 2000" to identify population health needs that should be addressed by both government agencies and private groups (U.S. Department of Health and Human Services, 1990). Although health care organizations have only recently begun to incorporate epidemiologic information into their strategic planning process, increased use of such information is likely as more organizations experiment with the delivery of specialized services to a subsegment of their defined population. An organization, for example, may realize that it has a high concentration of elderly in its service area. Through focused epidemiologic research, the organization can develop a set of services to address the special needs of this group. The organization could also design health education programs to offer in conjunction with services to increase their attractiveness among targeted consumers. The organization may conclude that packaging acute, long-term and subacute services with preventive, home-health services and social services would be an ideal set of services to offer the elderly, if priced appropriately. In this example, epidemiologic methods can be applied to assess the special needs of the elderly and further the organization's commitment to deliver appropriate care in the most economical environment and in a manner consistent with the overt intention of assisting the elderly to remain healthy and socially productive members of the local society.

In the past, epidemiologic approaches have been underutilized because clinical leaders within institutions have lacked sufficient understanding of their value because of a paucity of valid and reliable localized epidemiologic information and the low priority placed on epidemiology by universities involved in health professional education. Obviously, if a health care system is to take more responsibility for a population's health status, then the professionals comprising that system must be educated in the didactic and practical aspects of population-based medicine. Changes in the educational curricula of health professionals and a refocusing of research efforts would certainly seem necessary.

Strategically Developing New Services or Planning Changes in Existing Ones

Given the movement toward assumption of risk for a defined population, executives of health services should be cognizant of changing trends in both the natural history of diseases affecting their populations and medical practices designed to influence these trends. In the past, services would be initiated or expanded based primarily on anticipated profitability. The expected impact of new or expanded services on a population's health status was a secondary consideration. For example, the profit factor has caused the number of cardiac surgery programs to increase despite lack of planning encompassing consideration of population characteristics associated with need. The same disregard of population factors has occurred in the development of such "high tech" services as magnetic resonance imaging (MRI). In some areas, the addition of MRI units has not resulted in measurable improvement in the health status of the affected population. However, inappropriate utilization (or overuse) of the technology in question has been observed (Swedlow *et al.*, 1992).

Normatively speaking, services should be equated first with need and then with economic effects since there should be a direct relationship between the efficiency of a service and its long-term costs and benefits. In other words, it may be appropriate to assess the quality of a service by utilizing both effectiveness and efficiency parameters since "more is not necessarily better." Epidemiology-based surveys like the SF-36 can measure the changes in the status of a population's health as a result of the delivery of services provided by a health care organization or system. Epidemiologic analysis can also be utilized in conjunction with economic techniques such as cost-benefit and cost-effectiveness studies. The purpose of such studies is to determine the efficiency of an organization's services based on assessment of the appropriateness of services and the resources consumed relative to health outcomes within the population served. By using an epidemiologic framework, resources could be more rationally distributed on a value-added basis to the organization's community. Costs, like health status, could be measured over longer time horizons to derive lifetime-expected expenditures for a desired health status. Thus, a community could avoid a proliferation of tertiary services that have been found to have only marginal effect on health. Community energy could be directed, instead, to the development of a continuum of services designed to care for individuals throughout their life. In this scenario, an organization could measure its effectiveness by analyzing how *few* inpatient days per 100,000 population are experienced by its community and the magnitude of decreases in the number of lost work days caused by diseases or illnesses compared to increases in ambulatory services. In the end, new or expanded services should not be introduced unless there is an expected economic and health status "return on investment" for the population in question.

Projecting the Human Resources Necessary to Provide Health Care to a Population

In spite of decades of public and private investment, shortages, excesses, and maldistribution of skilled health professionals can still be found depending on the geographic area being studied (U.S. Department of Health and Human Services, 1986). With opportunities to practice in many different settings, health professionals have rarely been beholden to a single organization. Now the prospect of integrated systems has simultaneously increased the need for both generalist and specialized talent to provide a comprehensive continuum of services to a defined population. The anticipated structural changes in health care could potentially exacerbate manpower deficits in certain areas. For example, the need has become especially acute for primary-care physicians to serve as gatekeepers of large populations in a managed care setting. There is also substantial demand for allied health professionals, particularly physical and occupational therapists, to provide rehabilitation services to the aging population. Regardless of the final configuration of health reform, a population's need for health care services may not be met if the required resources are not identified, planned for, or attained (Donabedian, 1973). New partnerships must be developed between health professional educational programs and integrated health service systems, and epidemiologic data should be utilized to describe needs and to project the human resources required to address these needs.

The changes affecting resource requirements are contributing to a need among providers for an everexpanding set of skills and knowledge base. Health care is more complex and scientific in nature than ever before. Yet, it continues to depend on the value of human service. Although a "spirit of service" may remain entrenched in the field and supersede most organizational or policy changes, what remains lacking is the recognition that a single science or language could bind the various health professionals to each other, their institution, and their community. In fact, continuing struggles among these parties who have an influence on an institution's sometimes conflicting objectives may cause a human service organization to forget that its primary concern is to improve the health status of the population it serves.

In order to determine the optimal provider configuration based on consideration of cost and patient outcomes, the consensus of a wide variety of professionals is necessary. Epidemiology represents a science that can promote a common perspective among professionals and generate projections of the need for institutional or clinical services. For example, when determining the manpower needs of a new ambulatory surgery unit, the analysis can be pursued from an epidemiologic perspective by assessing the problem in terms of *who, what, where,* and *when.* Answers should be found to these questions: *"Who should provide the patient care?" "What tasks are performed in the delivery of care? Where are they performed (in the preop, recovery, or postop setting)? When are they performed?"*

Epidemiologic measures can also be used to establish the staffing patterns within an institution. A standard ratio for the number of professionals per 1000 persons served could be utilized to determine the appropriate number of physicians and nurses required to provide services to a defined population. This approach could be used, for example, to plan women's and children's services designed to offer care by a mix of physicians, nurse midwives, and nurse practitioners in the hospital, outpatient, and home locations.

Monitoring Institutional Performance with Respect to Population Health Status

In order to continuously evaluate the performance of a health system with respect to population health status, certain organizational structures and functions must be in place. First, the organization must have a system of planning, management and evaluation that incorporates consideration of the natural history of the diseases associated with the organization's services. Planning for clinical service lines should be based on the incidence and prevalence of a specified disease or related diseases, the availability of professionals, and the appropriate location for service delivery (Fig. 9.1). Measuring the success of an organization's efforts should involve assessing if the health status of those provided services improves more than would be expected if the services were not made available.

The second requirement for monitoring patient outcomes is the operation of an information system that links management and clinical data. Real-time availability of information from relational data bases can be useful for combining and maintaining data from different sources (e.g., institutional, departmental, local health department) for the purpose of continuous monitoring of the population's health. These data are also essential in assessing an organization's performance relevant to the objectives of total quality management. Common epidemiologic measures of organizational performance that should routinely be assessed by the health care manager are displayed in Table 9.3.

Finally, a health care organization should have resources and a process for analyzing the effect of medical therapies, technology, and changes in organizational practices on the population's health. An epidemiology unit or research center may be charged with performing these analyses, provided that input from management and provider representatives is obtained. Clinical and administrative data could be used to predict the utilization of resources, the expected effect on the population, and the financial implications associated with the delivery of services.

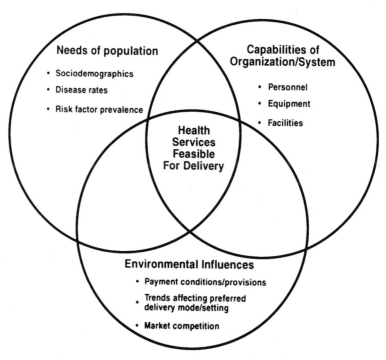

Figure 9.1.   Population-based health services delivery model.

Table 9.3. Epidemiologic Measures for Monitoring the Performance of Health Care Systems[a]

Mortality rates
    In-hospital overall, by procedure, by DRG, by clinical service
    Intensive care unit (SICU, NICU)
    Perioperative
    Cardiovascular disease
    Infant mortality
    Suicide
    Homicide
    Breast cancer
    Lung cancer
    Poisoning
Incidence (morbidity) rates
    Nosocomial infection overall, by service
    Adverse incidence (fall rates, medication error rates, etc.)
    Incidence of new cancer cases classified as "advanced"
    Tuberculosis
    Primary and secondary syphilis
    Measles
    Acquired immunodeficiency
    Hepatitis B
Prevalence rates of disease or risk factors
    Low birth weight
    No prenatal care during the first trimester
    Cigarette smoking
    Hypertension
    Hypercholesterolemia
    Obesity
Survival rates
    Cancer patient survival, by anatomic site and stage
    Patient and graft survival, by transplant procedure type
Other rates
    Pain control
    Cesarean section
    Vaginal birth after cesarean (VBAC) section
    Patient satisfaction with the organization, the environment, and services provided
    Unscheduled or unplanned readmission
    Canceled procedures
    Errors in patient identification
    Proportion of children 2 years of age who have been immunized with the basic series
    Proportion of women receiving a Papanicolaou smear at an interval appropriate for their age
    Proportion of women receiving a mammogram at an interval appropriate for their age

[a]Sources: Oleske (1993); The Governance Committee (1993a,b); Centers for Disease Control (1991).

Measuring the Success of Institutional Linkages and/or System Configurations to Effect Changes in the Health Status of the Population

An organization with an infrastructure for epidemiologic analysis will be able to mesh vertical (clinical service line) planning with the horizontal health needs of the population to create a model system designed to have positive health status impact. It will also be able to measure the effects of its interventions on the health of the population for which it claims responsibility by compiling data related to indicators of functional ability, morbidity, changes in life expectancy, quality of life, productivity, disability and death.

The organization must be cognizant of local, regional, and national health trends so that it can compare its impact with that achieved at various levels. In this way, the organization will be able to assess if its structural components and mode of operation are more or less adequate (based on consideration of the organization's ability to achieve better or less desirable results than other organizations or aggregations of these).

The expectations for a health care organization in a reformed health care environment is that it will be integrated (with adequate linkage between the components of a continuum of services), multisite, and capable of delivering services that are accessible and geographically well-distributed. However, an organization meeting these expectations will also be held accountable for achieving measurable change, in the intended direction, in the health status of the population it serves.

Conclusion

Regulators and planners have traditionally focused on population variables that were considered to be directly controlled or influenced by the patient and the health care system. There is considerable evidence that health care services have had a favorable impact on the populations served in terms of reducing mortality, in particular, from cancer, heart disease, infection, prematurity, and trauma (Goldberg *et al.*, 1986; Ornato *et al.*, 1985; Paneth *et al.*, 1981; Poikolainen and Eskola, 1986; Tabar *et al.*, 1985). Yet, supporters of health care reform argue that health status impact could be greater if health care organizations would more conscientiously assess population needs and offer specific services subject to certain constraints (e.g., economic and regulatory incentives, market conditions, and special characteristics of the populations in question). It has, in fact, already been demonstrated that a population's health status can be improved by decreasing preventable deaths and morbidity when appropriateness measures are linked to a provider's performance.

Who is to blame for the current unsatisfactory situation—the planners, institutional executives, physicians, government, the patients? All must share some of the responsibility. Without compliance to operational standards that can affect desirable health status changes, no system will be able to maximize its impact on the population served. Without coordination, public and private initiatives will fail to realize stated objectives to improve health. Without recognition of the strength of the interrelationships between and among characteristics of the population, their needs, and the configuration and delivery mode of the services designed to respond to defined needs, it is impossible to achieve the outcomes desired by patients and providers alike. After all, quality of care is related to the probability of attaining a desired outcome. Quality encompasses the provision of the appropriate level and mix of clinical services as well as the delivery of patient amenities in a "healing" environment. Unfortunately, we do not yet understand the true association between the process of care and the expected outcome. However, we do know that epidemiologic research can assist us in further exploring this relationship.

It is likely that the institutional executive in the future will be leading an effort designed to link providers across a variety of health settings with community-based services. Whether the services within this system will be provided by full-time, employed physicians or by a federation of independent practitioners is unclear. What is clear is the need to integrate objectives and align incentives such that organizations and their communities achieve a single-minded purpose—the provision of cost-beneficial services designed to improve the population's health status while decreasing both the unit and the lifetime costs of health care. To achieve anything less would be an abdication of the primary responsibility of a community organization. Epidemiologic methods should be utilized as tools for identifying, monitoring, and evaluating the results associated with this objective.

Case Studies

Case Study No. 1
Emergency Room and Hospital Resource Utilization

Dr. A. Robert Alexander, Chief of Medicine
Jokari Medical Center, USA

Dear Dr. Alexander:

This is just a note to let you know the status of the bed problem to date. The emergency room has continued to see many more patients than we ever imagined. Although the number of true emergencies is relatively low, the majority of the patients are presenting with minor ailments that could be treated by a private family physician, if they had one, or through one of the local clinics if they were open later into the evening or on weekends. The results is that these patients, although they certainly need to be seen by a professional, clog the emergency room and are forced to wait several hours as we treat the patients with life-threatening problems.

At the same time, the acutely ill patients must wait in the emergency room far too long while we locate a bed and make it available (have it cleaned and staffed). The problem here is that there never seems to be a bed available when we need one. In fact, the use of the hospital is such that, on occasion, we have had to resort to using hallways as staging areas until we can discharge patients or move them to other rooms.

To make the situation worse, consider the payment problem. Most of the emergency room visits are not being paid for, as these persons have inadequate or no insurance at all, and they certainly cannot afford to pay our charges from their personal incomes. The payment problem compounds if these persons require hospitalization. Health care has long since passed the time when it could be paid for out of one's disposable income.

I hope you will look into this situation and find some way we can do a better job of treating both our inpatients as well as our emergency room patients. There does not seem to be any rhyme or reason for the numbers of people using so many of our services. Then, when these patients are hospitalized, their lengths of stay are outside the parameters given to us by our various payers. Are we being inefficient? Perhaps. On the other hand, perhaps the patients have waited too long to see a physician and, thus, have many more complications than would normally be expected. Or, perhaps the patients don't have anyone to care for them at home so that discharge before the latter stages of their convalescence is not possible. Or, perhaps the patients just cannot afford our home health care services. Given the stress on our facilities and staff, I urge you to find a way to balance the needs of our patients with our available resources.

Sincerely yours,

Dr. Rebecca Michael
Director, Emergency Services

Ms. S. L. Berger, Hospital Director
Jokari Medical Center, USA

Dear Ms. Berger:

As you requested, I have attempted to resolve our constant shortage of beds through the means at my disposal. I have implemented split shifts of physicians and nurses, organized some of the patient care units into distinct geographic areas to care for patients of similar diseases, reorganized other units to allow hospitalization of a mix of patients, cross-trained staff to work on multiple units, extended the hours of the adult and pediatric clinics, and set up a triage area in the emergency room for more efficient after-hours care. Regardless of our actions, there seems to be no way to plan effectively for or project the number of people who will use our inpatient or outpatient services.

On any given day, we either see too many patients or not enough. We have applied all the traditional analytic techniques for smoothing out a demand curve, but none even comes close to providing us with a reasonable projection. And, once we hospitalize patients, their recovery period is not in line with their insurance benefits, if they have any insurance at all. Finally, our utilization management staff remind us that we should be discharging these patients to other types of more appropriate, less acute facilities. These patients do not have caregivers to provide assistance at home and home-bound services are not always available. In addition, the payment problem continues. We continue to attempt to reduce our expenses, but our inpatient and outpatient income does not even come close to covering our costs. Of course, we could streamline even more, but I am afraid of the gaps in service or the problems that would arise. As a last resort, we could always reduce the level of services that we provide our community.

If only we better understood the population we were serving, perhaps then we could do a better job of predicting their utilization, both initially and over the long run. We really need your help. I hope you can recommend an approach that we've not already used. We need to do a better job or providing our community with sorely needed health services.

Sincerely yours,

Dr. A. R. Alexander
Chief of Medicine

Q.1. What would you do to determine the current health status of the population served by the emergency room?

Q.2. What factors prompt utilization of the hospital's emergency room as a primary source of care?

Q.3. What could the hospital do to reduce unnecessary utilization of the emergency room?

Case Study No. 2
Poison Control Center

Austin Medical Center (AMC) provides poison information services to a population of seven million people located in the Northeastern portion of its state. The center is designated as the state's regional Poison Control Center. Telephone information services are provided by trained staff 24 hours per day, seven days per week.

Up until this year, the Poison Control Center received funding from a large, local philanthropic foundation. The foundation has changed its funding priorities and will no longer be a source of support for the Center.

Now AMC needs to reduce its operating expenses in order to compete more effectively for managed care contracts. One of the services it is considering eliminating is the Poison Control Center. With a budget exceeding $250,000, discontinuing this service would have a major impact on the hospital's cost per discharge.

Dr. Jacobson, Chief of Preventive Medicine, has expressed her disagreement with the proposed action of eliminating the Poison Control Center. She contends that the number of deaths from accidental poisoning has decreased significantly since initiation of the poison control program; data suggest that the results are especially notable for children under the age of 6 years. Thus, AMC has had a major effect on the health of the population by providing general information on poisoning, minimizing the effects after a poisoning incident, and minimizing disability from poisoning by its follow-up activity. "The social good of the Poison Control Center far exceeds its cost to AMC," she contends.

Q.1. What should the AMC Administration do with the recommendation to close the Poison Control Center?

Q.2. If the Poison Control Center is closed, what are the likely effects on the health status of the population served?

Case Study No. 3
Women's, Infants', and Children's Services

The William University Medical School utilizes Brown and Stein Hospitals for its teaching programs. Although medical students have an opportunity to take clerkships at either hospital, Brown is the larger and primary facility; consequently, most of the house officer programs are located there. In addition, students who receive guidance from the Medical School's faculty may rotate to Lee Regional Hospital, a quasipublic facility that is a primary provider of care to the indigent.

Through the development of the various clinical services, some programs are more (or less) prominent at each hospital. Over the years, the lack of interinstitutional cooperative planning has resulted in the duplication of expensive services at each facility. For example, full programs in obstetrics and pediatrics exist at both hospitals.

Through a special public–private partnership arrangement, an opportunity has been created to allow for cross-institutional planning under the aegis of the Medical School. Because the OB residency program has been under pressure from its accrediting agency to reduce the service load on the house officers and increase the time available for formal educational activities, OB was chosen as the pilot area for the new planning process. Although the labor and economic considerations certainly must be considered in the analysis, epidemiologic assessment of the needs of current and potential users of these services is warranted.

Q.1. What factors should be taken into consideration to assess the similarities/differences in the service populations of each hospital?

Q.2. What risk actors are prevalent in these populations that could affect the outcomes of newborn delivery?

Q.3. Propose epidemiologic measures to assess the effectiveness of the new plan on (1) organizational performance, (2) departmental performance, (3) normal deliveries, (4) high-risk deliveries, and (5) the prenatal program.

Q.4. Propose an epidemiologic study design to compare the two maternity centers with respect to the outcome measures you have proposed in response to Q.3.

Case Study No. 4
Indigent Care

The Lee Regional Hospital (LRH) has had a historic mission of serving the poor in the community. Within a six-county metropolitan area, it serves 2.5 million people, 14% of whom are uninsured. However, in the city the uninsured rate is 27%.

This 300-bed institution is funded by patient revenues, local governmental budget allocations, and an intergovernmental transfer payment (IGT). The IGT is predicated on the amount of money the local government allocates to LRH.

In the past 5 years, the amount of money made available by the city's mayor has decreased. Lee Regional Hospital has remained solvent only through special funding provided by the state. If Lee loses the city's funding entirely, the IGT will be forfeited as well. Lee will have to scale back substantially or close its doors. This situation poses a risk to the few remaining urban-based institutions that will have to bear the load of Lee's current patient care activities: 250,000 outpatient visits, 3000 obstetrical deliveries (many of them high-risk), 4000 medical–surgical admissions, and 50,000 emergency room visits.

The city is in the middle stage of development for a fully-capitated system. However, it will be several years before 40% of the population chooses such a capitated plan. Thus, while the poor must be cared for, volume remains the prevalent indicator for financial success; however, funds for indigent care are not readily available. All of this is occurring in a locale that is substantially overbedded (3.5 beds per 1000 population). A state-based health reform plan has been proposed, but state tax revenues are not projected to be great enough to cover all citizens for many years to come.

Your consulting firm has been asked to work with a special committee of the LRH Board to determine its future.

Q.1. What would be your first step?

Q.2. How would you determine the general and special health needs of Lee's service area population?

Q.3. How would you determine if health care could be handled in a setting other than the hospital?

Q.4. Can an incentive system based on managed care provisions be established to link responsibility for health status with financial risk, and would such a system be supported by the state and city governments?

References

Centers for Disease Control, 1991, Consensus set of health status indicators for the general assessment of community health status—United States, *Morbid. Mortal. Weekly Rev.* **40:**449–451.

Donabedian, A., 1973, *Aspects of Medical Care Administration: Specifying Requirements for Healthcare*, Published for the Commonwealth Fund by Harvard University Press, Cambridge.

Goldberg, R. J., Gore, J. M., Alpert, J., and Dalen, J. E., 1986, Recent changes in attack and survival rates of acute myocardial infarction (1975 through 1981), *JAMA* **255:**2774–2779.

The Governance Committee, 1993a, *Life of Fire: The Coming of Public Scrutiny of Hospital and Health System Quality*, Advisory Board Company, Washington, DC.

The Governance Committee, 1993b, *Vision of the Future*, Advisory Board Company, Washington, DC.

Hall, W. J., and Griner, P. F., 1993, Cost-effective health care: The Rochester experience, *Health Affairs* **12:**58–69.

Health Care Financing Administration, 1992, Medicare Hospital Information, U.S.G.P.O., Washington, DC.

Kaufman, A., and Waterman, R. E., eds., 1993, *Health of the Public, a Challenge to Academic Health Centers: Strategies for Reorienting Academic Health Centers Toward Community Health Needs*, Health of the Public Program, San Francisco.

Knaus, W. A., Wagner, D. P., Draper, E. A., Zimmerman, J. E., Bergner, M., Bastos, P. J., Sirio, C. A., Murphy, D. J., Lotring, T., Damiano, A., and Harrell, F., Jr., 1991, The Apache III prognostic system. Risk prediction of hospital mortality for critically ill hospitalized adults, *Chest* **100:**1619–1636.

Leitman, R., Blendon, R. J., Taylor, H., Kramer, E., and Klein, D., 1993, Rochester, New York: A model for health reform, *J. Am. Health Policy* **3:**49–54.

Lewin, L. S., 1993, Toward competitive advantage: Restructuring linkages and alliances, presentation to the Premier Health Alliance, Fairfax, VA, August.

Oleske, D. M., 1993, Linking the delivery of healthcare to service population needs: The role of the epidemiologist on the healthcare management team, *J. Health Admin. Ed.* **11:**531–539.

Ornato, J. P., Craren, E. J., Nelson, N. M., and Kimball, K. F., 1985, Impact of improved emergency medical services and emergency trauma care on the reduction in mortality from trauma, *J. Trauma* **25:**575–579.

Paneth, N., Kiely, J. L., Wallenstein, S., Marcus, M., Pakter, J., and Susser, M., 1981, Newborn intensive care and neonatal mortality in low-birth-weight infants: A population study, *N. Engl. J. Med.* **305:**489–494.

Poikolainen, K., and Eskola, J., 1986, The effect of health services on mortality: Decline in death rates from amenable and non-amenable causes in Finland, 1969–81, *Lancet* **1:**199–202.

Sedlow, A., Johnson, G., Smithline, N., and Milstein, A., 1992, Increased costs and rates of use in the California workers' compensation system as a result of self-referral by physicians, *N. Engl. J. Med.* **327:**1502–1506.

Tabar, L., Gad, A., Holmberg, L. H., Ljungquist, U., Fagerberg, C. J. G., Baldetorp, L., Grontoft, O., Lundstrom, B., Manson, J. C., Eklund, G., Day, N. E., and Pettersson, F., 1985, Reduction in mortality from breast cancer after mass screening with mammography, *Lancet* **8433:**829–832.

U.S. Department of Health and Human Services, 1986, *Fifth Report to the President and Congress on the Status of Health Personnel in the United States*, National Technical Information Services, Springfield, VA.

U.S. Department of Health and Human Services, 1990, *Healthy People 2000: National Health Promotion and Disease Prevention Objectives*, DHHS Pub. No. (PHS) 91-50213, U.S. Government Printing Office, Washington, DC.

10

Epidemiology and the Public Policy Process

Iris R. Shannon

The long-standing philosophical debate regarding government's role in health policy has heightened since the election of President Clinton. However, in reality, all levels of government have been significantly involved in health, especially, public health agencies. Governmental public health is responsible for assessment of population health needs, assurance that the services for the protection and promotion of health needed by a population are available, and development of policies to protect health. Epidemiologic methods and data are required to support each of these core public health functions. For this reason, public health is used as the contextual framework for illustrating the interrelationship between epidemiology and the public policy process.

Presented in this chapter are definitions and descriptions of terms and concepts associated with the policy process. Emphasis is given to the influence of epidemiology on the policy process. Case studies at the end of the chapter allow practice in applying epidemiologic concepts to the policy process.

A Contextual Framework for the Relationship between Policy and Epidemiology: Public Health

Definitions and parameters of public health used in this chapter are those published in a 1988 report from the Institute of Medicine, National Academy of Science (IOM/NAS). The report defines the "mission" of public health as **fulfilling society's interest in assuring conditions in which people can be healthy with contributions toward this end made by governmental and nongovernmental agencies**. The parameters for achieving this mission are the three core interdependent functions of governmental public health specified in the report: (1) assessment of the health needs of populations including the systematic collection,

Iris R. Shannon   Departments of Community Health Nursing and Health Systems Management, Rush University, Chicago, Illinois 60612.

Epidemiology and the Delivery of Health Care Services: Methods and Applications, edited by Denise M. Oleske. Plenum Press, New York, 1995.

analysis, and distribution of information on morbidity, mortality, and disability; (2) assurance that services to promote and protect the health of the public are provided directly or through others; and (3) development of policy for the protection of health grounded in scientific knowledge that will serve the public interest. To accomplish its mission, public health focuses on organized community efforts aimed at the prevention of disease and promotion of health and enlists the cooperation of governmental, private, and voluntary agencies in support of that goal. Epidemiology is identified in the IOM/NAS (1988) report as the science that links the multiple disciplines involved in the coordinated public health effort. Epidemiology provides a means of identifying the populations at risk for health problems, understanding causes of health problems, and suggests approaches for prevention that could be undertaken by public health and other agencies.

As mentioned above, one of the core functions of public health is policy formulation. Governmental public health develops policies based upon the assessment of health needs of the population. Epidemiology is a fundamental science that provides input into that function. Public health as the framework for this discussion represents policy in which epidemiology is used for decision making, and in which the public, through the political process, can participate in all aspects of the process.

Throughout the next decade, public health and public health policy will be guided by the National Health Objectives that are contained within the document, *Healthy People 2000* (U.S. Department of Health and Human Services, 1991). The objectives are organized according to broad categories that reflect the mission of public health: health promotion, health protection, preventive services, and surveillance, and data systems. Health promotion objectives concern those issues pertaining to life-styles that individuals control, such as nutrition, substance abuse, physical fitness, and for which educational and community based programs can be effective. Health protection objectives are related to environmental or regulatory measures that address large groups. Preventive objectives concern those activities provided in clinical settings and include screening, counseling, immunization, and chemoprophylaxis. Surveillance and data systems objectives pertain to the collection of public health data to understand the health status of populations and to evaluate programs and policies that emphasize the need for cooperation at all levels of government. A sample of the objectives is displayed in Table 10.1. For the most part, the objectives were based on epidemiologic data and studies concerning the occurrence, distribution and risk factors of disease, disability, and premature death in the population. In addition, each area contains objectives that have implications for "special populations." Special populations have been identified through epidemiologic data that indicate that they experience above-average incidences of death, disease, and disability. These populations include people with low incomes, some racial and ethnic minority groups, and people with disabilities.

It is important to understand that the National Health Objectives for the year 2000 are not public policy. They are described by the U.S. Department of Health and Human Services (1991) as opportunities and challenges for prevention, health promotion, and health protection. Specifically, they provide national direction for resource allocation and for the organization and delivery of public health activities. Therefore, it becomes particularly important for health professionals and students to understand the epidemiologic basis for the objectives and their application to local populations. Implementation guidelines for attaining the National Health Objectives before the next decade have been made available through the American Public Health Association (APHA) in cooperation with the Department of Health and Human Services and other interested groups (APHA, 1991).

Table 10.1. Selected National Health Promotion and Disease Prevention Objectives Pertaining to Violent and Abusive Behavior[a]

Health status objectives
7.1   Reduce homicides to no more than 7.2 per 100,000 people.

Homicide Rate (per 100,000)	1987 Baseline	2000 Target
7.1a Children ages 3 and younger	3.9	3.1
7.1b Spouses ages 15–34	1.7	1.4
7.1c Black men ages 15–34	90.5	72.4

Risk reduction objectives
7.10   Reduce by 20% the incidence of weapon-carrying by adolescents age 14 through 17.

Services and protection objectives
7.12   Extend protocols for routinely identifying, treating, and properly referring suicide attempters, victims of sexual assault, and victims of spouse, elder, and child abuse to at least 90% of hospital emergency departments.

[a]Source: Department of Health and Human Services (1990).

Public Policy: An Interactive Process

A **public policy** is a law or other actions legitimized by government officials, including legislators and judges, and involves decisions regarding the allocation of resources to accomplish a stated goal or purpose. Public policy is a response to demands made by an assortment of organizations and individuals. An important characteristic of public policy is that it includes outputs or what must be actually implemented and evaluated.

The **public policy process** is usually highly interactive and includes the following elements:

1. **Problem identification** defines the nature of the health care issue and who is affected.
2. **Formulation** utilizes epidemiologic data and studies, expert discussions, anecdotes, public opinions, and published viewpoints.
3. **Implementation** is the change directed by rules and regulations, or allocation of resources that follows a policy mandate.
4. **Evaluation** assesses the outcomes, including both costs and effects, of policy implementation and determines the degree to which the results of the program matched the anticipated goal.

The policy process is congruent with the nation's political and economic belief systems and provides the public opportunity to participate directly or indirectly in the process. When the policy process is interactive and open, input of the public and epidemiologic data can be used in any of the elements. However, when the policy process is closed, policy outcomes are more likely to reflect the values and preferences of an official elite. Limiting public input may also limit public support and funding.

The Interrelationship between Epidemiology and Public Policy

Support of policy makers, health professionals, and the public for policies that impact the public's health is influenced, in part, by the strength of the scientific evidence presented. Terris (1985) discussed the value of epidemiology in the policy process:

> Epidemiology, the study of the health of human populations, is by definition a social science. Its theory and practice have been profoundly influenced by society—by economic, social and political developments. Conversely, epidemiology has become a powerful force in the evolution and transformation of human populations and their social organization. (p. 15)

Terris posited that the powerful impact epidemiology has had on the improvement of health status of human populations resulted from applying appropriate methodological epidemiologic tools to understanding effects of social, environmental, and occupational conditions. Epidemiologists have provided the reasoning upon which most health policy is based and the bases for "powerful weapons to prevent many of the major causes of illness, disability, and death" (p. 29). Specifically, epidemiologic data and methods are used in the policy process to:

1. Prioritize health problems.
2. Assist in the planning and improvement of health services.
3. Monitor policy effectiveness in terms of changes in the rates of occurrence of new problems and in the rates of mortality.
4. Identify risk factors that effect the health and well-being of populations, particularly of vulnerable populations.
5. Aid in choosing among alternative policies and allocating resources.

This interrelationship between epidemiology and public policy is conceptualized in Fig. 10.1. However, one must keep in mind that this schematic does not reflect the total policy process.

Examples of public policies that have utilized epidemiology are provided. One example of a public policy concerns injury prevention. Injuries are a major public health problem according to epidemiologic data and were the fourth leading cause of death in 1991 (National Center for Health Statistics, 1993a). One of the priority areas of the Injury Prevention Council is the reduction of fire fatalities (Hemenway, 1991). Botkin (1988) in describing the epidemiology of fire injuries reported that as much as half of the deaths from fire injuries are attributable to cigarettes. Additionally, two-thirds of these are associated with intoxicated smokers, rendering prevention, through behavior modification or education, less likely to have immediate wide-spread effectiveness. Design modifications of cigarettes in laboratory studies have been shown to reduce ignition potential of cigarettes without elevating the inhalation of toxic compounds they presently represent. With epidemiologic analysis, coupled with laboratory studies, public health advocacy, and cooperation among professionals, government, and the industry, the Fire-Safe Cigarette Act of 1987 was passed. The intent of this policy was to put in place national standardized testing procedures for ignition propensity of cigarettes. A Technical Study Group created by Congress determined that a fire-safe cigarette was technically feasible. Congress subsequently passed the Fire-Safe Cigarette Act of 1990 ordering the Consumer Product Safety Commission to oversee the establishment of federal testing procedures for fire-safe cigarettes. With a standard test in place at the national level, the likelihood of states mandating the fire-safe cigarette is increased. In addition, this increases the probability of product liability suits against companies who do not produce fire-safe cigarettes (Hemen-

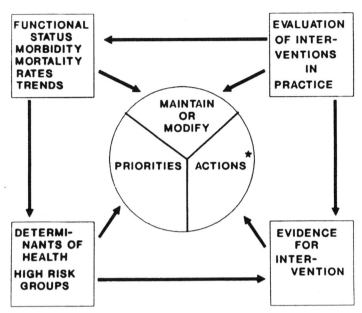

Figure 10.1. Intersections of epidemiology and public policy, from development of health-related information to action and evaluation. * Legislative, regulatory, and programmatic. Reprinted from Shapiro (1991) with permission of The Johns Hopkins University School of Hygiene and Public Health, copyright, 1991.

way, 1991). Subsequent policy initiatives to require manufacturers to comply with fire safety standards are being examined.

The second example concerns federal policy regarding immunizations. In 1989–1990, the nation experienced the greatest number of measles cases in more than a decade. Profound differences by age and race with respect to measles incidence were observed (Fig. 10.2). Low immunization levels were a major reason for the outbreak, particularly in inner cities, with less than 65% of 2-year-olds being immunized. Black and Hispanic children were found to have lower immunization levels than white children (Gindler *et al.*, 1992). This epidemiologic data provided the basis for the Comprehensive Child Immunization Act of 1993. The intent of this policy included: funding for universal purchase of vaccine for all children, public and provider education, community outreach, the extension of hours at local health departments, and the establishment of an immunization registry that would help ensure that children receive vaccines at the appropriate time.

Epidemiology has also had input into the formulation of social policy, which is a form of public policy. Social policy, as public policy, influences health because of its impact on social and environmental management. Increasingly, the health consequences of social problems are being identified by epidemiologic studies. Among the most devastating social problems is poverty because of strong epidemiologic evidence for its association with increased morbidity and mortality rates. Particularly affected are: diabetes and heart disease rates; prevalence of risk factors known to be associated with high morbidity and mortality rates, such as low birth weight, a correlate of infant mortality; and environments high in lead concentrations, which is associated with impaired mental and physical development (Nersesian *et al.*, 1985; Haan *et al.*,

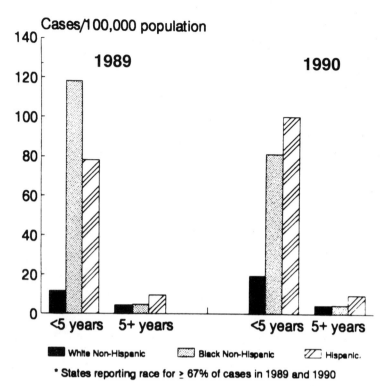

Figure 10.2. Measles attack rates by race/ethnicity and age in 22 states, 1989 and 1990. Reprinted from Gindler *et al.* (1992) with permission from The Johns Hopkins University School of Hygiene and Public Health, copyright, 1992.

1987; Evans *et al.*, 1987; McCord and Freeman, 1990; Boring *et al.*, 1992; Rowland, 1994). The bulk of those living in poverty represent four groups: children, single mothers, the aged, and the disabled, each of which are expected to increase in numbers (Najam, 1993). Lashof (1992) reports that the number of American children in poverty were 13 million in 1990 and are projected to reach 14.8 million by the year 2000. The absence or inadequate presence of social determinates to support good health outcomes become measures of populations at risk. For example, Wagner (1988), characterized infant mortality as a social problem with health consequences. As one response to this problem, federal policy provided the funds to initiate the Healthy Start Program. The Healthy Start Program is a comprehensive initiative involving nursing, social services, and case management to provide well-baby, well-child, and maternity services to low-income women with the goal of reducing infant mortality. Therefore, cities and regions with persistently high infant mortality rates including Washington, D.C., Chicago, Detroit, Cleveland, Milwaukee, Gary, Indianapolis, and others were targeted sites for this program. Infant mortality rates for the years 1986–1990 reported in Chicago, one of the program sites, showed a decline since the city's participation in that program (16.5 deaths under one year of age per 1000 live births in 1986; 16.6 in 1987; 15.2 in 1988; 17.0 in 1989; and 15.5 in 1990) providing some evidence of the program's impact (City of Chicago, 1991). Epidemiologic data, in particular infant mortality rates, will be used to monitor Healthy Start's efficacy.

Epidemiologic data have continued to be a primary source of information for policy makers to identify health threats to populations and to develop legislative responses to such threats. Responses are usually targeted to those populations at greatest risk of disease, disability, and premature death.

Discussions regarding health care reform reflect the dynamic relationship between epidemiology and health care policy. Health care reform is being driven by a number of factors, including increasing health care costs and percentage of the gross domestic product devoted to health care; the 35 million Americans, mainly workers and their families, reported to be uninsured; and the additional millions reported to be underinsured (Himmelstein et al., 1992). Absence or lack of third-party coverage for health care often results in more serious health problems and more costly treatment. The Robert Wood Johnson Foundation (RWJF) (1991), in their analysis of the uninsured, reported that the health care costs of the uninsured and underinsured are subsumed by higher taxes, cost-shifting medical care charges, and insurance premiums.

Himmelstein and Woolhandler (1994) reminded readers that the rise of national health costs were in spite of 20 years of cost-containment policies. Acknowledging that the United States spends more on health care than any other nation, they offered the following predictions: costs will exceed 14.4% of the Gross National Product (GNP) to about $900 billion in 1993 and 18.1% of the GNP ($1.74 trillion) by the year 2000.

Most states have organized health programs stimulated by the need to increase access to care. The much publicized Oregon approach involved the community in determining what services would be available in that state's program. Kitzhaber (1990–1991) described the prioritizing of health services as a process that included public input through hearings held around the state. Another method used in Oregon was a formula "that considers the benefit likely to result from each procedure, the duration of that benefit and the cost involved" (p. 62). To determine what efficacious measures should be available in the state's program, opinions of physicians were sought and the literature reviewed to determine the effectiveness and efficiency of specific procedures. In essence, the list, upon which decisions would be made primarily reflected efficacious procedures based on epidemiologic investigation.

An important consideration in the debate of the role of the government in health policies concerns the impact of existing policies such as Medicare and Medicaid. Medicare is an example of a public policy that provides health care to persons aged 65 and over and by doing so generates revenue for hospitals, home health agencies and health care providers. The American Association of Retired Persons, representing a very large constituency of Medicare users, keeps their members informed about policy changes and the political processes surrounding those changes. The organization is considered by politicians and others interested in health coalitions and networks as an effective force and important in promoting political action.

Health policy is not only developed, implemented, and evaluated in an interactive process but one that is enigmatic, and responsive to scientific, political, and market forces. Governmental public health, in fulfilling functions of assessment, policy development, and assurance, is dependent on epidemiology to provide a basis for sound decision making. In our democratic and pluralistic society, the evolution of any national health policy attempting to address access, cost control, funding, universality, comprehensiveness, equity and quality, must reflect input from the public. In addition, providers and producers of health care as well as health care advocates are major contributors to the policy process. Political processes facilitate education regarding population needs and preferences, stimulate and influence public support, and provide opportunities for consensus building.

Ethical Considerations of Policy Decisions and Their Relationship to Epidemiologic Data

Policy decisions will be influenced by ethical and ideological frameworks in which issues of fairness, equity and social justice* are raised. Thus, ethical concerns questions arise in the policy process. Given that resources are finite, epidemiology can provide objective data needed for debate and clarification of distributional issues.†

According to Stiller (1987), one dimension of an ethical problem is manifested when the effects of an action may put others at risk, harm others, lead to a violation of rights, or have other ethical implications. In health care, when disparity in the health status is detected, an ethical concern is triggered. Causes of this disparity may emerge because of how services are distributed, the evenness of access to care, and the quality of care. For example, the disparities in health status between minority and nonminority populations in the United States have been the subject of extensive physiological and sociological studies. Two epidemiologic measures are useful for assessing this disparity. One measure is **life expectancy**. Of concern is the persistent wide gap in life expectancy between blacks and whites (Fig. 10.3). The other measure is **excess risk**, which is the absolute difference between two measures of risk. Although either incidence or mortality rates can be used to compute excess risk, excess mortality is the measure typically used for health policy purposes. To reduce the disparity among population subgroups, the strategy is to identify the leading causes of death responsible for contributing to the differences. Using data from Fig. 10.4, the excess death rate for heart disease among those 45 to 64 years of age among blacks relative to whites is 182 per 100,000

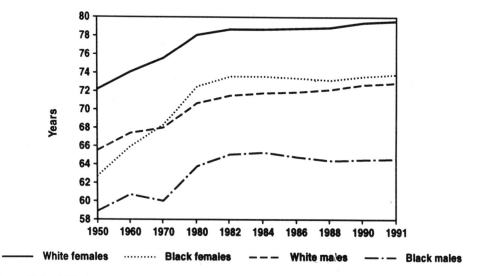

Figure 10.3. Life expectancy at birth by race and gender, United States, 1950–1991. Source: National Center for Health Statistics (1993c).

*Within a public health framework, social justice is the use of resources so that preventable death and disability are minimized (Hanlon and Pickett, 1984).
†The costs and benefits associated with the distribution of goods and services are determined by society. Different theories influence distributional decisions made by society, e.g., entitlement, utilitarian, maximum, or egalitarian theories (Stanhope and Lancaster, 1988).

(426 per 100,000, blacks, minus 289 per 100,000, whites). This means that 182 more deaths in 100,000 persons are occurring among blacks than whites from heart disease. Both epidemiologic measures suggest that there may be inequities in the distribution, access, or quality of health care resources attributable to current policies that need to be corrected.

The complexities involved in any discussion regarding ethics and health care cannot be addressed in this brief chapter. Literature regarding ethics in health care has increased over the years and should be explored by the reader for a more in-depth discussion of the contemporary issues involved in ethical decision making. One such report from the Institute of Medicine, National Academy of Sciences (1981) concluded that there was considerable evidence that racial and ethnic factors were associated with less-good care for minorities and that the average need for medical care among these groups was greater than for whites. In a statement of ethical concerns, the Report of the National Leadership Commission on Health Care (1989) established guidance for the examination of such issues:

> Since health care is a universal need essential for people to function in society, it follows that society has an obligation to provide for access to an adequate level of care for all its people. No society can be healthy if its members are not healthy. (p. xxxiii)

> Since resources for health care are finite, major moral issues arise over the allocation of resources between health and other social goods such as education, security, and housing. Similarly, allocating resources among health care needs also raises ethical issues concerning primary versus tertiary care, caring for the young versus the elderly and prevention versus cure. (p. xxxvi)

The Commission recognized that, in a democratic society, it is imperative to have public participation in the solutions that will protect the common interest. Governmental public health is representative of a public interest approach and, as indicated earlier, the context for this discussion.

Dougherty (1988) reminds us that until America has a health policy that establishes and defines health care as a universal right, the questions for public debate will continue to include: "Do all Americans have a right to health care?" If yes, "To what kinds of health care do Americans have a right? To how much care do they have a right? Who is duty bound to provide this care? How is it to be delivered and paid for? (p. 23)."

Although data support the continuing improvement of the nation's health, analysis of the data indicates certain groups in the population such as African-Americans, other ethnic minorities, and those in poverty, are not benefiting as much as others from these gains. In 1989, only 43.5% of the households in poverty were covered by Medicaid (the state and federal government program designed to provide health care for the poor). These issues raise distributional questions regarding how resources are allocated.

Issues of access and equity are predominate in national discussions surrounding health care reform. Epidemiologic data provide participants in policy debates explanations of disease, its prevention, and its variability among populations.

Summary

The concepts discussed in this chapter are not meant to be inclusive of the many that impact the policy process. This author agrees with those who acknowledge that specific medical procedures and the expansion of medical services have had little effect on the overall health of populations. But rather, information and behavioral changes stimulated by the enactment of policies based on epidemiologic data have contributed greatly to the prevention

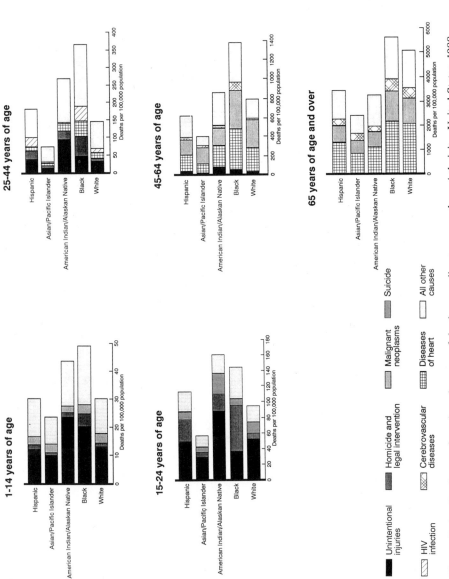

Figure 10.4. Death rates for selected causes of death, according to age and race/ethnicity, United States, 1988. Reprinted from Fingerhut and Makuc (1993), Mortality among minority populations in the United States, *Am. J. Pub. Health*, Vol. 82, No. 8, p. 1169, with permission from the *American Journal of Public Health*, copyright 1992.

of disease and disability. However, not all population groups have experienced the same improvements in health. The reasons for this disparity are complex; however, the challenge for the nation is to reduce the risks among groups in our society who are experiencing excess health risks. Public policies targeting disparities among population groups must be based on sound epidemiologic data and must have the political support necessary for success. Health care managers and health care professionals are key members of the community able to interpret to policy makers and the public the need and relationship of proposed policies to the health of the community. The translation of epidemiologic data is a critical component in the debate. Data are needed for sound decision making in public policy and for information that will educate the public and professions. In essence, it is critical in the resolution of what is currently characterized as the crisis in health care.

Case Studies

Case Study No. 1
Assessment of Selected National Health Program Legislative Proposals

As an organization whose members are mainly health professionals from varied disciplines and levels, and persons interested in public health issues, APHA has been taking positions on public health issues since 1872. In order for resolutions and position papers to become Association policy, they must go through a prescribed process that includes acceptable evidence of sound scientific principles, successful public hearings at Annual membership meetings and acceptance by the Association's Governing Council. Nationally, over 50,000 health workers are represented by APHA and the views and cooperation of the Association are sought by and shared with policy makers at national, state, and local levels. The largest affiliate groups of APHA are the autonomous state public health associations who, through their memberships and contacts, provide opportunity for effective involvement in the policy process. Because of the public health orientation of APHA, epidemiologic studies and approaches are frequently used to substantiate policy.

A set of Association principles relative to a national health approach was seen as necessary given the continuing absence of a national health policy and the increasing public interest in the development of such a policy. Using content analysis as a method, APHA's principles were extracted from existing Association policies. These principles are used to measure the congruence of proposed national health care reform legislation to APHA's policies embodied in the principles. The thirteen principles included in the process include: (1) universal coverage; (2) comprehensive benefits; (3) elimination of financial barriers; (4) equitable financing; (5) public accountability mechanisms and a major role for governmental agencies; (6) quality and efficiency assurances; (7) payment mechanisms; (8) ongoing planning and evaluation with consumer and provider participation; (9) disease prevention and health promotion; (10) education and training of health workers; (11) affirmative action for health workers; (12) non-discrimination in service delivery; and, (13) consumer education.

Q.1. Given the above principles, discuss how the effectiveness of a national health plan may be evaluated using epidemiologic data.

Case Study No. 2
Infant Mortality among African-Americans

Gains in knowledge and technology and socioeconomic conditions have contributed significantly to the reduction of infant mortality over the last 35 years. The rate has decreased from 30 deaths per 1000 live births in 1950 to 9.7 per 1000 live births in 1989. One of the national health objectives for the year 2000 is to reduce infant mortality in the United States to seven deaths per 1000 live births. Epidemiologic analyses indicate that the infant mortality rate among African-Americans is twice that among whites. This disparity is strongly associated with low birth weight (infants weighing less than 2,500 g or 5.5 pounds at birth)—a condition influenced by physiological, sociological, demographic, and behavioral factors. Efforts to reduce low-birth-weight problems have met with limited success. Infants who have been compromised before birth by drugs, AIDS, or other maternal conditions are at increased risk of low birth weight and associated illness, disability, and premature death.

Several maternal factors are identified with low birth weight, including age (over 35 years), race (African-Americans are at the highest risk), poverty, marital status (unmarried), low educational achievement, poor weight gain during pregnancy, poor nutrition, smoking, substance abuse, multiple gestation pregnancy, and history of a previous low-birth-weight infant. Improved access to prenatal care increases opportunities for reduction of low-birth-weight babies. Poverty, disproportionately experienced in African-American populations, contributes to poor health outcomes. The excess infant deaths among African-Americans, as a continuing disparity, represent an ethical dilemma.

Governments at all levels have funded comprehensive programs for populations at risk of poor pregnancy outcomes. One such program is the State of Illinois' Families with a Future program (Infant Mortality Reduction Initiative). In place since 1985, this comprehensive approach included family-focused health, social, and educational services, community management and control, case finding, case management, and emphasized prevention and health maintenance. A report on infant mortality released by the Chicago Department of Health (1993) indicates that African-American infant mortality rate is declining in Chicago, but it remains twice the rate of white infant mortality. Comparing the years 1988 to 1992, African-American and white infant mortality rates per 1000 live births were respectively 21.1 and 9.9 in 1988, 23.3 and 11.6 in 1989, 23.1 and 8.9 in 1990, 22.4 and 9.0 in 1991 and 19.3 and 8.1 in 1992. Data in 1992 represent a reduction in Chicago's infant mortality rate per 1000 live births from 15.1 in 1991 to 13.3 in 1992. Although the disparity between African-American and white infant mortality has decreased somewhat, African-American infant mortality rate remains almost twice the rate of white infant mortality. Distributional solutions such as those that consider quality education, full employment, adequate day care, national health program, and affordable housing are just a few of the approaches that could reduce infant mortality and improve the quality of life for Americans who are identified in the national health objectives for the year 2000 as "special populations."

Q.1. Propose an epidemiologic study to identify new risk factors for infant mortality.

Q.2. Discuss the evaluation of a program designed to reduce a community's infant mortality.

Q.3. Describe how the effectiveness of this program may be addressed using epidemiologic methods.

Case Study No. 3
Women, Infants and Children (WIC) Program

Voices for Illinois Children (1992) included a report on the Women, Infants, and Children (WIC) food supplemental program. The focus of the report was the underfunding of this and other programs by the Illinois General Assembly although WIC saves Illinois tax payers money in the long run. The WIC program was created in the 1970s to provide nutritious foods, nutritional information, and access to health care for low-income pregnant women, new mothers, and children under five years old.

According to the report, scientific data support that good nutrition during a women's pregnancy increases her chance of delivering a healthy, full-term baby and results in the reduction of infant mortality, premature births and low-birth-weight babies.

Studies have also shown WIC to be cost effective. For example for every dollar spent on prenatal care, up to three dollars were saved in hospital costs for low-birth-weight babies. According to *Voices*, "despite the program's proven success and cost-effectiveness, a lack of funding keeps approximately half of the eligible women and children in Illinois from participating in WIC" (Corrigan, 1992).

The Illinois General Assembly cut $5.8 million in state funding for WIC for the 1993 fiscal year. Although 210,000 women and children participated in the WIC program during 1992, it was estimated that twice that number of women and children are eligible. The State was reported to have contributed $5.8 million of the $82.7 million spent on WIC. The remainder of the funds were federal. Although the federal funds for FY 93 are expected to increase to between $85.9 and $90 million, the state's elimination of its contribution will reduce the number of new families added to the program. The WIC programs are vital because they also facilitate childhood immunizations and referrals for other needed services.

Q.1. What type of epidemiologic data could be used to persuade legislators about the efficacy of WIC in order to stimulate the restoration of funding?

Case Study No. 4
The Resurgence of Tuberculosis

Tuberculosis was once considered a disease that had the potential for eradication. However, it has reemerged in the 1990s as a formidable communicable disease complicated by the rise in drug-resistant tuberculosis cases (Shubert, 1993). The problem is further compounded by the epidemic nature of human immunodeficiency virus (HIV). The disease results in damaged immune systems and is associated with immense social problems such as drug abuse, homelessness, and poverty—particularly among racial and ethnic minorities in poor urban areas. Since tuberculosis is a reportable disease, the Centers for Disease Control receive information on all new cases from health departments. Gittier (1994) reports that beginning in the 1950s to 1985, the number of new cases of tuberculosis in the United States had been on the decline. The lowest rate of 9.3 per 100,000 population (22,201 cases) was reported in 1985; however, by 1992, 26,673 cases had been reported representing a rate of 10.5 per 100,000 population. In 1992, New York City had the highest rate of 52.0 per 100,000 population (3811 cases) with Central Harlem reporting 256 cases (240.2 per 100,000 population).

Multidrug-resistant tuberculosis outbreaks have occurred in institutional settings such as hospitals, jails, and prisons and involved tuberculosis patients, health care providers, inmates, and guards. Large cities, because of their population density and concentrations of poor and minority groups, have reported increase incidence of the disease. A breakdown in the "public health infrastructure" was associated with insufficient resources for tuberculosis control from federal, state, and local sources over an extended period of time. Infrastructure problems are also attributed to a dearth of public health workers with tuberculosis expertise, separation of public health functions resulting in fragmentation of services and lack of effective relationships between the public and private health sectors. The increase in immigration from countries where tuberculosis is prevalent has been associated with the "upsurge" of cases reported after 1985. One study reported that 27.3% of the reported cases involved foreign-born persons who had been in the United States 5 years or less.

Government has responsibility for enacting and enforcing tuberculosis control laws. However, the primary public health goals in the control of tuberculosis were described by Gittier as three pronged: (1) finding and treating active cases of tuberculosis; (2) finding latent tuberculous infections and preventing the progression of the disease; and (3) preventing the spread of the disease. The failure of tuberculosis patients to adhere to a treatment program is "a chief cause of the development of drug-resistant strains of TB" (p. 118). Given the high risk of tuberculosis among urban poor who are disproportionately represented by minority groups, noncompliance may be a function of barriers related to their socioeconomic status. Many approaches have been developed that consider such barriers. For example, one approach is offering food and clothing as an incentive and another program presently being used by several urban health departments, is directly observed therapy (DOT). The core of the latter program is to observe the patient's taking of the medications. "Patients may go to hospitals or clinics for DOT; alternatively, DOT may take place in a patient's home, workplace, or other locations where the patient is to be found" (p. 120).

Public policy issues are focused on governmental intervention as a measure of tuberculosis control. Emphasis has been on voluntary cooperation whenever possible however, the policy debate is centered on issues of individual versus community rights. As the issues are delineated in the Gittier article, compulsory tuberculosis treatment programs may curtail the individual's rights to privacy, autonomy, and liberty in the short term, but in the long term, such treatment will "enhance" those same rights. Some legal challenges to public policy have been made by persons with tuberculosis, particularly in conformity with the Americans with Disabilities Act that has an impact on employment and other concerns. The Court, under such circumstances, considers whether persons with tuberculosis represent a risk to the public's health as assessed by public health officials. Considering the increased risk of patients with HIV to develop tuberculosis, control measures must reflect issues of stigmatization and the discrimination associated with HIV patients. Tuberculosis and HIV are very different diseases. HIV is primarily transmitted through blood-borne contact, and tuberculosis is primarily transmitted through the air. Tuberculosis can be treated and cured, whereas HIV is considered a fatal disease.

Public health-control measures for tuberculosis have had a direct correlation with levels of public funding for such activities. Patterns of fiscal crises at all levels of government have "compounded" the problems of funding for public health programs. One estimate is that for every dollar spent on the control of tuberculosis the return in savings is three to four dollars in the treatment of tuberculosis. The return of tuberculosis and the emergence of HIV are indications that control of communicable diseases remains a challenge. To protect the public and meet these challenges, the nation will need an effective public health enterprise.

Q.1. Propose an epidemiologic study to determine if there is an association between tuberculosis and poverty.

Q.2. Given the differences in the transmission of HIV and tuberculosis, their management, and differences in reporting requirements, how would the impact of a policy to control these disease be evaluated?

Case Study No. 5
Use of Firearms in Homicides

Violence is a major concern for many Americans and has priority status on the public policy agenda. It is considered a public health problem requiring public health measures for its prevention and control. One of many dimensions of this problem is that not all guns are at equal risk of being used in violent crime.

The use of handguns in homicides of law enforcement officers in the United States between 1980 and 1989 was investigated by Wintermute (1994). "This group is at high risk for occupational homicide, with rates of 20 to 25 homicides per 100,000 officers per year" (p. 564). Most involved the use of firearms. Two data sources were used in the study. The Uniform Crime Reporting Program of the Federal Bureau of Investigation provided information on all firearm homicides of law enforcement officers. The Bureau of Alcohol, Tobacco, and Firearms provided information on new hand-gun availability according to manufacturer, importers and according to caliber. Absolute and relative risk for gun types (revolver or pistol and caliber) were estimated for involvement in fatal shootings.

This study generated life tables for each year's cohort of new hand guns to generate estimates regarding gun-years at risk for rate and relative risk calculations. The research reported 735 firearm homicides of law enforcement officers in the study years of which 59% (435) were committed with 428 criminal handguns. Sixty-nine percent (296) were revolvers, 24% (104) were pistols, and 7% (28) were unknown. Most of the guns were medium caliber and manufactured in the United States. The relative risk (RR) for the involvement of hand guns in homicides of law enforcement officers was lowest for .22 caliber handguns and greatest risks were .32 caliber handguns (RR = 15.3; 95% CI = 3.56, 14.5). Analysis of the data indicated revolvers were at greater risk than pistols (RR = 1.40; 95% CI = 1.10, 1.77). Another finding was related to the predominance of short-barreled handguns. As expected, a high frequency of such guns was found in the study because of their concealability. Limitations of the study included the absence of a national data base on the prevalence of handguns in circulation, the representiveness of the guns in the study to those used for in other homicides and those used in nonfatal assaultive violence.

Among the researcher's recommendations was the use of soft armor for protection against .38 caliber handguns used at close range. He also concluded that his data indicate "that restrictions limited to imported firearms—a characteristic of much of American firearms policy—will not be effective" (p. 564).

Q.1. How do you think that the Wintermute epidemiologic findings can influence public policy regarding firearms?

Case Study No. 6
Trauma Care

> Injury kills more people under age 45 than any other single cause. It is the fourth leading
> cause of death among all Americans, killing about 140,000 annually. Estimates of the cost
> of initial hospitalization for severe injury—trauma—in 1988 were as high as $6 billion.
> (U.S. General Accounting Office, 1991, p. 2)

In May 1991, the United States General Accounting Office (GAO) reported on trauma care to the Chairman, Subcommittee on Health for Families and the Uninsured, Committee on Finance, United States Senate. The report was prepared in response to a request by the Chairman of the Subcommittee to examine the reasons for trauma center closures in major urban areas.

The trauma care systems made up of groups of hospitals with specialized facilities and personnel were established to provide timely and appropriate medical care to reduce death and disability among trauma victims. Centers are classified by levels of care: level I centers are the primary hospitals in the trauma system and provide immediate 24-hour care by in-hospital surgeons and other on-call physicians; level II centers provide 24-hour care, but not the same level of sophisticated care as represented by level I centers; and level III are rural trauma centers that lack the resource requirements of level I and II centers. Catchment areas for trauma centers are determined by the time it takes to transport an injured patient, not to exceed 20 min. At the time of the study, about 60 trauma centers had closed in the proceeding 5 years. Urban areas were particularly hard hit by the closings. Legislation passed in 1990 encouraged the development of more regional trauma systems at the state level. (Trauma Care Systems Planning and Development Act of 1990 was initially authorized for $60 million.) However, states could apply for a waiver to use some of the federal funds as reimbursement for uncompensated trauma care.

The GAO study included centers in Chicago, Detroit, Los Angeles, Miami, San Diego, and Washington, D.C. Data were collected and analyzed from interviews, financial and/or statistical records from 35 designated trauma centers. The investigators found that closures were the result of financial losses associated with uninsured patients and patients covered by Medicaid and other government-assisted programs. Annual losses among hospitals able to measure them ranged from $100,000 to $7 million. In the face of rising urban violence, remaining trauma centers face growing financial losses.

Public policy requires that most hospitals with emergency facilities treat all emergency patients without screening for ability to pay. An increase in the number of uninsured between 1977 and 1988 "exacerbated financial losses." Investigators reported that in 1989, 80% of the gunshot and stabbing victims treated in some urban trauma centers were uninsured. When urban trauma centers close, the remaining centers take the uninsured and government-assisted program patients, resulting in additional trauma centers closing.

Trauma care is efficacious. Examples included in the report were a 50% reduction in trauma deaths over a 5-year period in Washington, D.C., and San Diego County experienced a 55% reduction in death rate after the first year of implementation of a countywide system. According to the report, proficiency levels can be maintained if a trauma center treats a minimum of 350 trauma patients per year, and each physician treats at least 50 patients per year.

Public policy targeted at improving emergency care includes categorical grant programs associated with the 1966 Highway Safety Act and the 1973 Emergency Medical Services Systems Act. During the 1980s, the federal government shifted its leadership to the states by "folding the Emergency Medical Services Systems Act into the Preventive Health and Health Services block grants." In 1986, public policy required all hospitals participating in the Medicare program and equipped to do so to treat all persons who presented for emergency care.

Congress authorized the establishment and financing of trauma care systems in 1990. "Trauma centers' financial well-being is related to their location and type of injuries they treat" (p. 21). Inner-city trauma centers experience larger percentages of penetrating injuries from gunshots and other weapons. These patients are more likely to have a negative impact on reimbursement. The GAO report further explained the problem by indicating that trauma centers that have a poor payer mix find it difficult to recover costs. However, when privately insured patients received care, they generated revenues ($22 million), but this amount did not make up for the shortfall of $47 million from serving uninsured and government-assisted program patients. Medicaid as a federal/state medical assistance program is particularly problematic. In most of the cities covered in the GAO report, Medicaid program reimbursements did not cover trauma care costs and ranged from $58,000 to $3.3 million annually.

Q.1. What epidemiologic data should be presented with economic data to better explain how trauma center closures impact the public?

References

American Public Health Association, 1991, *Healthy Communities 2000: Model Standards*, APHA, Washington, DC.
American Public Health Association, 1994, Comparison of key Congressional health care reform bills—1993, *Nation's Health* **14**:14–16.
Boring, C. C., Squires, T. S., and Health, C. W., Jr., 1992, Cancer statistics for African Americans, *CA* **42**:7–17.
Botkin, J. R., 1988, The fire-safe cigarette, *JAMA* **260**:226–229.
City of Chicago, Department of Health, 1993, *Infant Mortality in Chicago 1991–1992*, unpublished report, February 16.
Corrigan, P., 1992, Neglect of prevention programs for children proves expensive for Illinois taxpayers, *Voices Illinois Child.* **5**:1.
Dougherty, C. J., 1988, *American Health Care—Realities, Rights and Reforms*, Oxford University Press, New York.
Evans, R., Mullally, D. I., Wilson, R. W., Gergen, P. J., Rosenberg, H. M., Grauman, J. S., Chevarley, F. M., and Feinleib, M., 1987, National trends in the morbidity and mortality of asthma in the US. Prevalence, hospitalization and death from asthma over two decades: 1965–1984, *Chest* **91**(6 Suppl):65S–74S.
Gindler, J. S., Atkinson, W. L., and Markowitz, L. E., 1992, Update—The United States measles epidemic, 1989–90, *Epidemiol. Rev.* **14**:270–276.
Fingerhut, L. A., and Makuc, D. M., 1992, Mortality among minority populations in the United States, *Am. J. Public Health* **82**:1169.
Gittier, J., 1994, Controlling resurgent tuberculosis: Public health agencies, public policy, and law, *J. Health Pol. Policy Law* **19**:107–147.

Haan, M., Kaplan, G. A., and Camacho, T., 1987, Poverty and health. Prospective evidence from the Alameda County Study, *Am. J. Epidemiol.* **125:**989–998.

Hanlon, J., and Pickett, G., 1984, *Public Health Administration and Practice*, C.V. Mosby, St. Louis.

Hemenway, D., 1991, Injury prevention, *J. Public Health Policy* **12:**23–24.

Himmelstein, D. U., and Woolhandler, S., 1994, *The National Health Program Book*, Common Courage Press, Monroe, ME.

Himmelstein, D. U., Woolhandler, S., and Wolfe, S. M., 1992, The vanishing health safety net: New data on uninsured Americans, *Int. J. Health Serv.* **22:**381–396.

Institute of Medicine, National Academy of Sciences, 1981, *Health Care in a Context of Civil Rights*, National Academy Press, Washington, DC.

Institute of Medicine, National Academy of Sciences, 1988, *The Future of Public Health*, National Academy Press, Washington, DC.

Kitzhaber, J., 1990–1991, A healthier approach to health care, *Issues Sci. and Technol.* **7:**59–65.

Kronick, R., Goodman, D. C., Wennberg, J., and Wagner, E., 1993, The marketplace in health care reform, *N. Engl. J. Med.* **328:**148–152.

Lashof, J. L., 1992, Poverty is a public health issue, *Nation's Health* **January** 1992:2.

McCord, C., and Freeman, H. P., 1990, Excess mortality in Harlem, *N. Engl. J. Med.* **322:**173–177.

Najman, J. M., 1993, Health and poverty: Past, present and prospects for the future, *Soc. Sci. Med.* **36:**157–166.

National Center for Health Statistics, 1993a, *Advance Report of Final Mortality Statistics, 1991. Monthly Vital Statistics Report*, Vol. 42, No. 2, Public Health Service, Hyattsville, MD.

National Center for Health Statistics, 1993b, *Monitoring Health Reform*, Public Health Service, Hyattsville, MD.

National Center for Health Statistics, 1993c, *Health United States, 1992*, Public Health Service, Hyattsville, MD.

National Leadership Commission on Health Care, 1989, *For the Health of a Nation—A Shared Responsibility*, Health Administration Press Perspectives, Ann Arbor, MI.

Nersesian, W. S., Petit, M. R., Shaper, R., Lemieux, D., and Naor, E., 1985, Childhood death and poverty: A study of all childhood deaths in Maine, 1976 to 1980, *Pediatrics* **75:**41–50.

Rowland, D., 1994, Lessons from the Medicaid experience, in *Critical Issues in U.S. Health Reform* (E. Ginzberg, ed.), pp. 190–207, Westview Press, San Francisco.

Shapiro, S., 1991, Epidemiology and public policy, *Am. J. Epidemiol.* **143:**1058.

Shubert, V., 1993, Overcoming barriers to TB prevention and treatment, *Health/PAC Bull.* **16:**21, 1993.

Stanhope, M., and Lancaster, J., 1988, *Community Health Nursing*, C.V. Mosby, St. Louis.

Stiller, J., 1987, A practical guide to legal considerations in ethical issues, in *Health Care Ethics—A Guide for Decision Makers* (G. R. Anderson and V. A. Glesnes-Anderson, eds.), Aspen Publications, Rockville, MD.

Terris, M., 1985, The changing relationships of epidemiology and society: The Robert Cruikshank Lecture, *J. Public Health Policy* **6:**15–36.

The Robert Wood Johnson Foundation, 1991, *Challenges in Health Care*, RWJF, Princeton, NJ.

U.S. Department of Health and Human Services, 1991, *Healthy People 2000—Full Report with Commentary*, U.S. Government Printing Office, Washington, DC.

U.S. General Accounting Office, 1991, Trauma care—Lifesaving system threatened by unreimbursed costs and other factors, GAO, Washington, DC.

Wagner, M. G., 1988, Infant mortality in Europe: Implications for the United States, *J. Public Health Policy* **9:** 473–484.

Wintermute, G. J., 1994, Homicide, handguns, and the crime gun hypothesis: Firearms used in fatal shootings of law enforcement officers, 1980 to 1989, *Am. J. Public Health* **84:**561–564.

Suggested Answers to Selected Case Studies Questions

Chapter 1

Case Study No. 1: Service Population in an Urban Public Hospital

A.1. Several factors could explain this. The need for health care services in the community in which the new facility was opened was not previously being met by CCH. Also, service population, which is most likely to use CCH, has continued to increase because of increased birth rate and number of immigrants moving into the area served by CCH who are younger and likely to be uninsured.

A.2. The less seriously ill patients were more likely to be treated at the community hospital. The patients admitted to CCH continue to be high-risk patients, i.e., have multiple diagnoses.

Case Study No. 3: Effectiveness of Comprehensive-Care Programs in Preventing Rheumatic Fever

A.1. Program eligibility was defined by the census tract. In addition, census tracts provide detailed information on the numbers of persons in a defined geographic area according to age, gender, and race. This information is used for determining the denominator of the rate measure used to evaluate program effectiveness.

A.2. The outcome measure was felt to be easily quantifiable from medical records, and the condition is one that health services delivered in the community could prevent. That is, rheumatic fever is known to be preventable by prompt identification and adequate treatment of streptococcal infections.

A.3. Persons at high risk for the condition could have moved out of the community. Social, nutritional, and environmental conditions may have improved. Changes in medical practice might have occurred such that individuals with rheumatic fever are treated on an outpatient basis.

Chapter 2

Case Study No. 1: Measuring Quality of Life

A.1. The Functional Assessment of Cancer Therapy Scale-General (FACT-G) is a health index intended to measure the QL of adult cancer patients (Cella *et al.*, 1993). The FACT-G is a 38-item survey form with subscales that measure physical, functional, social, and emotional well-being in addition to satisfaction with treatment. The measure can be self-administered or administered through interview. Responses to items are in Likert-type format (1 = agree to 5 = disagree) and can be recorded using paper and pencil or via interactive computer entry. Data for a reference sample consisting of in- and outpatients and individuals seen at a free-standing, community cancer patient support center are available. The instrument can be obtained from the author. Scoring is an arithmetic sum of the subscales on the form.

A.2. Content validity was determined by oncology specialists (MD or RN) with at least 3 years' experience with treating at least 100 patients. The specialists were asked to rate each item with respect to relevance to QL. The test–retest correlation coefficient for the physical well-being subscale of the FACT-G was 0.84, indicating reliability over time. Convergent validity was evaluated by comparing the scores of the FACT-G with similar measures administered at the same time. For example, the Pearson correlation coefficient from the comparison between the FACT-G and the Functional Living Index–Cancer (Schipper *et al.*, 1984) was 0.79, supporting convergent validity.

Case Study No. 3: Inappropriate Emergency Department Visits by Members of a Health Maintenance Organization

A.1. $P_o = (257 + 1411)/1745 = 0.96$

$P_e = \{[(277 \times 314)/1745] + [(1468 \times 1431)/1745]\}/1745 = 0.72$

$\kappa = (P_o - P_e)/(1 - P_e) = (0.96 - 0.72)/(1 - 0.72) = 0.86$

   The *kappa* statistic of 0.86 indicates that there was excellent agreement between the two physicians. Therefore, the lists help in promoting the achievement of reliability.

A.2. The *kappa* statistic was used because the independent variables (physician type, emergency room physician/primary care physician) and dependent variable (appropriateness, yes/no) are represented as binary variables.

Case Study No. 4: A Breast Cancer Screening Program

A.1. First, compute the number of women with breast cancer:

250,000 × 0.3% = 750 women.

Next, find the number of true positives:

750 × 99/100 = 742

A.2. Continuing with the information from A.1., obtain the number of women without breast cancer:

250,000 − 750 = 249,250.

Determine the number of false positives:

$249,250 \times (1 - 99/100) = 2,492$.

The data from A.1 and A.2 result in the following 2×2 table:

	Breast cancer	
	Yes	No
Mammography result		
Positive	742	2,492
Negative	8	246,758

A.3. Yes. The specificity and sensitivity are both high, thus, you have a high probability of accurately classifying a woman who is positive from mammography screening to truly have breast cancer. You also have a high probability of determining that if a woman tests negative she does not have the disease; only 8 women show false-negative results.

A.4. Yes. Because a large number of women are expected to test positive, a procedure should be in place to supplement the results of the initial screening, such as a physical exam by a physician or nurse practitioner.

Chapter 3

Case Study No. 1: In-Hospital Mortality from Hip Fractures in the Elderly

A.1. Age-specific mortality rates:

$\text{Rate}_{65-69 \text{ years of age}}$ per 100 = $68/2542 \times 100 = 2.68$ per 100
$\text{Rate}_{70-74 \text{ years of age}}$ per 100 = $140/3842 \times 100 = 3.64$ per 100
$\text{Rate}_{75-79 \text{ years of age}}$ per 100 = $216/5374 \times 100 = 4.02$ per 100
$\text{Rate}_{80-84 \text{ years of age}}$ per 100 = $297/6541 \times 100 = 4.54$ per 100
$\text{Rate}_{\geq 85 \text{ years of age}}$ per 100 = $618/9071 \times 100 = 6.81$ per 100

Race- and gender-specific mortality rates:

$\text{Rate}_{\text{white males}}$ per 100 = $392/4970 \times 100 = 7.87$ per 100
$\text{Rate}_{\text{white females}}$ per 100 = $847/20,675 \times 100 = 4.10$ per 100
$\text{Rate}_{\text{black males}}$ per 100 = $38/506 \times 100 = 7.51$ per 100
$\text{Rate}_{\text{black females}}$ per 100 = $62/1209 \times 100 = 5.13$ per 100

The mortality rate increases with advancing age. White males are at highest risk for death, followed by black males, black females and white females.

A.2. The higher death rate among males may result from a higher proportion of the injuries being associated with more serious injuries incurred in motor vehicle accidents, assaults, and falls from heights.

A.3. Because there are a small number of deaths in the cells resulting from the cross-tabulation of age group, gender, and race, this was done in order to have stable rates in the population subgroups examined.

A.4. Death certificates.

A.5. Deaths may not have been recorded on the hospital discharge abstract, as there may not be a legal requirement for doing so, since death certificates are viewed as the standard mechanism for reporting this event. This would underestimate the inpatient mortality rate. Persons with a hip fracture may be readmitted for management of the hip fracture. This could also underestimate the rate because these persons would artificially increase the denominator. If procedure codes are not used concurrently with diagnosis code, persons with hip fracture may be missed. If in-hospital death occurred in the unidentified case, the rate could also be underestimated; otherwise the rate would be overestimated.

Case Study No. 3: Risk Factors for Coronary Artery Disease

A.1. RR = 12.6 per 100 pop./7.7 per 100 pop. = 1.64

A.2. An RR of 1.64 means that smokers are 1.64 times more likely to develop CAD than nonsmokers.

A.3. PAR% $= [P_e (RR - 1)]/[1 + P_e (RR - 1)] \times 100\%$

$= [0.42(1.64 - 1)]/[1 + 0.42(1.64 - 1)] \times 100\%$

$= 21\%$

A.4. In this case, the RR helps define causation and provide an estimate of the degree to which a risk factor plays a role for an individual. The RR indicates that smoking elevates one's chances of developing CAD, and, therefore, health promotion services should include methods for assisting an individual in quitting smoking.

Chapter 4

Case Study No. 1: Strategic Planning for a County Health Department

A.1. Yes. Although the situation is one full of change, there is no evidence of a crisis situation. Strategic planning could help the Health Department effectively address these changes and chart its future direction.

A.2. No. The Executive Director is new; he lacks a sense of the organization's history, and he received mixed messages when members of the Health Department's Board shared their vision of where the Department should go in the future. Staff of the organization have never had the opportunity to reflect formally on the organization's mission. There is a policy and procedures manual that was compiled some time ago. It describes the mandates of Health Departments if they are to receive state monies as local public health agencies. The role the Department has taken on as a provider of mental health services (a role not essential for Health Departments) was not addressed in the dated publication (which rarely had been removed from the shelf in recent years anyway). Developing consensus on a mission for the Health Department is a step appropriate for inclusion in the strategic planning process.

A.3. The types of data appropriate for review by the Health Department include the following: financial data pertinent to funding of the Department's programs and service-specific income and expense data; statistical reports that present data relevant to trends in the utilization of services and to the characteristics of those served; county and statewide morbidity data for reportable diseases and vital statistics (contained in reports prepared by the Illinois Department of Public Health); census data for the county and other data describing the demographic and socioeconomic characteristics of county residents; reports by state agencies (such as the Department of Mental Health and Developmental Disabilities) that provide an inventory of services available for treatment of acute and chronic illnesses and other dysfunctions and present data pertinent to the assessment of unmet health needs (for a range of medical treatment, habilitative, and supportive services); and data pertinent to the availability of health personnel (such as child psychologists, certified addiction counselors, and therapists of various kinds).

Because some Board members expressed the opinion that the Health Department should do more to monitor and improve the environment, it is also appropriate that data be compiled to assess the status of the county's environment against standards for land, air, and water quality. Sources of data may include results from periodic testing of soil, water, and air by the Health Department, governmental reports, and studies of "watchdog" and consumer advocacy organizations. Morbidity and mortality data for the county could also be reviewed to determine if the county has a higher incidence of diseases that appear to have a link to environmental pollutants.

A.4. The data identified above could be utilized to gain awareness of the health status of the county's population relative to a meaningful comparison group (such as the population of the state) and to assess possible causes for discrepancies from the norm. The data can facilitate an understanding of the variables (such as age, economic and occupational status, and environmental conditions) that influence health needs and demands.

A.5. Members of the County Board, the Executive Director, and staff (all or some) should certainly be involved in the process. Representatives of local businesses, other service agencies, and the community at large may also be invited to participate in the process. There is no standard answer to this question, but it is important to have a basis for justifying selection of planning participants. A process that is open and democratic probably has a better chance of success than one that appears closed and autocratic.

A.6. The case does not suggest evidence that the Health Department has personnel knowledgeable about strategic planning. The Executive Director and Board President should evaluate the capabilities that can be applied to a strategic planning process. If the commitment to undertake the process is sufficient, the Executive Director and the Board can agree to seek expert help and contract with consultants who can assist in the process. Other potential problems could be avoided if adequate attention is given to planning the planning, to selecting a process tailored to the needs of the organization, and to establishing other conditions that are associated with effective strategic thinking and action.

Case Study No. 2: Strategic Planning for Inpatient Rehabilitation Services

A.1. A comprehensive feasibility study could include assessment of the following factors:

- The need for comprehensive rehabilitation among the population in communities traditionally served by the hospital (with consideration given to sociodemographic variables such as age and income levels) as well as epidemiologic variables (causes of morbidity and mortality, incidence of work injuries, and illnesses that could increase the need for work rehabilitation programs).
- The diagnoses of patients currently utilizing the hospital (to assess if the hospital was already providing acute-care services to substantial numbers of patients who were likely candidates for rehabilitation and to determine the impact of more aggressive need identification on occupancy).
- Financial implications of operating a larger, exempt unit.
- The perceived need among the hospital's physicians for expansion of inpatient rehabilitation services, and the physicians' willingness to refer patients to the hospital's rehabilitation service rather than identifying other resources in the community for meeting the needs of patients.

- Competitors in the rehabilitation business (their levels of success, the programs offered, and those not available).
- The unit's current ability to achieve established clinical outcomes and to satisfy other quality standards and expectations of consumers and stakeholders.

A.2. No. It made a decision to involve consultants to expedite the process. This was probably a responsible decision, considering that the management team lacked adequate time and expertise to address the problem itself. There is no absolute formula for success in strategic planning. However, the management team worked with consultants to design a process with a high probability of success. The consultants did the research and analytic work usually associated with a situational analysis. However, the management group maintained involvement in the process and carefully reviewed the work of the consultants to ensure that there would be adequate confidence in conclusions and ownership of recommendations. The hospital's management team became more educated and informed of the issues as the process proceeded; this facilitated good judgment and decision making on their part. The management team also gave full consideration to what needed to be done to begin implementation of some of the recommendations of the consultants.

A.3. There's no right or wrong answer to this question. Certainly, other approaches might have worked as well or better. The hospital wanted to get a Certificate-of-Need permit, which was necessary to achieve formal recognition of the unit and to gain authorization of capital expenditures that the hospital had budgeted to improve the physical environment of the unit. It obtained the permit, but not without difficulty, because it initially failed to give attention to the politics associated with the CON regulatory process. The hospital wanted the rehabilitation unit to gain exemption and to achieve a more favorable "*bottom line*." Both of these objectives were also attained. Therefore, unless the management team had other objectives that were not accomplished, the process worked.

Chapter 5

Case Study No. 1: Mandated Evaluation of the Elderly in Preferred Provider Organizations

A.1. Since the program is about to begin and Medicare recipients can exercise choice in selecting a program, a quasiexperimental design is appropriate for comparing HMO, PPO, and FFS arrangements.

A.2. Health status and functional status are important criteria to consider.

A.3. The prevalence rate of specific screening tests (visual and hearing acuity, fecal occult blood test, mammography, pap smear) and physical examinations (pelvic, breast, digital rectal exam) and other preventive procedures (e.g., immunization for influenza) can be determined by a review of the medical records, and comparisons can be made across payment systems.

A.4. A cross-tabulation of each preventive health care practice by payer category can be prepared. From this, odds ratios and 95% confidence intervals representing the likelihood of performance of each of the preventive health care practices can be computed.

	Payer	
	HMO	PPO
Mammography		
Yes	a	b
No	c	d

In this example, the OR of mammography in an HMO relative to a PPO = $(a/c)/(b/d)$.

Multiple logistic regression can also be used for this same purpose if the effects of age, gender, marital status, and duration of time in the plan need consideration.

A.5. Comparisons can be done of HMO versus FFS and PPO versus FFS. Comparisons can also be done by population subgroups of interest, for example, young–old versus old–old, or those with versus those without supplemental insurance.

Case Study No. 2: Impact of a Hospital-Based AIDS Program

A.1. An assessment of the magnitude of the incidence of AIDS and the prevalence of HIV among persons in the community is the initial step. An estimate should also be made of the number of individuals in various risk groups (e.g., homosexuals, public safety and health care workers potentially exposed to bodily fluids, users of illicit intravenous drugs). A local or state health department may already have this data for the community.

A.2. A cross-sectional design can be used. In this design, a random sample of persons in the hospital and in the community would be surveyed regarding awareness of AIDS risk factors. The data would then be crosstabulated by population subgroups, and it could be determined if AIDS awareness differs among hospital employees by job category. The results of the study can identify groups that should be targeted for intervention.

A.3. First, the intervention and evaluation criteria must be specified. The intervention may consist of radio and television announcements about the danger of acquiring AIDS from intravenous drug use. This would be a quasiexperimental design, since persons cannot be randomized, and it is not feasible to have a control group. Appropriate evaluation criteria could include the percentage of the population reporting knowledge of this risk factor (in a repeat survey after the ad campaign) and the incidence of AIDS cases among intravenous drug users.

Case Study No. 4: Evaluating a Community-Based Hypertension Control Program

A.1. Changes in the prevalence of hypertension, prevalence of controlled hypertension, and cardiovascular mortality rates are appropriate criteria.

A.2. This is a quasiexperimental design because of the inability to randomize persons in the community into an intervention or a control group.

A.3. Factors other than the intervention could contribute to the outcome experienced by the population over time.

A.4. The program was effective. The prevalence of hypertensives who were controlled significantly increased in only the intervention counties. In addition, the percentage of the population with hypertension declined in the intervention counties but not significantly in the control group.

A.5. An audit of the process could have been done and accounted for in the follow-up survey. That is, attention could have focused on delineating the types of interventions for high-blood-pressure control to which those surveyed were exposed. It would also be relevant to assess how long survey respondents had lived in the county (to assess the duration of exposure to the various intervention approaches).

Chapter 6

Case Study No. 1: An Epidemic in a Neonatal Unit

A.1. When a manager suspects the occurrence of an epidemic within a patient care unit, the first step would be to contact the hospital epidemiologist to confirm that an epidemic exists.

A.2. The ill babies should be geographically separated from the well babies. Separate equipment and supply areas for each group of babies should be maintained. The separation in terms of location and functions should reduce the likelihood of cross-contamination of the infants. Policies and procedures regarding infection control should be reviewed with all staff on the unit as well as those ancillary personnel who enter the unit. Since hands are the most common means by which infection is transmitted in the health care setting, the review of policies and procedures regarding handwashing should be emphasized. Monitoring of staff compliance to these procedures subsequent to the review should be done. The hospital infection-control nurse can assist in monitoring.

A.3. Nursing staff should be separated into those who will be caring exclusively for the ill babies and those who will be caring exclusively for the well babies. This measure should also reduce the likelihood of cross-contamination. The nurse who had tested positive for MRSA should be removed from duty in the special care unit and should receive treatment from employee health for her dermatitis. The nurse should then either remain at home or be reassigned to non-patient-care activities until a medical determination is made that her dermatitis has been cleared. The manager in consultation with the hospital epidemiologist should determine if more than one nurse had developed dermatitis. If more than one nurse developed dermatitis, the cause may be either the handwashing system or the gloves used. This may necessitate a change in the product(s) used.

A.4. The epidemic continued because of the influx of the use of agency nurses who may not have been properly trained in the policies and procedures regarding infection control in the neonatal intensive care unit. In addition, the census of the unit was maintained at 45 babies, allowing for the possibility of continued cross-contamination.

A.5. The manager should limit the census (not accept new admissions) until no new cases of MRSA are identified. Agency nurses should receive training regarding the unit's policies and procedures on infection control prior to beginning work on the unit. Retraining of staff and ancillary personnel should be done with particular attention to any staff who had missed the previous session.

Case Study No. 3: Prevention of Needlestick Injuries in Hospital Employees

A.1. To obtain the needlestick injury rates for each job category, divide the number of needlestick injuries by the number of FTEs and multiply by 100. Part-time nursing personnel, regardless or whether they are RNs or LPNs, and night-shift housekeeping personnel are at highest risk.

A.2. Institute training and retraining programs regarding disposal of sharps, particularly of part-time (which would include agency personnel), and third-shift employees. Establish a surveillance system for identifying all needlestick injuries within the organization. Periodically, conduct auditing of on-site clinical performance with respect to disposal of sharps. Ensure that appropriate puncture-resistant receptacles are on all patient-care units. An analysis of needlestick injuries by hospital area should also be done as a means of determining which areas may not be complying with practices regarding prevention.

Case Study No. 4: An Outbreak of TB Infection in an HIV Unit

A.1. Patients infected with HIV are immunocompromised and, therefore, are more susceptible to co-infection with other opportunistic diseases.

A.2. Because of an immunocompromised state, HIV patients are more likely to have a shorter incubation period than a healthy individual.

A.3. All patients admitted with active TB should be placed in isolation. The air exchange systems should be tested daily to ensure proper air-flow levels in order to decrease the concentration of infectious droplet nuclei in the environment. The patient should be restricted to the isolation area and should leave only when necessary for testing and treatment that cannot be performed in the room. The patient should be masked during movement around the unit and organization.

A.4. All patients who display signs of active infection should be separated from others and placed into isolation. Diagnostic testing should begin immediately to rule out active TB. If tests are positive, the patient should remain in isolation, and immediate treatment should begin. If test results are negative for active TB infection, the patient should be removed from isolation, and further testing should be continued to determine the etiology of symptoms.

A.5. The HCW should be immediately relieved of direct patient contact, tested for confirmation of active TB, and initiate treatment upon confirmation.

A.6. Since the spread of a second strain of TB occurred, further education should be provided to HCWs to assist them in correctly identifying signs associated with active TB infection. Policies should be reviewed with the HCWs to inform them of proper steps to take in order to decrease added risk to patients and staff once active TB infection is suspected.

Chapter 7

Case Study No. 1: Extracorporeal Shock-Wave Lithotripsy for Kidney Stones

A.1. The optimal study design would be a randomized controlled experiment.

A.2. Criteria could be disease recurrence rates, complication rates, and patient satisfaction.

A.3. High patient dropout rate, follow-up rates different between the treatment groups, and sample size lower than required might compromise the study.

Case Study No. 2: Chorionic Villus Sampling

A.1. Diagnostic accuracy is the number of true positives plus the number of true negatives divided by the total number of persons evaluated. Diagnostic accuracy is determined from comparing the results of CVS testing to an expected outcome, in this case, the outcome at birth (defects or no clinical defects observed at birth). The sensitivity and the specificity of the test results should be computed. Ideally, the sensitivity, specificity, and diagnostic accuracy should all be 100%.

A.2. Factors that influence diagnostic accuracy include adequacy of the tissue sample, physician skill level and experience with the procedure, and technician and equipment error.

A.3. The offering of this technology depends upon the demographic characteristics of the population served and the prevalence of maternal risk factors associated with an increased likelihood of genetic abnormalities. For example, the incidence of congenital malformations in infants born to women over 35 years of age is high. Thus, if the HMO has a high proportion of women in this age group, CVS may be introduced as a routine prenatal procedure. The past performance of amniocentesis (an alternative procedure) in this population needs to be compared to CVS. In addition to comparing the sensitivity and specificity of the two procedures, the fetal loss rates and the incidence of limb malformation (which could be linked to CVS) may also be examined.

A.4. Ethical issues that should be considered are: Do parents have a right to choose the sex of the child to be born? Should the pregnancy be terminated for nonfatal birth defects (e.g., limb malformation)?

Case Study No. 3: Ambulatory Uterine Monitoring

A.1. A randomized clinical trial can be done in which pregnant women in the health plan are randomized into one of two groups: one group receives either the uterine monitoring device to wear at home; the other group would be followed per the routine office visit schedule.

A.2. Epidemiologic measures may include the cesarean birth rate, birth weights, and admission rate to the hospital for false labor.

Case Study No. 4: Positron Emission Tomography

A.1. Diagnostic imaging technologies include magnetic resonance imaging (MRI), spectroscopy, single photon emission computed tomography (SPECT), and CT scanning. Factors to consider include (1) acquisition cost, (2) maintenance/staffing cost, (3) patient processing time, (4) obsolescence, (5) medical staff wants/needs, (6) competitive market position, and most importantly, (7) the specificity, sensitivity, and predictive value of each imaging technology.

A.2. The ideal study design would be a prospective, blinded, randomized trial, that would compare images obtained by PET and an alternative technology. The two sets of images would then be interpreted by several radiologic experts blinded to the diagnosis and treatment strategy suggested by each set of images for a patient. The consistency of responses and the alteration of an expected course of therapy would be outcomes of interest in evaluating the study.

Case Study No. 5: Thrombolytic Therapy

A.1. Drug administration protocols (e.g., dose, duration, route of administration), patient exclusion criteria, ancillary treatments (e.g., CABG, PTCA, antithrombotics), and outcome measures (e.g., vessel patency, morbidity, mortality).

A.2. Absolute risk reduction equals 1.1% (7.4 minus 6.3). Relative risk reduction equals 14.9% $[(7.4 - 6.3)/7.4] \times 100\%$

Chapter 8

Case Study No. 1: Reducing the Nonacute Inpatient Days at Random Medical Center
for DRG 182 (Esophagitis, Gastroenteritis, and Miscellaneous Disorders;
Age > 17 Years with Complications)

A.1. Construct a control chart of the average length of stay (ALOS) by month for DRG 182 for the past 5 years, utilizing a 99% confidence limit (Fig. A.1). The control chart of the average length of stay shows that the process is in statistical control; the upper 99% confidence limit is exceeded only in one month in year 1. Therefore, common rather than special causes are the source of the variation. The control chart suggests that the delivery process itself must be redesigned to eliminate nonacute days. Strategies could include preadmission processing of patient information (e.g., medical history, lab tests) and improved speed in processing laboratory results when requested during the hospital stay.

   Construct a histogram of the distribution of patient length of stays for the 5-year period overall and for each year studied. The histogram revealed that 25% of patients in DRG 182 were hospitalized for more than 7 days. The characteristics of these persons should be more closely examined. This process should be repeated for each nursing unit which cares for patients in DRG 182 to determine if there are differences with respect to nursing efficiency.

   Construct a cause-and-effect diagram to assist in developing hypotheses regarding root causes (Fig. A.2). The cause and effect diagram should depict the influence of patient comorbidities, physician characteristics, and laboratory ordering patterns on the length of stay (LOS).

A.2. Construct a pareto chart of LOS by specialty of attending physicians (Fig. A.3). Such a chart could be utilized to assess if LOS is substantially longer when the attending is not a digestive specialist or when no digestive consultation is requested.

A.3. The team decided to establish guidelines for delivering care to these patients and represent these as a critical path. To do this, a subcommittee of qualified members and clinicians from the digestive subspecialties was formed. In constructing the critical path, each inpatient day is planned so that diagnostic tests and digestive consults (if the attending physician is not a digestive subspecialist) are accomplished in a logical sequence early in the stay. This subcommittee would also be given the responsibility of training other physicians on the use of the critical path.

A.4. A 1-year prospective study could be conducted comparing the length of stay of those patients in DRG 182 whose physicians reported following the critical path to those whose physicians reported that they did not follow the critical path. An independent review of the charts of the patients would be performed to validate the physician report and obtain information on length of stay from administrative records.

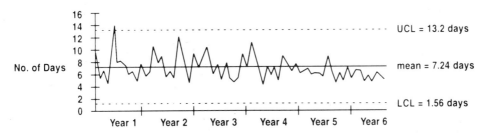

Figure A.1.   Control chart of average length of hospital stay by month for patients in DRG 182.

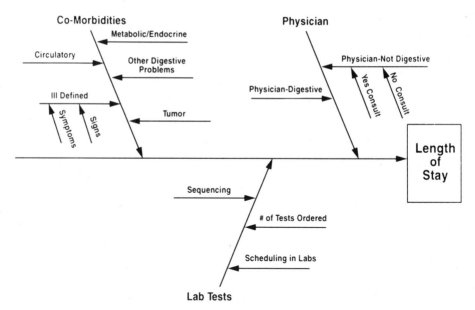

Figure A.2. Cause-and-effect diagram of factors contributing to the length of hospital stay for patients in DRG 182.

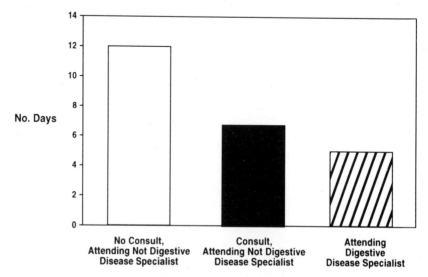

Figure A.3. Pareto chart of average length of hospital stay in days by type of physician attending patients in DRG 182.

A.5. The results of the SF-36 medical outcomes survey, patient satisfaction surveys, rates of unscheduled readmissions, rates of complications, mortality rates, and lengths of stay would be compared in the group that received care according to the critical path and those who did not. The data should ideally be severity adjusted to make valid comparisons.

A.6. If the results indicate that the variation in LOS can be reduced while quality is maintained, then the critical path evaluated should be broadly implemented within the hospital. Quality management requires ongoing monitoring of the effectiveness, appropriateness, and efficiency of care. Thus, the subcommittee that developed the critical path should also be trained in the use of CQI and epidemiologic methods to improve the critical path. The subcommittee could complete additional PDSA cycles, each time incorporating feedback from outcomes assessment. For example, improvements in the clinical path may be made by focusing on the last few days of the inpatient stay for DRG 182 to determine if outpatient or home care therapy could be incorporated into the critical path.

Case Study No. 4: Reducing Infant Mortality

A.1. The qualifications and performance of specialists contracted through an HMO are important. Because the employee population is largely female and of childbearing age, aspects of the quality of obstetrical services provided through an HMO should be critically assessed. For example, evidence suggests that the availability of neonatal intensive care can reduce the risk of infant death. However, since the expected impact of improved neonatal care is probably much smaller than that of improved prenatal care, the benefits manager should focus on indicators of primary prevention. The manager should ask for the results of clinic record audits and seek information about the proportion of prenatal care patients whose urine was checked for proteinuria, or the proportion of cases with elevated blood pressure or low hematocrit in which follow-up took place. The manager should also look for clinical guidelines or algorithms that are utilized to manage women in labor as a means of avoiding unnecessary surgery among those who are at high risk for a cesarean section.

A.2. Process measures of the timeliness, frequency, and content of prenatal care are probably most appropriate. Outcome measures of the rate of LBW births are useful for monitoring progress in process improvement, as long as the rate is adjusted for maternal age, comorbidity, socioeconomic status, ethnicity, and complexity of the pregnancy (e.g., multiparity).

Case Study No. 5: Assessing Quality of Care
for Chronic Illness in a Health Maintenance Organization

A.1. No. The prevalence of asthma may not be randomly distributed among health plans. Therefore, a high or low asthma admission rate may not be a reliable measure of quality. In addition, the lack of severity adjustment may also bias the data. A more sensitive method would be to include in the denominator only those who have been dispensed asthma medication during the year on an ambulatory basis. In using this measure as a monitoring device, the Benefits Manager should trend the data over time rather than look at isolated points.

A.2. Asthma is but one of many chronic illnesses that afflict a population. Perhaps Sunnyside's quality of care for chronic illness varies according to disease types or other factors. Because asthma is more common in children than in adults, it is important to obtain quality data for the treatment of chronic illnesses common to older members of the plan as well. For example, another HEDIS measure related to the quality of care for chronic illness would be the annual rate of diabetic retinal exam, which is the percentage of diabetics who have had a retinal examination during the preceding calendar year. Diabetics can develop severe eye disease, and early identification and treatment can reduce the likelihood of blindness. The rate is calculated from the denominator (those who are in ICD-9 codes of: 250.xx; 357.2x with 250.xx; 362.0x–362.x, with 250.xx; or 366.41 with 250.xx) and the numerator (those with CPT-4: 99201–99275, ophthalmic services, exams, or ophthalmoscopy). Although the rate measure is an acceptable quality indicator of performance, assuming a correlation between early detection and intervention, it does not answer the question of the effectiveness or the appropriateness of the treatment.

A.3. No, since the rates are not severity adjusted, and the prevalence of asthma may differ systematically among plan populations.

A.4. No. An HMO is organized to care for its members as a defined population (with financing and delivery of care combined). The HMO has the data required to compute the numerator and de- nominator. However, a hospital may not serve a defined population under contract, so it would be impossible to calculate an accurate rate.

Chapter 9

Case Study No. 1: Emergency Room and Hospital Resource Utilization

A.1. Ask your marketing or planning office to identify the population of potential users of ER services by geographic, political, or commuting area. For the target population, obtain information from the state and local bureau of the budget or office of economic development (or the census data) concerning the population profile, i.e., numbers of persons in service areas by age, sex, and race/ ethnicity, employment status, educational level, and median incomes. Obtain vital statistics data from state and local health departments on all causes of mortality, by age, race, and sex. Also obtain information regarding any special vulnerable populations that could influence utilization patterns of the ER, such as the prevalence of females of childbearing age covered by Medicaid or with no insurance, asthma incidence, and trauma rates.

A.2. Perceptions vary among the population of potential users of ER services regarding severity of the health problem. There is a lack of knowledge and awareness about the prevention of health problems and the early recognition of the onset of serious health problems among the population. Barriers limit access to primary health care, including unavailability of primary care providers, inability to pay, language barriers, and geographic distance.

A.3. Increase the level of knowledge about preventable or controllable medical conditions (e.g., diarrhea, diabetic ketoacidosis) and methods of prevention. Encourage primary care providers to increase their efforts to ensure that treated persons and their caregivers are knowledgeable about their conditions and their management in the home setting. Collaborate with local associations and health units to promote healthy behaviors associated with those health problems most commonly linked with emergency room use, e.g., passenger restraints, caution in alcohol consumption. Create linkages with community-based agencies to provide a smooth transition from primary to acute to subacute care facilities. Work with businesses and payers to change reimbursement systems so that they reward prevention and health promotion. Enjoin students in the health professions to provide needed primary care and clinical and social services to the community as a part of their course work.

Enlist the assistance of a school of business or public health to measure the changes in the health status of the population of potential service recipients.

Case Study No. 4: Indigent Care

A.1. Determine the size, distribution, and characteristics of the inpatient and outpatient populations served by LRH. For determining distribution, utilize LRH's administrative data base and construct a frequency distribution of discharges (for inpatient population) and of visits (for outpatients). If required data are not available, contact the state agency and request hospital discharge data, which it is required to collect. With respect to patient characteristics, data should be compiled for age, gender, and race/ethnicity at the very least.

A.2. Vital statistics data should be compiled to indicate the mortality and morbidity rates for the geographic area in which the service population resides. Mortality data (e.g., infant mortality) can be obtained from the state department of health. Morbidity data (incidence of communicable diseases, etc.) can be obtained from the local health department. If possible, a determination of the prevalence of risk factors leading to the highest rates of morbidity, mortality, and hospitalization should be examined. A wealth of data on the prevalence of risk factors may be available if the state is participating in the Behavioral Risk Factor Surveillance System (BRFSS) of the Centers for Disease Control (see Chapter 3 for a description of the BRFSS).

A.3. Determine number and percentage of emergency room visits involving the need for nonurgent care that could be provided in a primary-care setting. One way of validating this approach would be to have two physicians review the records. A *kappa* statistic can be computed (see Chapter 2) to measure the amount of agreement between physicians regarding the appropriate site of care. A frequency distribution of the reasons for emergency room use should also be constructed. A comparison should be made of the area's ratio of primary-care providers to the patient population against national standards in order to evaluate potential manpower shortages. Utilization rates of the LRH population at federally or locally supported clinics should be examined, along with the reasons for use.

A.4. If the population has special needs that could be measured, the capitated payment system should be risk-adjusted. Risk-adjustment variables include age, gender, race, principal and comorbid diagnoses (from the HCFA groups, Health Care Financing Administration, 1992), admission type (emergent or elective), source of admission (e.g., nursing home, transfer), preadmission functional status (ambulatory, wheelchair, bedridden), and a severity measure (e.g., APACHE II, Knaus *et al.*, 1985).

A baseline level of the special health education needs of the population should be determined, and efforts to address these needs should implemented as a means of preventing morbidity.

Chapter 10

Case Study No. 1: Assessment of Selected National Health Program Legislative Proposals

A.1. Epidemiologic data may include percentage of mothers receiving prenatal care in first trimester, percentage of mothers receiving late or no prenatal care, percentage of women aged 35 and over who ever had a mammogram, percentage of the population aged 20–74 years with high serum cholesterol (≥ 240 mg/dl), and number of work-loss days associated with various acute conditions per 100 currently employed persons ≥ 18 years. These data need to be monitored over time.

Case Study No. 2: Infant Mortality among African-Americans

A.1. A prospective (longitudinal) concurrent study should be done involving a special group (females aged 13–15 years) from various health risk populations in a defined geographic area for a period of 10 years to assess and compare pregnancy outcomes. Data on the following confounding factors would be collected: education, income, family responsibilities and decision structure, community safety (drugs, crime, and violence), awareness and use of community resources, housing, number and spacing of pregnancies, health status, and health beliefs and behaviors.

A.2. Preventable health problems seem a likely place for intervention. These causes include infectious diseases, accidents, and homicides. Access to prenatal care should be provided for early recognition, counseling, and treatment of infectious diseases, including sexually transmitted diseases, tuberculosis and AIDS, for prompt treatment of accidental injuries and counseling and education to prevent accidents, and for counseling and screening related to abusive relationships. Case finding and other case management system activities should be used to ensure early intervention and continuous contact.

A.3. Epidemiologic measures to determine the effectiveness of the prevention programs would include those demonstrating impact on modifiable risk factors associated with infant mortality (e.g., decrease smoking and increase the proportion of high-risk mothers participating in prenatal care activities).

Case Study No. 3: Women, Infants, and Children Program

A.1. Epidemiologic data that could be used are hospitalization rates, immunization rates, and incidence of low birth weight. Efficacy could be demonstrated if, among the population served by the WIC program, the hospitalization rates for pregnancy complications are lower, immunization rates are higher, and the incidence of low-birth-weight babies is lower than that in a comparable population without exposure to this program. The results of the impact must be conveyed to state law makers to restore and increase funding as an investment that will, in the long run, save its citizens money. To develop broader public support, information regarding the advantages of the program must be shared with the public in terms its economic savings.

Glossary

Adjusted rates   The value derived from weighting population specific rates for a confounding variable by the percentage (or number) of persons in the specific stratum of that variable in a standard population and summed across all strata. This removes the confounding effect of population characteristics on an outcome to permit comparison of groups of individuals or populations with respect to incidence or mortality rates.

Alpha level   An arbitrary value set by the investigator that indicates the threshold probability for rejecting a true null hypothesis. Also known as the "level of significance."

Alternative hypothesis (H_A)   A statement about the values of population parameters that is phrased to contradict the null hypothesis.

Attributable risk   The proportion of excess risk of disease or health problem that is associated with exposure to a risk factor.

Beta level   Probability of accepting a false null hypothesis.

Bias   Any difference between an observed parameter and the true value.

Carrier   An infected person or other vertebrate who harbors a transmissible agent without discernible clinical disease and who serves as a potential source of infection.

Case-control study   Individuals are selected on the basis of the presence or absence of an outcome. Evidence of a factor suspected as causative of the outcome is sought by comparing its prevalence among those who have the outcome factor (cases) to those who do not (controls).

Case-fatality rate   Number of persons dying of a condition divided by the number diagnosed with the condition within 1 year or less.

Causative factor   A variable that is linked to producing an effect, either by itself or in combination with some other factor. It must precede the effect in a time interval consistent with the anticipated effect.

Clinical outcomes   The health status changes or effects that individual patients experience resulting from the delivery of health care; they are measured in terms of the patient's perspective as morbidity, mortality, functional abilities, satisfaction with care.

Coefficient of variation   Relates the variability of a set of scores to the average size of the set of scores (as a percentage). Coefficient of variation equals standard deviation divided by the mean, times 100%.

Cohort   Group of individuals who share a common experience or event and who pass through time together. Cohorts could be defined by birth year, death year, or exposure to a common source (e.g., atomic bomb survivors).

Competitor   An individual, group, or organization that competes for the same customers or valued resources or otherwise interferes with the ability of another entity to engage in exchange with a targeted market.

Competitor analysis   An assessment of an organization's position in the marketplace relative to other entities (individuals, groups, or organizations) that may compete for the same customers or valued resources or otherwise interfere with an organization's ability to serve its selected markets.

Confidence interval   A range of values for a point estimate of a parameter (mean, proportion, odds ratio, difference between means) within which the true population parameter is expected to lie within a given level of probability.

Crude death rate   All deaths in a calendar year per population at midyear, times a factor of 10. It represents the probability of dying from all causes and is affected by the age distribution of the population under consideration.

Customers   In a health care situation, those individuals utilizing services offered by a health care provider; a term frequently favored over the term "patients," as it is suggestive of a scenario in which the consumer has a choice among alternatives for the satisfaction of a health-related need or want.

Demand   In the context of health care, the amount of service actually utilized or the amount of service considered necessary to meet need as perceived subjectively or as determined "objectively" by application of a formula.

Demography   The study of human populations in reference to such variables as size, distribution, and composition and to the dynamics of fertility, mortality, and migration.

Dependent variable   The variable that is altered as a result of some antecedent or independent variable. Sometimes called the response or outcome variable.

Double-blinded   The administration of an intervention in which neither the person receiving the intervention nor the person administering the intervention knows the nature of the treatment.

Effectiveness   The impact of an intervention in practical application, such as a community setting.

Efficacy   Whether a medical technology or other intervention technique works under controlled conditions, ideally as determined through a randomized clinical trial.

Endemic   The usual or constant prevalence of a disease or infection in a human population in a defined geographic area.

Environmental scanning   An organizational function designed to ensure that the organization is aware of change relative to the forces and character of its environment so that both the threats and opportunities inherent in the environment are recognized.

Epidemic   The occurrence of cases in excess of expected. Expected values are defined from historical rates in the population, or the occurrence of two or more cases of a condition not normally expected in a population.

Etiology   The sum of knowledge regarding the cause of a disease.

Excess risk   The arithmetic difference between two measures of risk.

External environment   Individuals, groups, or other organizations that exist outside the boundaries of a focal entity as well as the political, economic, social, and technological forces that impact the entity's operations.

False-negative probability   Probability of an outcome in those whose test results are negative for that outcome. Inversely related to sensitivity.

False-positive probability   Probability of absence of an outcome among those whose test results are positive for that outcome. Inversely related to specificity.

Gap analysis   An analysis that attempts to quantify a deficit by comparing an ideal situation with the current situation or the situation as it would be in the future without some form of intervention.

Goal A broad statement indicating the general direction toward a desired future state.

Hazard rate The number of persons having an adverse outcome before time $t + 1$ who were outcome-free until time t divided by the number at risk between t and $t + 1$ times. Synonym is failure rate.

Health outcomes Injury and disease morbidity and mortality resulting from the intervention of health care services.

Health promotion Activities related to individual life-style to prevent disease, disability, and injury, e.g., physical fitness, nutrition counseling, tobacco-cessation programs, family planning.

Health protection Environmental or regulatory interventions aimed at large groups, e.g., air quality standards, seat belt laws, water fluoridation.

Herd immunity Populations protected from infection as a result of the presence of immune persons. The degree of protection achieved depends on age of immunity, season of the year, timing of introduction of susceptibles, and disease reproduction rate.

Immunity Resistance of the host associated with the presence of antibodies or cells having a specific action on the invading microorganism or on its toxin.

Inapparent infection Presence of infection in a host without the occurrence of recognizable clinical signs and symptoms.

Incidence Number of new cases.

Incidence rate Number of new cases at time t, divided by the population at risk at $t \times 10^k$, where t is a time period and k is some power of 10. A change in the incidence rate means that there is a change in the balance of etiological factors, some naturally occurring fluctuation, or possibly the application of an effective control program.

Incubation period Time between the entry of a microorganism into a host and the first signs or symptoms of disease.

Independent variable The variable that is manipulated to cause or influence an outcome. In experimental studies, this is the intervention. Sometimes called the antecedent variable.

Infection The entry and multiplication of a transmissible agent in a host resulting in cellular injury.

Internal environment The situation of an organization as characterized by its structure and resources or inputs; the elements associated with an organization's internal environment are generally those under direct control and within defined organizational boundaries.

***Kappa* statistic** A measure of agreement (reliability) beyond chance alone. $\kappa = 1$ indicates perfect agreement. The significance of the *kappa* statistic is assessed with a z score.

Likelihood ratio Ratio of the probability that persons with an outcome have an observed value of a test to the corresponding probability among people without the outcome. Likelihood ratios (LR) are expressed as odds. They do not vary with prevalence. Good for examining likelihood of outcome at various levels of a test.

Longitudinal study Individuals are selected in consideration of varying degrees of exposure to suspect factor but are not known to possess the outcome associated with the factor under study. The purpose of this study is to examine the rate of occurrence of a particular outcome with various levels of some causative factor(s). The group selected for study can be a sample from the general population or a select group, e.g., individuals in certain occupations. It is also possible to conduct a longitudinal study (also known as a prospective study) by defining a past date for a specific group (e.g., HMO enrollees) investigation. Follow-up information concerning the outcome is reconstructed, if necessary, through a number of sources including death certificates and hospital records. This latter approach may be also termed historical prospective or retroprospective.

Market   The set of all people who have an actual or potential interest in a product or service.

Market analysis or audit   An analytic process associated with planning that is initiated for the purpose of defining and characterizing the market and its needs, wants, or preferences.

Market area   The place or location associated with the actual or potential markets (or customers) that an organization targets or selects for delivery of one or more products or services.

Marketing   A managerial function encompassing planning, analysis, implementation, and control activities that is undertaken to bring about the voluntary exchange of valued resources between two or more parties; a set of activities designed to facilitate the satisfaction of the resource-dependency needs of an organization.

Market segment   A subset of a larger market (or set of all people who have an actual or potential interest in a product or service); members of such a subset are homogeneous in regard to defined demographic, geographic, psychographic, or behavioristic variables and adequately distinct from other market segments to justify delineation of specific marketing strategies.

Medical technology   Therapeutic or diagnostic devices, medical or surgical procedures, pharmaceuticals, or combinations thereof.

Meta-analysis   A systematic method using statistical analyses that combines data from independent studies to obtain a quantitative estimate of the summary effect of an intervention and to determine the variability of effect among studies examined.

Mission statement   A statement that describes an organization's reason for being, its business, the products or services it offers, the market(s) it intends to serve, and features that distinguish the organization from others.

Morbidity   The condition of being affected by a disease, illness, or symptoms. It may be newly onset case (incidence) or an existing condition (prevalence).

Mortality rate   Number of deaths in a time period divided by the population at risk, times a power of 10.

Negative predictive value   Probability that a person with a negative test result does not have the outcome. It is the same as the posttest likelihood or posterior probability of no disease.

Nosocomial infection   An infection in a patient or staff member emerging as a result of exposure to a source within a health care facility.

Null hypothesis (H_o)   A statement about the value of a population parameter to be statistically evaluated, phrased to negate the possibility of a relationship between the independent and dependent variables.

Objective   A specific statement that indicates in measurable terms what an organization intends to accomplish and when in order to progress toward fulfillment of a goal objective.

Odds   Ratio of the occurrence of an attribute in a sample or population relative to its absence.

Odds ratio (OR)   Is the ratio of one odds to another. In a case-control study, the odds ratio compares the odds of exposure among the cases to that in the controls. The odds ratio in longitudinal and cross-sectional studies compares odds of outcome among the exposed to that among those not exposed. The OR is a descriptive measure of the strength of the relationship between a risk factor and outcome.

Open-systems theory   A theory that recognizes the importance of the interface or optimum fit between an organization and its environment and attempts to explain organizational behavior by viewing the organization as an open system that must interact with other entities in its environment in order to acquire resources and disburse its goods or services.

P **Value**   The probability associated with a test statistic. Indicates how much observed values differ from expected ones. A *p* value of less than 0.05 generally is accepted as meaning that the results of the statistical test are unlikely to result from chance alone. It also means that a test statistic with a *p* value of less than 0.05 is less than 5 times out of a 100 to be as extreme as the one observed.

Pathogenicity   The ability of a biological agent to cause disease in a susceptible host.

PESTs   An acronym for the political, economic, social (demographic), and technological forces that exist in an organization's external environment and determine the nature of the threats and opportunities confronting an organization.

Population   The universe of all possible observations given a set of rules.

Position   In the context of marketing, a comparative measurement of the standing of an organization or of each of its products and services relative to competitors and their products or services.

Positive predictive value   Probability that a person with a positive test result has the outcome. Used to assess yield of cases for screening efforts. It is the same as the posttest likelihood of disease or posterior probability of disease.

Prevalence   Is the number of individuals in a population with the attribute of interest. Prevalence includes both previously diagnosed as well as new cases of a disease. Prevalence is a function of both the incidence and duration of the disease. It is also the proportion of individuals in the population with a characteristic at a specified point or period of time and the same as the pretest likelihood of disease or the prior probability of disease. The lower the prevalence rate, the lower the predictive value of a positive test.

Prevalence rate   Total number of new and old cases at time t, divided by the total population at t, times 10^k, where t designates a time interval and k is some power of 10.

Prognostic factor   A variable that affects the course of a disease or other health problem.

Random sample   A subset of observations drawn from a populations in such a way that each observation contained in population has an equal chance of being included in the sample.

Receiver operating characteristic (ROC) analysis   A graph of pairs of true positive and false positive cases used to evaluate the accuracy of a diagnostic test. The x axis is $1-$ specificity or $1-$"true negatives"; the y axis is sensitivity or "true positives." A way to determine the optimal cutoff point in consideration of diagnostic error. The optimal curve (test with the least diagnostic error) is one in which the x and y coordinates are maximal at the upper left of the graph.

Relative risk (RR)   Ratio of the incidence rate among exposed individuals divided by the incidence rate among the nonexposed. If the RR is greater than 1, a "positive" association is said to exist. If RR is less than 1, exposure is protective against the outcome.

Research hypothesis   A statement about a presumed relationship between an independent variable(s) and a dependent variable within a population, e.g., that fewer adverse patient incidents will occur with more RN staff.

Resource dependency   A facet of open-systems theory that holds that the behavior of an organization is influenced by the need to relate to other organizations in the environment in order to obtain resources essential for organizational survival and for production of outputs (or the goods and services of the organization).

Risk   The probability that an event will occur within a defined population during a specified time.

Sample   A subset of observations drawn from a population.

Secondary data   Data that already exist, having been collected for another purpose; these data may contribute to the understanding of a situation or problem, although they may not be entirely responsive to the information needs of a current situation because the data were previously collected for some other reason.

Sensitivity   The ability of a screening test to give a positive finding when the person tested truly has the disease. It equals the number of persons with the disease identified by the screening test, divided by the total number of persons with the disease, times 100%.

Situational analysis   An assessment of an organization's situation in terms of its market(s), the forces in its external environment, competitors, the internal aspects of the organization associated with its resources and capabilities, and the performance of the organization relative to expectations.

Specificity   The ability of the test to give a negative finding when the person tested is free of the disease under study. It equals the number of persons without the disease who are negative to the screening test, divided by the total number of persons without the disease, times 100%.

Specified rate   Rate pertaining to a segment or subgroup of a population.

Stakeholder   An entity (individual, group, or organization) that has an interest in or influence on a specified organization.

Sterilization   The complete destruction of biological agents on or in an object, usually by means of heat (e.g., autoclave) or chemicals.

Strategic planning   A systematic process for setting future direction, developing effective strategies, and ensuring that an organization's structure and systems are compatible with long-term survival and success.

Strategy   A set of decision rules developed for the purpose of guiding an organization's behavior under varying circumstances; a pattern or plan for integrating an organization's mission, resources, and activities into a cohesive whole.

Surveillance   The scrutiny of all those at risk for a particular condition regarding occurrence of the condition to promote prompt and early recognition of disease and to prevent occurrence and/or spread of disease. Surveillance involves systematic data collection, analysis, and dissemination of findings.

Survival curve   Graphic representation of the cumulative probability of death, survival, or other endpoint determined from the follow-up of a defined group of persons at risk for the event.

SWOT analysis   An assessment of the strengths and weaknesses of an organization (as represented by the resources under the organization's control and the resulting organizational capabilities) and the opportunities and threats (SWOT) existing in an organization's external environment and determined by the political, economic, sociodemographic, and technological forces in that environment.

Technology assessment   The evaluation of the safety, effectiveness, efficiency, and appropriateness of devices, medical and surgical procedures, and pharmaceuticals as promoted for improving a patient's condition or quality of life.

Type I error   This results when a true null hypothesis is rejected. It may occur when the sample is too large.

Type II error   This results when a false null hypothesis fails to be rejected. It occurs when the sample is too small.

Index